Adventuring along the
Lewis and Clark Trail

Adventuring along the Lewis and Clark Trail

MISSOURI

ILLINOIS

IOWA

NEBRASKA

SOUTH DAKOTA

NORTH DAKOTA

MONTANA

IDAHO

OREGON

WASHINGTON

ELIZABETH GROSSMAN

SIERRA CLUB BOOKS • SAN FRANCISCO

Published by Sierra Club Books
San Francisco, California
www.sierraclub.org/books

Produced and distributed by the University of California Press
Berkeley and Los Angeles, California
www.ucpress.edu

LIBRARY OF CONGRESS CATALOGING-IN-PUBLICATION DATA
Grossman, Elizabeth, 1957–
    Adventuring along the Lewis and Clark Trail / by Elizabeth Grossman.
        p. cm.
    Includes bibliographical references
    ISBN 1-57805-067-7
    1. Lewis and Clark National Historic Trail — Guidebooks. I. Title.
    F592.7 .G76 2003
    917.804'34 — dc21   2002026974

Series cover and book design by Bonnie Smetts
Cartography by Bill Nelson

10 9 8 7 6 5 4 3 2 1

For my nieces, Jane and Olivia,
and for all those working to protect wildlands,
rivers, and oceans and all that they give life to

The concept of conservation is a far truer sign of civilization than that spoilation of a continent which we once confused with progress.

— Peter Matthiessen, *Wildlife in America,* 1959

The West of which I speak is but another name for the Wild; and what I have been preparing to say is, that in Wildness is the preservation of the World.

— Henry David Thoreau, *Walking,* 1862

Contents

Acknowledgments

My thanks to Jim Cohee and Helen Sweetland and their colleagues at Sierra Club Books for thinking of me for this project, and to all of those who shared information, advice, expertise, suggestions, and enthusiasm along the way — not just about the Lewis and Clark Trail but also about natural history and the protection of wildlife, rivers, and wildlands west of the Mississippi River.

Those to whom thanks are due include Sierra Club staff members and volunteers Jonathan Bry, Chase Davis, Ann Eggebrecht, David Ellenberger, Nick and Holly Forrest, Kathryn Hohmann, Mary Kiesau, Kirk Koepsel, Mari Margil, Ken Midkiff, Heather Morijah, John Osborne, Wayde Schafer, Carmen Schwisow, Paul Shively, Roger Singer, Tracie Weber, and Jim Young — apologies to anyone there I have inadvertently overlooked. For help with information on endangered species, forests, grasslands, tribal issues, wild salmon, wilderness protection, and places to explore, thanks to Sybil Ackerman, Susan Ash, Rick Brown, Nicole Cordan, Kathy Crist, Bill Cunningham, Brett Dufur, Cal Elshoff, Katie Fite, Charles Hudson, Marilyn Hudson, Joan Jewett, Andy Kerr, Gilly Lyons, Sam Mace, Regna Merritt, Ken Olsen, Allen Pinkham, Mark Salvo, Kathleen Sayce, Chad Smith, Kieran Suckling, Jenny Valdivia, Amie Wexler, and Wendell Wood, and to additional staff members at Alliance for the Wild Rockies, American Lands Alliance, American Rivers, Center for Biological Diversity, Earthjustice, Oregon Natural Resources Council, and Save Our

Wild Salmon. Special thanks to Ric Bailey, Susan Ewing, Kevin Gorman, John Haines, and Carol Porto, who were kind enough to look over my manuscript, and to Edward Wade for his attention to the details of turning a manuscript into a book.

Special thanks also to paddling companions John Haines, Esther Lev, Burt Lloyd-Jones, Jill Ory, Debbie Sohm, and Ted, Laurel, and Lydia Wolf; to traveling companions Monica Allen, Linda Anderson, Susan Ewing, Lisa Miles, and Margot Thompson; to Dick Manning and Tracy Stone-Manning for their wisdom and generous hospitality; to the folks at the Virgelle Mercantile; and to Jack and Jessie Priley for their generosity at Judith Landing. My thanks also to the many Bureau of Land Management, Forest Service, National Park Service, and U.S. Fish and Wildlife Service, state parks, fish, game, wildlife, recreation, and natural resource department employees who answered my numerous questions.

And thanks to my parents, Alvin and Sari Grossman, for encouraging my desire to make life an endless voyage of discovery.

Why This Book?

There are so many books about the Lewis and Clark expedition, and so many editions of their journals that they easily fill a small library. So why this book? What makes this book different from other guidebooks, coffee-table books, and accounts of the journey?

For one, this book aims to get readers out of their cars and into the landscape of the Lewis and Clark Trail to sense how that country might have looked when the Corps of Discovery ventured through. Mindful of the enormous changes America's use of this land and its rivers has wrought over the past two centuries — and what we now know about how those changes have affected the ecological integrity of the landscape — I have designed this book to help readers understand the importance of conserving what is left of that original landscape. This is not a whistle-stop guidebook that whisks readers from one historic landmark to the next but a guide for travelers who like to get off the highway, away from convenient access to cold drinks and rest rooms, and who are willing to learn about and become actively engaged with the places they visit.

Thomas Jefferson commissioned the Lewis and Clark expedition to extend the commercial reach of the United States. He also envisioned it as a journey undertaken in the interests of geography and science. Travel the Lewis and Clark Trail today, and the expedition's commercial success is all too apparent. Most of the Missouri, Snake, and Columbia Rivers are dammed. Much of the Missouri River's floodplain has been drained and ditched for farming. Railroads run along many riverbanks of the Lewis and Clark Trail.

Also in Jefferson's mind when he dispatched Lewis and Clark was to see how the "vacant lands" of the West could be parceled out in accordance with his notions of an agrarian democracy. In time, these western lands were indeed divided and settled, and the native people — most of whom were not farmers — eventually restricted to reservations. Today the Great Plains and prairies have lost most of their native vegetation and are almost all planted with row crops as far as the eye can see. Only 1 percent of the native tallgrass prairies remains.[1] Over 90 percent of the Missouri's natural floodplain is now gone, having been converted to agriculture.[2] In Idaho, Oregon, and Washington, at least 90 percent of the sagebrush grasslands have now been lost.[3] Oil and gas drilling threaten plant and animal habitat in the Greater Yellowstone region — as they do across much of the West. Mining and industrial waste continue to leave a toxic legacy of polluted rivers, streams, and underground aquifers. Ninety percent of old-growth forests are now gone from Oregon and Washington.[4] Motor vehicles now have access to more of the Pacific Northwest in the United States than do salmon or trout.[5] In the same part of the country, between 1982 and 1997, sprawl consumed one acre of land every four minutes.[6] Idaho's national forests now have more than enough roads to circle the planet.[7]

Yet this is still amazing and spectacular country well worth reveling in. Many open, undeveloped, and wild places remain, including millions of acres of roadless land. As our understanding of this astounding continent's ecological workings has grown, we have become acutely aware of what we risk losing — or may have already lost — if we do not curtail the pace of development that has marked every year since Lewis and Clark completed their journey.

One of the best ways to appreciate the landscape Lewis and Clark explored and to learn the natural history of the places they visited is to get out into the backcountry. Examine the wildflowers along a hiking trail, paddle a river, camp in the mountains, bike a riverside path, watch for birds and wildlife. Doing so, you will become intimately acquainted with the rise and fall of the land, the location of plant communities, the bends of rivers, the squelch of wetlands, and the sounds of animals and insects. This book is designed to pique your curiosity, to make you want to learn still more, and with the hope that you will begin to care for the places you have visited.

The western United States has vast expanses of public land — land that belongs to every citizen, and of which we are all stewards. We also have a system of laws that allows citizens to be actively engaged in protecting our natural resources. The bicentennial of the Lewis and Clark expedition presents an opportunity to look critically at what parts of this landscape need preserving and restoring — and to renew efforts to restore their ecological integrity. Protecting and restoring rivers, endangered species, and damaged landscapes and conserving roadless areas requires enormous effort on the part of a great many people. It requires decisive action as well as patience and humility, and it entails changes that will not please everyone.

Currently there is debate — mostly in academic circles, but this discussion has edged into politics as well — over the nature of wilderness in this country. The Wilderness Act of 1964 defines land worthy of its legislative protection as that which is "untrammeled by man" and "where man himself remains but a visitor." Some argue about the usefulness and authenticity of drawing lines around such places, about the utility and philosophical merits of keeping humans and "nature" separate. Humans have lived throughout the river valleys and lands traveled by Lewis and Clark since well before most record keeping began. Yet only within our country's history has technology allowed us to alter that landscape in ways that make its recovery problematic. As readers travel the Lewis and Clark Trail, I hope they will gain a greater appreciation for what wilderness protection can achieve, as well as for the value of conservation, restoration, and ecologically compatible land-use practices. Also, please take the time to learn the history and culture of the people who lived here before white settlers arrived, with the understanding that those histories and cultures are not artifacts of the past but are very much a part of America today.

Many of the explorations suggested here will take readers into undeveloped country — wilderness areas, remote forests, mountain ranges, wild and scenic stretches of river. Others are in parks, in wildlife refuges, and along developed trails. Because following the Lewis and Clark Trail demands at least some allegiance to visiting historic landmarks, some of the explorations are designed to take in those locations, many of which are far from wild.

The route Lewis and Clark followed is the natural transportation corridor from the confluence of the Missouri and Mississippi Rivers to the Pacific Ocean. It follows paths long familiar to natives of those regions. Where Lewis and Clark walked into territory previously unknown to European Americans, there are now major roads, railroads, and rivers dammed for barge traffic. To get present-day travelers away from this well-beaten path and into wilder country, some explorations are a bit removed from the trail itself. The explorations are all muscle-powered adventures. They include hiking — day hikes and backpacking trips, as well as shorter walks — flat-water paddling by canoe or kayak, possibilities for white-water rafting and kayak trips, some bike trips, and cross-country ski and snowshoe trails. I have not included mountain biking, rock climbing, technical mountain climbing, or daredevil rapids running, although all are possible in many locations, as are horseback trips. This is not, however, a guidebook for wimps. The idea is to be able to admire the view and appreciate the place rather than to be preoccupied with gear or speed of descent.

Although the 200th anniversary of the Lewis and Clark expedition inspired Sierra Club Books to commission this guide, this book is intended not to encourage an all-out recreational assault on the landscape but to help people gain a deeper understanding of this countryside, whenever they choose to go. Some of the hoopla surrounding the expedition's bicentennial envisions hordes of tourists chugging across the western United States in minivans and motor homes. Indeed, from the Wood River and the Illinois banks of the Missouri River to Ilwaco, on Washington's Pacific coast, commemorative sites and interpretive centers are preparing for an influx of visitors. There are historical dioramas, models, memorabilia, artifacts, murals, and interactive displays. Many offer a window onto perspectives of often-overlooked local history and a solid introduction to expedition history and geography. This book will help travelers delve a little farther into the landscape itself. It points them toward open spaces where they will confront the elements and discover things for themselves: places where they can watch a pelican sliding into the water by the bow of their kayak, see a monkey flower in bloom by a mountain stream, glimpse a salmon in its spawning dance, listen to prairie dogs chattering into the silence of the sunset, walk among old-growth trees in a Northwest forest, or realize that the view from their campsite on the Missouri has not changed for over 200 years.

Whether you live in a crowded city or a quiet rural community, whatever region of the country you call home, how America treats the landscape of the Lewis and Clark Trail will affect your future. These rivers nourish the land. The mountains, forests, and grasslands harbor plants, animals, and streams without which those rivers — and our lives — are not complete. The first 200 years of calling this land "ours" in the United States has been an era of using natural resources as if there were no tomorrow. Learning the landscape's history, its ecology and biology — and how beautiful it can be — should help us live in a way that ensures that this land not merely persists but truly continues to thrive. This book takes advantage of this occasion to nudge a few more people in that direction.

PART I

The Country
of Lewis and Clark

CHAPTER 1

Introducing the Lewis and Clark Expedition

The object of your mission is to explore the Missouri river, & such principal stream of it, as, by it's course & communication with the waters of the pacific Ocean, may offer the most direct & practicable water communication across this continent, for the purposes of commerce," wrote President Thomas Jefferson to Captain Meriwether Lewis on June 20, 1803. Ever since he had been a congressman twenty years earlier, Jefferson had been trying to organize an expedition to explore America west of the Mississippi — territory that, until barely six months before Lewis and Clark set out, was claimed by countries other than the United States.

Throughout much of the eighteenth century, France and Spain had laid claim to the Louisiana Territory, originally described as the western half of the Mississippi River Basin but later expanded to include the northern extent of the Missouri. In 1762, as part of settling the Seven Years' War, France had ceded possession of Louisiana to Spain. But in 1800, hoping to secure his empire a place in North America, Napoleon pressured Spain into signing the Treaty of Ildefonso, which would return the Louisiana Territory to France. The Mississippi River and port of New Orleans were considered strategic assets for any nation hoping to assert its power in North America, and so Louisiana became something of a pawn between France and England at the onset of the Napoleonic Wars.

The new United States also considered control of the Mississippi vital to its future success, and by the time the transfer of Louisiana from Spain to France took place in 1802, the United States, led by President Thomas Jefferson, had begun to maneuver for the territory. After negotiations aimed to avert embroiling the United States in conflict with the warring European nations, and in a move designed to thwart England's chances of expansion in North America, France agreed to sell the United States not only the city of New Orleans but also the whole Louisiana Territory. The price was three cents an acre.[1] Thus in October 1803, the United States made the Louisiana Purchase, immediately doubling the nation's territory. "The consequences of the cession of Louisiana will extend to the most distant posterity," wrote Jefferson.[2]

To explore this new territory and find a path to the Pacific, Jefferson selected Meriwether Lewis. Lewis was then twenty-nine years old, an army captain who had served in the militia during the Whiskey Rebellion of 1794 and had spent the past four years working as Jefferson's private secretary. William Clark, under whom Lewis had served briefly in rifle command, was Lewis's choice as co-commander. Histories of the expedition recount how, in defiance of standard military procedure, Lewis insisted that he and Clark — who was thirty-three at the time of the expedition and technically not a captain by rank — serve as equals on the mission.[3] Their congeniality set the tone for the expedition and its telling in their journals.

Jefferson persuaded Congress to fund the "Corps of Discovery" as a commercial venture, but he stressed the importance of the expedition's "literary" interests — those of natural history, science, geography, and what we would today call anthropology. The "literary" investigations also provided important diplomatic cover for the mission's ultimate, if unstated, political aim of extending America's commercial reach west of the Continental Divide and the United States' territory to the Pacific.

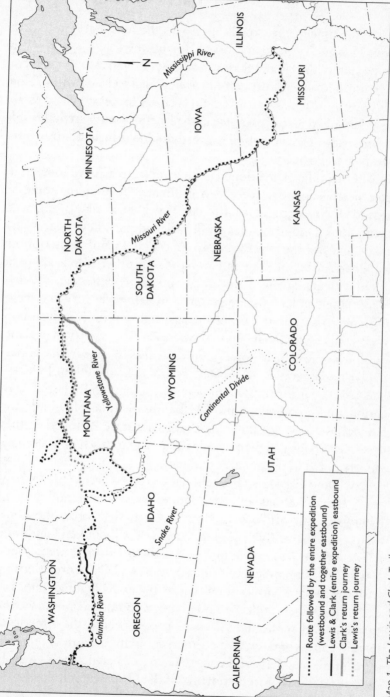

Map 1 The Lewis and Clark Trail.

At the time of the expedition it was thought that if a "North-west Passage" — one that crossed North America by water — were to be found, the United States could gain dominance in the lucrative northern fur trade and improved access to trade with China. The Corps of Discovery found no such route, yet it helped establish the United States' presence in the Pacific Northwest and firmly set the stage for the nation's already marked inclination toward westward expansion.

Although the expedition may have failed to achieve some of its commercial goals, it succeeded brilliantly in bringing home an extraordinary account of the country it explored, along with meticulous hand-drawn maps. In their journals, Lewis and Clark made many of the first European American scientific descriptions of native American flora and fauna. "Your observations are to be taken with great pains & accuracy," instructed Jefferson, and they were. Jefferson had a strong interest in natural history and meteorology, so among the details he asked Lewis and Clark to note were nuances of climate and "the dates at which particular plants put forth or lose their flowers, or leaf, times of appearance of particular birds, reptiles or insects." Before the expedition, Jefferson had sent Lewis for training in botany, zoology, and celestial navigation, and both Lewis's and Clark's observations of wildlife and landscape are vivid and remarkably accurate. Altogether they described about 178 plant species and 122 animal species not previously noted in the annals of science.

Lewis and Clark also brought back detailed accounts of a great many Indian nations and their languages, customs, and politics, including those of the Mandan, Blackfeet, Nez Perce, Shoshone, Sioux, and the many Columbia Basin and Chinookan bands and tribes. Jefferson's instructions to Lewis called for "friendly and conciliatory" treatment of "the natives." And Clark's relationship with the Indians was so good that he became a favored ambassador to the tribes. Still, the underlying assumptions of those relationships — that the natives were people whom the Americans might "endeavor to civilize & instruct" in the culture of domestic agriculture that Jefferson considered key to civilization — can be seen as an uneasy foreshadowing of the history that followed.

In the winter of 1803, the Corps of Discovery gathered supplies and prepared for its journey from a camp at the confluence of the Mississippi and Wood Rivers, not far from St. Louis. The permanent party numbered around thirty. When the expedition set out, it included two interpreters, three sergeants, about two dozen privates, Clark's slave York, a half dozen men who accompanied the expedition as far as the Mandan villages in what is now North Dakota, and some additional boatmen. When the expedition continued on from its winter camp at Fort Mandan in April 1805, it was accompanied by the interpreter Toussaint Charbonneau and his Shoshone wife, Sacagawea, along with Sacagawea's baby Pompey, who was born in the Mandan camp that February. Also accompanying the party was Lewis's black Newfoundland dog, Seaman.

In the expedition's initial outfitting were a 55-foot-long keelboat equipped with a sail and twenty-two oars, two pirogues with three or four sets of oars, and two horses. Careful lists have been kept of the expedition's provisions, which included "12 Pipe Tomahawks," "12 doz. Pocket Looking Glasses," and "72 ps. Strip'd silk ribbon" as "Indian Presents," along with one magnet, one 6-inch pocket telescope, a quarter pound of India ink, and six brass inkstands.

The expedition left Camp Wood in May 1804, and the journey was officially under way when it set out upriver from St. Charles, Missouri, on May 21, 1804. The Corps of Discovery reached the Pacific Ocean in November 1805 and returned to St. Charles at the end of its homebound journey in September 1806. The crew suffered many minor casualties along the way, but the only fatality was Sergeant Charles Floyd, who is believed to have died of a ruptured appendix. From start to finish the first official American exploration of the country between the Mississippi and Columbia Rivers covered about 8,000 miles over the course of twenty-eight months.

The journals of Lewis and Clark contain what are arguably the most extensive written descriptions of the western United States' landscape before European American settlement. Despite the enormous and ecologically destructive changes development has brought to that country, many places remain as Lewis and Clark described them. Now, as we try to preserve what is left of America's wild lands, rivers, and their native species and attempt to restore fragmented and degraded landscapes, the journals of Lewis and Clark can serve as a guide to what that country once was. Perhaps the fecundity of the landscape they encountered — the vast herds of bison, pronghorn, and elk, the rivers teeming with salmon and skies flocking with birds — can inspire us to turn the corner on a new chapter of American history in which environmental exploitation will be replaced by conservation and restoration.

CHAPTER 2

Chronology
of the Expedition

Meriwether Lewis and William Clark and what came to be called the Corps of Discovery began their journey in May 1804. They had spent the previous five months preparing for the expedition from Camp Wood — named for the Wood River — near the east bank of the confluence of the Missouri and Mississippi Rivers, not far from St. Louis. The initial crew for the expedition included close to four dozen men. The permanent party — the group that continued west from the Mandan villages in what is now North Dakota — was about thirty in number. The expedition pushed off on May 14, 1804, at four o'clock in the afternoon, under what Clark described as "a jentle brease." Lewis, who had been in St. Louis, joined the group on May 20. Lewis and Clark called the Wood River by its French name, Dubois, so some editions of their journals describe the first leg of the journey as "from the River Dubois to the River Platte." On May 20, 1804, Captain Lewis wrote from near St. Charles, Missouri,

> the first 5 miles of our rout laid through a beautifull high leavel and fertile prairie which incircles the town of St. Louis from N.W. to S.E. the lands through which we then passed are somewhat broken less fertile the plains and woodlands

are here indiscriminately interspersed untill you arrive within
three miles of the vilage when the woodlands commences
and continues to the Missouri the latter is extreemly fertile.

The expedition left St. Charles — a city established by French
traders in 1769 — on May 21 and continued upriver toward what
is now Jefferson City, the capital of Missouri. On May 25, about
60 miles upriver, it passed the village of La Charrette, which was
then the westernmost white settlement on the Missouri. During
the first week of June 1804 the party made its way through the
country of the Osage and Kansas Nations and camped near
Rocheport and what is now the site of Arrow Rock State Park.
The men hunted for deer, elk, and bear, encountered pelicans and
a den of rattlesnakes, and saw buffalo on the plains above the
river. By the end of June the expedition had reached the Kansas
River, where Kansas City, Missouri, is now located. It was hot and
buggy, the water muddy. Near the river were wild grapes, goose-
berries, and hazelnut, plum, and cherry trees. In the bluffs above,
the men noted some burial mounds left by Missouri Indians. By
mid-July they had reached the Little Nemaha River on the edge of
the Great Plains, just north of present-day St. Joseph, Missouri. As
Captain Clark noted on July 15, 1804,

> I had at one part of the Prarie a verry extensive view of all the
> Countrey around and up and down the river a Considerable
> distance . . . those Hills have but little timber, and the Plain
> appears to Continue back of them. I saw Great quantities of
> Grapes, Plums of 2 kinds, Wild Cherries of 2 Kinds, Hazel-
> nuts, and Goosberries.

The expedition reached the Platte River on July 21, 1804, a river
Lewis and Clark described as "being much more rapid than the
Missourie." In the evening there were wolves near their camp. This
was the country of the Oto and Missouri. As they continued
upriver, Clark made frequent mention of the mosquitoes, which
were "thick & troublesom." One of the party killed a badger, an
animal they had not encountered before. The men caught catfish
and hunted turkey and geese. About a week after reaching the
Platte, they floated the stretch of the Missouri River that now flows

between the cities of Omaha, Nebraska, and Council Bluffs, Iowa — home of the Omaha and a gathering point for the Oto, Sioux, Missouri, and other Indian nations. A few days later, on August 3, Clark wrote,

> The Situation of our last Camp *Councile Bluff* or Handsom Prarie, (25 Days from this to *Santafee*) appears to be a verry proper place for a Tradeing establishment & fortification The Soil of the Bluff well adapted for Brick, Great deel of timber above in the two Points — many other advantages of a small nature. . . . perhaps no other Situation is as well Calculated for a Tradeing establishment.
> The air is pure and helthy so far as we can judge.

On August 20, 1804, the Corps reached what is now Sioux City, Iowa, where Sergeant Charles Floyd was taken ill and died. A tall obelisk now commemorates his grave site in Sioux City.

From here, the upstream path of the Missouri leads west into what are now Nebraska and South Dakota. On August 23, a hunting party shot a buffalo. Elk were seen swimming in the river, and prairie wolves were spotted. Just north of the river, not far from the present-day cities of Vermillion and Yankton, South Dakota, in the country of the Sioux and Ponca, Lewis and Clark visited a place known as Spirit Mound, from where Captain Clark wrote on August 25, 1804:

> The Surrounding Plains is open Void of Timber and leavel to a great extent, hence the wind from whatever quarter it may blow, drives with unusial force over the naked Plains and against this hill; . . . One evidence which the [Indians] give for believeing this place to be the residence of Some unusial Sperits is that they frequently discover a large assemblage of Birds about this Mound.

In the following week, the expedition followed the river upstream through what is now the impoundment formed by Gavins Point Dam to where the Niobrara River flows into the Missouri. It was here that the expedition met with the Lakota, and Captain Clark described the lands of the various "Tribes or bands of the Sceoux." He wrote on August 31, 1804,

This Nation is Divided in 20 Tribes, possessing Seperate interests. Collectively they are noumerous say from 2 to 3000
men, their interests are so unconnected that Some bands are
at war with Nations [with] which other bands are on the most
friendly terms. This Great Nation who the French has given
the Nickname of Suouex, Call themselves Dar co tar
[Dakota].

Near the Niobrara members of the Corps saw their first prairie
dogs, which Clark described on September 7, 1804:

a Village of Small animals that burrow in the grown. . .
contains great numbers of holes on the top of which those
little animals Set erect and make a Whistleing noise and
whin allarmed Step into their hole.

The party continued upstream, through the sections of the
Missouri now flooded by the impoundment created by Fort
Randall Dam. The plains here were filled with great numbers of
buffalo, deer, elk, and other wildlife. On September 14, near what
is now Chamberlain, South Dakota, Lewis described a white-
tailed jackrabbit and his first sighting of a black-billed magpie.
Here Lewis and Clark also saw their first pronghorn — sometimes
referred to in the journals as "goats." Both described the pronghorn meticulously, Lewis remarking that "The agility and fleetness
of this animal . . . was . . . really astonishing."

On September 17, near present-day Oacoma, South Dakota,
Lewis noted that "the country in every direction for about three
miles intersected with deep reveenes and steep irregular hills . . . at
the tops of these hills the country breakes of[f] as usual into a fine
leavel plain extending as far as the eye can reach." There was a vast
prairie dog town here, along with "immence" herds of buffalo,
deer, elk, and antelope and numerous large wolves. The vegetation
of the plains became drier as the expedition moved west, with the
growing aridity marked by great quantities of "Prickley Pear."

On September 25, 1804, near what is now Pierre, South
Dakota, Lewis and Clark met and had an altercation with the
Teton Sioux, who controlled trade going north along the river —
and who attempted to seize one of the expedition's boats. A Teton

chief known as Black Buffalo helped defuse the situation, and the Corps of Discovery continued upstream unharmed.

The Indians of the upper Missouri River, including the Teton Sioux, were known for stopping trading parties, demanding high payment for safe passage, and paying low prices for goods. Making diplomatic peace with the Omaha, Arikara, Teton, and other upper Missouri tribes would be essential to settlement of the United States west of the Mississippi. But the peace and diplomacy were viewed very much from the European American perspective, and for the tribes of the Great Plains, very little of either ultimately prevailed.

In late September and early October, the Corps continued upriver, past the Cheyenne and Grand Rivers through the country of the Arikara — a stretch of the Missouri now inundated by the Oahe Dam. On a river island, Clark noted on October 8, were fields where the Indians "raise their Corn Tobacco Beens &c." The next two days were cold, windy, and wet. The Arikara, Clark wrote, "Live in warm houses, large and built in an oxigon [octagon] form forming a cone at top which is left open for the smoke to pass." The Arikara grew squash and pumpkins and made willow baskets and buffalo skin canoes. They gave the expedition's men a "rich & verry nurrishing" bread made from beans and corn. Lewis and Clark presented the Arikara with various gifts and met with a council of their warriors and chiefs. Near here, Lewis and Clark saw great numbers of grouse, black-tailed deer, elk, pronghorn, and buffalo.

By the third week of October 1804, the expedition had reached Mandan and Hidatsa country, where the Knife River meets the Missouri, near present-day Bismarck, North Dakota. "I walked out on the Hills & observed Great numbers of Buffalow feeding on both Sides of the river," Clark noted in his journal on October 19. The next day he wrote, "our hunters killed 10 Deer and a Goat [what they called pronghorn] and wounded a white Bear, [what they called the grizzly] it was very cold and I saw several fresh tracks of those animals which is 3 times as large as a mans track." By October 23 the ground was covered with snow.

On October 24 the expedition reached the large Mandan and Hidatsa villages, like those whose remains can be seen today near

Washburn, North Dakota. On the 31st the expedition was received by the chief of the Mandan with whom the men smoked a pipe and who told them "he believed what we had told them, and that peace would be general, which not only gave him Satisfaction but all his people." On November 2, after a week spent camping and meeting with the Mandan, Captain Clark and four of his men set about looking for a "proper place to winter." The next day they began building what came to be called Fort Mandan, about a mile downstream from the Mandan villages near the confluence of the Knife and Missouri Rivers.

On the night of November 6, the "Sergent of the Guard" woke the party to see the Northern Lights. Ice was noted in the river on November 13. A week later the Corps moved into its newly completed huts at Fort Mandan, a location noted as 47°21′47″ latitude, at a "computed distance from the mouth of the Missouri" of "sixteen hundred miles."

The Corps of Discovery spent the winter at Fort Mandan, embarking upstream on the Missouri again on April 8, 1805. Over the long, cold winter (the temperature often fell well below zero), Lewis and Clark visited and conferred with the Mandan, with whom the men of the expedition went hunting. To guard against the extreme cold, Clark lined his gloves with lynx fur. On January 15 Clark noted the details of a lunar eclipse. The icy weather continued, and on February 3 Lewis bemoaned the fact that their boats were "firmly inclosed in the Ice and almost covered with snow." The supply of meat laid in during November and December was running low. The expedition traded some of its blacksmithing iron for Mandan corn. On February 11 Sacagawea, the Shoshone wife of interpreter Toussaint Charbonneau, gave birth to a baby boy. The wintry weather continued well into March, but by then river ice had begun to break, and great chunks were observed floating downstream.

On April 1 Clark noted the first rainstorm the party had witnessed since October 15. A day earlier he had watched ducks and geese flying upriver. Spring was on its way, and the Corps began preparing for the journey west. Before leaving Fort Mandan on April 8, Lewis and Clark sent a large collection of flora and fauna specimens back to President Jefferson. The collection included "4

Buffalow Robes, and a ear of Mandan Corn," antelope and bear skins, "1 Tin box containing insects mice &c. ... 4 liveing Magpies ... a liveing hen of the Prairie," a "Specimon of a plant, and a parcel of its roots highly prized by the natives as an efficatious remidy in cases of the bite of the rattle Snake or Mad Dog," and elk and bighorn sheep antlers.

Some of the Corps — about a dozen men — traveling on the large keelboat, returned to St. Louis and points east with correspondence and the natural history items. It was at the Mandan villages that Toussaint Charbonneau and his Indian wife, Sacagawea — being the most legendary of the expedition's interpreters and guides — and her baby joined the expedition, as did another interpreter, George Drewyer (or Drouillard), and a Mandan man who promised to accompany Lewis and Clark as far as the home of the Snake Indians, serving as interpreter and guide. The expedition's vessels now "consisted of six small canoes, and two large perogues," wrote Lewis on April 7. "This little fleet altho' not quite so respectable as those of Columbus or Capt. Cook," Lewis went on to say, "were still viewed by us with as much pleasure as those deservedly famed adventurers ever beheld theirs; and I dare say with quite as much anxiety for their safety and preservation." The party was reported to be in excellent spirits, eager to proceed, and Lewis pronounced the anticipation of the next morning's departure "among the most happy of ... [his] life."

The 180 or so miles of the Missouri the expedition traveled before reaching the Yellowstone River are now flooded by the impoundments of the Garrison Dam. Strong winds blew up great quantities of sand from the riverbanks and churned up waves on the river, causing great discomfort and slowing progress upstream. In early April large numbers of lesser snow geese were seen flying upriver, followed a few days later by cranes. In the first several days out of Fort Mandan, Lewis and Clark met up with some Frenchmen trapping beaver — beaver that Lewis called the "best" he had ever seen.

On April 15 Lewis noted the first frog song of the season, as well as sharp-tailed grouse. The country was full of buffalo, elk, and pronghorn. Bald eagles, beaver, deer, wolves, and a curlew were also observed.

The expedition reached the Yellowstone, on what is now the border between North Dakota and Montana, on April 26, 1805. Clark measured both the Yellowstone and the Missouri above their confluence. A few days later, Lewis and one of the crew shot a grizzly, which he noted "is a much more furious and formidable anamal" than the black bear. They feasted on what was probably wild golden currant and saw great numbers of pronghorn, as well as buffalo, elk, deer, wolves, geese, ducks, and crows. It was here that the expedition made its first description of an American avocet. Snow fell on May 2, and the temperature dropped, freezing the boats' oars. A "verry extraordernarey climate," Clark wrote, "to behold the trees Green & flowers spred on the plain, & Snow an inch deep." But the weather soon warmed, and two days later Lewis noted that the frost had barely affected the cottonwood, willow, wild roses, or honeysuckle.

On May 5 Captain Clark "found a den of young wolves in the course of his walk." Lewis's journal describes both the gray wolf and the coyote and recounts the killing of the largest brown bear (grizzly) the party had yet encountered. Beaver burrowed in the riverbanks, and Lewis wrote of seeing a great number of bald eagles as they approached the Milk River. He also described in detail a root they called the "white apple," which the Indians called bread root. "I have no doubt but our epicures would admire this root very much, it would serve them in their ragouts and gravies in stead of the truffles morella," he wrote. Lewis noted having killed "four plover" of a "different species" than any he had seen before — they were willets. The men saw large numbers of elk, antelope, mule deer, bighorn sheep, and buffalo as they continued upriver through the stretch of the Missouri that flows through what is now the Charles M. Russell National Wildlife Refuge, much of which is flooded by Fort Peck Dam. Lewis noted several plants with which he was not familiar, including what is now called greasewood, a wild cherry, and an "arromatic herb on which the Antelope and large hare feed," which is sage. On May 14 the men in two of the party's rear canoes had a frightening close call with a large brown bear. All but the bear escaped unharmed. On May 20 the expedition reached what the Minnetare — now known as the Hidatsa — called the Musselshell River.

On May 25 the travelers saw a number of bighorn sheep and spotted the Bear Paw and Little Rocky Mountains, mistaking them for the Rockies themselves. On May 28 they reached the Judith River, which Lewis originally called the Bighorn and which was renamed by Clark in honor of his cousin Julia Hancock, whom he later married. Nearby, Lewis noted the remains of an Indian buffalo hunt at a buffalo jump, where the bison were killed by being run off a steep cliff. Many "circumstances indicate our near approach to a country whos climate differs considerably from that in which we have been for many months," wrote Lewis on May 30. The air was drier and clearer. The "banks and sides of the bluff were more steep than usual and were now rendered so slippery by the late rain that the men could scarcely walk."

Rocks tumbled off the "immence high bluffs," and the mud was "so tenacious that [the men were] unable to wear their mockersons." On May 31 they reached the great White Cliffs of the Missouri Breaks. "The bluffs of the river rise to the hight of from 2 to 300 feet and in most places nearly perpendicular; they are formed of remarkable white sandstone which is sufficiently soft to give way readily to the impression of water," wrote Lewis, who went on to describe the sculpted stone formation of the cliffs and their canyons. "As we passed on it seemed as those seens of visionary inchantment would never have and [an] . . . end; . . . so perfect indeed are those walls that I should have thought that nature had attempted here to rival the human art of masonry had I not recollected that she had first began her work."

On June 2 they reached a fork in the river. Much of the party thought the north fork would be the main stem of the Missouri, which would take them to the Columbia and on to the Pacific. Lewis and Clark themselves were not so sure but decided to explore this apparent "north fork" — which they spent nearly a week doing — before deciding which way to go. Choosing the south fork as the main stem, they named the northern tributary — which Lewis declared "a noble river" — the Marias River, after Lewis's cousin Maria Wood.

On June 8 the expedition set off again toward the Great Falls of the Missouri, reaching them on June 13, with Lewis scouting ahead to make sure they were indeed following the Missouri's main stem. Sacagawea was seriously ill for about a week, and both Lewis and Clark tended to her with various medicaments. By the time the expedition had reached the Great Falls of the Missouri, she was much improved.

> [M]y ears were saluted with the agreeable sound of a fall of water and advancing a little further I saw the spray arrise above the plain like a collumn of smoke . . . which soon began to make a roaring too tremendious to be mistaken for any cause short of the great falls of the Missouri. . . . I hurryed down the hill . . . to gaze on this sublimely grand spectacle,

wrote Lewis on June 13, 1805. The falls were some 80 feet high, and the sun created rainbows in the spray and mist of the water tumbling down the cliff. Lewis lamented that he lacked the artistic ability to adequately sketch the falls or a "camera obscura" to capture the impressive scene, which he ventured "to ascert is second to but one in the known world."

In the river near the Great Falls, Private Silas Goodrich caught half a dozen cutthroat trout, of which Lewis made the first European American identification. That evening they had a "sumptuous" meal of "buffaloe's humps, toungues and marrowbones" and "fine trout."

Over the next several days, Clark and the rest of the party arrived, and they began to scout and make their portage of the Great Falls and the several other falls just upriver. They cached some of their supplies and built carts to haul the rest of the gear. The terrain was difficult, with many steep ups and downs. The carts broke and required frequent repair, and gear often had to be hauled by hand. Prickly pears underfoot added to the distress. "I am apprehensive . . . that the portage is longer than we had calculated on," wrote Lewis on June 20. Three days later Clark wrote, "to state the fatigues of this party would take up more of the journal than other notes which I find scercely time to set down."

On June 29 a severe storm blew in, bringing rain and hail. The expedition's only compass was lost in the torrential downpour but was later found at the bottom of a ravine. "I begin to be extremely impatient to be off as the season is now waisting a pace nearly three months have now elapsed since we left Fort Mandan and not yet reached the Rocky mountains," wrote Lewis on June 30, 1805. It would be another full two weeks before the men completed the portage. It was mid-July when they rejoined the Missouri at the mouth of the Smith River near the present-day town of Ulm.

On the morning of July 15, Lewis rose early to oversee the reloading of the boats — they now had eight boats between them — and they were under way again by 10:00 A.M. Prickly pear and sunflowers were blooming, and there were currants, serviceberries, and buffalo by the river. But "the Musquetoes are extreemly troublesome," wrote Lewis. By July 18 they had reached the next major tributary upriver of the Smith, naming it Dearborn's River after the United States' secretary of war. Lewis wrote that they were anxious to meet with the Shoshone or Snake Indians so they could learn more about the geography of the country ahead. "I saw a great maney Ibex," wrote Clark in his journal that day.

On July 19 — another day of troublesome mosquitoes — the expedition reached the remarkable river canyon Lewis called "the gates of the rocky mountains," now known as the Gates of the Mountains, near Helena, Montana. Clark and three other men proceeded on foot to see if they could find any Shoshones, since they saw evidence of hunting camps. But the expedition's hunting shots had alarmed the Shoshones who had been nearby at the time, causing them to retreat into the mountains.

On July 20 Lewis noted swans, geese, sandhill cranes, and an unfamiliar kind of woodpecker that today is known as Lewis's woodpecker. On July 22 the men added "about half a bushel" of wild onions to their breakfast fare. That day Lewis wrote that the "Indian woman recognizes the country and assures us that this is the river on which her relations live, and that the three forks are at no great distance." On July 25, 1805, the expedition reached what is now Three Forks, Montana, where the Jefferson (named after "that illustrious personage Thomas Jefferson"), the Madison (named in honor of James Madison), and the Gallatin Rivers (this last named after Albert Gallatin, secretary of the treasury) join the headwaters of the Missouri. Many of the men had blisters and were stuck with prickly pear thorns. Captain Clark was ill with fever and chills.

> We begin to feel considerable anxiety with rispect to the Snake Indians. If we do not find them or some other nation who have horses I fear the successful issue of our voyage will be very doubtfull or at all events much more difficult in its accomplishment. we are now several hundred miles within the bosom of this wild and mountainous contry, where game may rationally be expected shortly to be scarce and subsistence precarious without any information with rispect to the country not knowing how far these mountains continue, or wher to direct our course to pass them to advantage or intersept a navigable branch of the Columbia,

wrote Lewis on July 27, 1805.

On August 8 the expedition reached the landmark called the "beaver's head" — now known as Beaverhead Rock — between present-day Twin Bridges and Dillon, Montana. Sacagawea recognized the place because it was near the "summer retreat of her nation." She assured Lewis and Clark that they would find "her people on this river or on the river immediately west of its source." Snow-covered mountains were visible from this vantage point. In the next few days, the expedition found a cove in which to cache the canoes until the return journey the following year.

On August 12, after seeing, but not succeeding in meeting, an Indian they took to be Shoshone, Lewis and several of the men climbed up to the "top of the dividing ridge" — the Continental Divide at Lemhi Pass on the Montana-Idaho border. There they "discovered immence ranges of high mountains still to the West . . . their tops partially covered with snow." On the west side of the ridge they hiked down the steep slope to the Lemhi River. Here, wrote Lewis, "I first tasted the water of the great Columbia River."

A few days later Lewis met a party of Shoshones in the Beaverhead Mountains just west of the Continental Divide, not far from the present-day town of Tendoy, Idaho. On the evening of August 13, 1805, Lewis's party dined with the Shoshones. The Indians had little to eat besides berries, yet they shared some fresh roasted salmon with Lewis, who wrote in his journal: "this was the first salmon I had seen and perfectly convinced me that we were on the waters of the Pacific Ocean."

Lewis spent a couple of days with the Lemhi Shoshones, who took the men antelope hunting on horseback. Lewis was able to convince a chief named Cameahwait to accompany his party back to where Clark and the rest of the expedition were camped. The reunion on August 17 was particularly joyful, as Lewis noted in his journal, because "the Indian woman . . . proved to be a sister of the Chief Cameahwait." There was also delight in discovering that these Indians had with them shells "resembling perl," which was procured "from the nations resideing near the Sea Coast." Lewis and Clark were also grateful to have met up with the Shoshones because they knew they would need horses to cross the mountains ahead. That evening Clark described the conversation with the Shosones in his diary:

> we made a number of enquires of those people about the Columbia River [actually the Lemhi which flows into the Salmon, a tributary of the Snake River] the Country game &c,
> The account they gave us was verry unfavourable, that the River abounded in emence falls, one perticularly much higher than the falls of the Missouri & at the place the mountains Closed so Close that it was impracticable to pass, & that the ridge Continued on each Side of perpendicular Clifts inpene-tratatable, and that no Deer Elk or any game was to be found in that Countrey, aded to that they informed us that there was no timber on the river Sufficiently large to make Small Canoes.

August 18 was Lewis's thirty-first birthday. On the morning of August 19 there was frost as Clark and several men set out with Cameahwait to scout the way ahead along the Salmon River. The route along the Salmon, as the Shoshone described it to Lewis, passed through steep, rocky, and mountainous as well as dry desert country. The latter is the high arid Lemhi and Pahsimeroi Valleys that lie to the south of the huge mountains surrounding the Salmon River. Lewis then asked "by what rout the Pierced nose indians" (the Nez Perce) traveled from their country to the Missouri. He was told of a pass through the mountains along a river to the north — the Lochsa River, which flows from the Bitterroots toward the Snake across what is now the southern portion of Idaho's panhandle. Clark's scouting party returned nine days later convinced that the route along the Salmon was indeed too difficult, and that the party should instead take the more northerly path, even though the Shoshones cautioned that "road was a very bad one."

So, in the last days of August, the expedition, accompanied by a Shoshone guide named Old Toby, set out to reach this northerly pass that would lead them to the waters of the Columbia. To do so, the travelers first had to make their way north to the Bitterroot River. The travel was arduous. In the first days of September 1805, the party traveled through Lost Trail Pass on the Continental Divide. The hills were "high & rockey on each Side," Clark noted on September 3. The horses were in constant danger of slipping on the steep slopes, especially when they encountered a storm that left about 2 inches of snow on the ground, followed by rain and sleet. On September 4 they visited with the Flathead Indians near the headwaters of the Bitterroot close to present-day Sula, Montana.

"We continued our rout down the W. side of the river about 4 miles," wrote Lewis on September 9, 1805, the day they reached the Bitterroot (which they originally called Clark's River). Having been told by Old Toby that they would be leaving the river to head west at this juncture, Lewis was "determined to halt the next day . . . and take some scelestial Observations." This they did at a place they called "Travellers rest," site of present-day Lolo, Montana. On the eleventh they proceeded west along a creek Lewis and Clark called "Travellers rest Creek," now called Lolo Creek.

By September 14, traveling the steep terrain above the Lochsa River, the expedition reached the Clearwater River, which the Flatheads called the "Koos koos ke," west of Lolo Pass on what is now the Montana-Idaho border. There were "high rug[g]ed mountains in every direction as far as I could see," wrote Clark on the fifteenth. The next morning it began to snow well before dawn, and the snow continued all day. Travel was miserably difficult through the steep, snowy mountains. The horses stumbled, occasionally dumping gear down the slopes. The men were exhausted and hungry, their feet freezing. "I have been wet and as cold in every part as I ever was in my life," wrote Clark on September 16. There was little game apart from birds and squirrels, so to provide the party with meat, they killed two colts.

On September 20 Lewis had his first sight of a Steller's jay and noted the differences between blue grouse, spruce grouse, and ruffed grouse. That day Clark encountered a Nez Perce village at what is now Weippe, Idaho. The Nez Perce shared dried fish, roots, and berries, which Lewis and Clark's party received and consumed gratefully — and a little too enthusiastically, for Clark noted he felt unwell "from eateing the fish & roots too freely."

"the pleasure I now felt in having tryumphed over the rockey Mountains and decending once more to a level and fertile country where there was every rational hope of finding a comfortable subsistence for myself and party can be more readily conceived than expressed," wrote Lewis on September 22.

On the twenty-fourth the expedition camped on a river island near what is now Orofino, Idaho. The Nez Perce drew maps of the river country that lay ahead. Several of the expedition's men were ill, so they rested while Clark set out with a Nez Perce chief named Twisted Hair and two young men to find trees that would be suitable for building canoes. One of the young Nez Perce men "killed 6 fine salmon," two of which they roasted and ate. Over the next four days, while some members of the expedition recuperated and others continued to suffer gastrointestinal distress from the diet of roots and fish, all those who could worked on the canoes. By October 5 they had finished and launched two canoes. One canoe was declared "verry good," the other "a little leakey." On the seventh, when they launched their new canoes down the Clearwater with its many rapids to the Snake, most of the party was still feeling under the weather. It is worth noting that for the first time on the journey the Corps of Discovery was floating with rather than against the current.

On October 10 the expedition reached the confluence of the

Clearwater and Snake Rivers, where the city of Lewiston, Idaho, now sits. From this point, the Nez Perce indicated, the river was "navagable about 60 miles up with maney rapids at which places the Indians have fishing camps and Lodges . . ." The next day the party set out early and proceeded downstream on the Snake. By the end of the day the party had passed "nine rapids all of them great fishing places," wrote Clark. The canoes had taken on a lot of water in the process — one had sunk — and time was taken to dry what could be dried. On October 14, after negotiating more difficult rapids, Clark noted that he had "a good dinner of Blue wing Teel." Two days later the expedition reached the confluence of the Snake and Columbia Rivers.

> In every direction from the junction of those rivers the
> countrey is one continued plain low and rises from the water
> gradually, except a range of high Countery which runs from
> S.W. & N.E. and is on the opposite Side about 2 miles distant
> from the Collumbia and keeping its direction S.W. untill it
> joins a S.W. range of mountains,

wrote Clark on October 16, 1805, in a description that would be recognizable by any visitor to the region today.

The expedition camped above the Snake about a quarter mile from a Nez Perce encampment. There, wrote Clark,

> a Chief came from this camp . . . at the head of about 200
> men singing and beeting on their drums Stick and keeping
> time to the musik, they formed a half circle around us and
> Sung for Some time, we gave them all Smoke, and Spoke to
> their Chief as well as we could by signs informing them of our
> friendly disposition to all nations.

The next day Clark killed a sage grouse and penned that bird's first European American description. Lewis took down a vocabulary of the Wanapum and Yakama. Clark described lodges of Indians drying salmon. "The number of dead Salmon on the Shores & floating in the river is incrediable to say — and at this Season they have only to collect the fish Split them open and dry them on their Scaffolds on which they have great numbers," he wrote. It was fall spawning season.

On October 18 a number of Yakama Indians came down the river by canoe and had "a council" with Lewis and Clark's party. "The Great Chief" of the Yakama sketched a map of the Columbia and the tribes living on its banks. The expedition then "proceded on down the great Columbia river," wrote Clark. From this point in the Columbia Basin the travelers could glimpse the snow-covered peaks of the Cascade Mountains. The same day Clark described a mountain, which he does not name. It was Mount Hood.

On October 19 they reached the mouth of the Umatilla River and climbed up to a cliff above the river. From there they saw a snow-capped "conical mountain," which they took to be Mount St. Helens — named by George Vancouver when he surveyed the Pacific Northwest coast between 1792 and 1794 — but was actually Mount Adams, a bit farther southeast in the Cascades. By October 21 the expedition had reached the mouth of the John Day River, where the men purchased some wood for their cooking fires from the Indians camped there. Clark noted that the Corps of Discovery dined on dog meat and fish.

The next day they arrived at the mouth of the Deschutes River just upstream from Celilo Falls. "I beheld an emence body of water compressd in a narrow chanel . . . fomeing over rocks maney of which presented their tops above the water," wrote Clark on October 22. The expedition landed and walked down "accompanied by an old man to view the falls" — Celilo Falls — to scout a portage route around the rapids. At the lower end of the rapids were five large Indian lodges where people were drying fish. There were great stacks of dried, pounded salmon and baskets lined with fish skins to secure drying fish. The Indians — among them Wallawalla, Yakama, and Wanapum — gave Lewis and Clark's party filberts and berries and helped portage the heavier gear around the falls. Over the course of the next two days, the expedition negotiated the narrows and rapids of the Columbia River near what is now The Dalles, Oregon.

Below this point in the river, cliffs of the Columbia River Gorge began to rise, and they could see the "rocky and hilley" foothills of the Cascades. On October 26 Clark wrote that "one man giged a salmon trout [steelhead] which we had fried in a little Bears oil which a Chief gave us yesterday and I think the finest fish I ever tasted." On October 31 the expedition passed a rock near the north bank of the river, which Clark estimated to be 800 feet high and 400 paces around. He called it Beacon Rock, the name it carries today. On the southern shore of the river — today's Oregon side — the party passed a "Great Shute or falls," which were the cascades, for which Cascade Locks, Oregon, was named. There were harbor seals in the river — Clark called them "sea otters." In his journal, Clark wondered about the Indians who lived at this part of the river, who seemed to trade mainly pounded fish, bear grass, and roots — things that he found difficult to consider "objects of commerce." Along the Columbia, between The Dalles and the ocean, lived at least a dozen different Chinook-speaking tribes, all of whom were known for canoe building. Salmon was central to their culture and diet, but they also hunted and gathered berries and roots in the uplands. Among them were the Wahkiakum, Cathlamet, Clatsop, Chinook, Multnomah, Wasco, and Wapato.

On the morning of November 3, 1805, there was thick fog as the expedition approached what it called the "Quick Sand river," known today as the Sandy River. Clark noted that the Columbia had risen during the night — the effects of the tide. Nearing the stretch of the Columbia that flows through what is now Portland, Oregon, they saw "A Mountain which we Suppose to be Mt. Hood" as well as Mount St. Helens. (They were right about both. It should be noted that by the time Lewis and Clark reached the mouth of the Columbia, British and American sailing ships had already begun arriving on the Pacific Northwest coast.) The next day the party landed at a Chinookan village near present-day Vancouver, Washington. Along the Columbia near what is now north Portland, Lewis and Clark admired a finely painted and carved canoe belonging to Chinookan Indians close to what is now Sauvie Island — which Lewis and Clark originally called "Image Canoe Island." There were noisy ducks and geese and lots of steady rain.

Over the next several days they proceeded downriver along the north shore of the Columbia toward what is now Skamokawa, Washington. On November 7, 1805, they camped near Pillar Rock near today's tiny town of Altoona, Washington. Clark noted that the Indian women wore clothes woven from cedar bark. There was dense fog, and the party needed an Indian guide to help them find the main channel of the river. The river here widens dramatically, and the tide and wind whip the water. That day Clark wrote in his diary, "Great joy in camp we are in view of the Ocian this great Pacific Octean which we have been so long anxious to See." In fact, they were still some twenty miles from the coast, but the river's mouth is so wide here, it is easy to see how they could have mistaken the great bays of the Columbia River estuary for the ocean itself.

"Some rain all day at intervals, we are all wet and disagreeable as we have been for Several days past and our present Situation a verry disagreeable one," wrote Clark on November 8. The ocean flow makes the water quite salty at this point along the river, and the shoreline hills above the river made for difficult camping, especially with the tidal rise and flow. Rain continued, and the wind "blew with great violence immediately from the Ocean," endangering the party and its canoes. "Pine of the fur [fir] species, or spruce pine grow here to an emence size & hight maney of them 6 & 7 feet through and upwards of 200 feet high," Clark noted on November 12. Everything was soaked, including clothes and bedding. But salmon and steelhead were plentiful. In addition to catching their own, the men purchased sockeye from the Indians in exchange for "fishing hooks & some trifling things." On November 15 Clark described the high waves of the Pacific Ocean crashing onto the rocks at Cape Disappointment.

While camped for about ten days just east of what is now the town of Chinook, Washington, the crew explored the stretch of the coast from what is now called the Long Beach peninsula in southwest Washington down toward Tillamook Head in Oregon. The men saw a whale and killed a bird they called a "Buzzard," but that was actually a California condor. They dined on goose, pounded fish, and venison roasted on sticks over an open fire. Clark named a river that flows into the Columbia there after his "particular friend Lewis." The party bought cranberries, woven mats, salmon, dried sturgeon, baskets, and basketry hats from the Chinook, as well as some roots, which they used in lieu of potatoes and bread. The men also traded with the Clatsop, who came from the south bank of the river. Among their trades was a robe made out of sea otter fur, which Lewis and Clark obtained in exchange for a belt of blue beads that Sacagawea had been wearing.

On November 24 the entire Corps of Discovery voted — including York and Sacagawea, which was notable for the time — on where its "Winter quarters" should be. The majority chose the south side of the Columbia, a place that came to be called Fort Clatsop, near what is now Tongue Point just upstream from Astoria, Oregon. They thought the elk hunting might be better on the south side of the river, and that there would be better access to the ocean for salt making. Fort Clatsop would be the expedition's home base until the third week of March 1806, when they began their eastward journey back to St. Louis.

By Christmas, all of the expedition's meat was spoiled, and there was little else to eat but pounded fish. Among Clark's Christmas gifts were socks from Lewis and two dozen weasel tails from Sacagawea. The whole party was tormented by fleas. Despite these difficulties, the fort was completed on December 30, 1805. On December 31 the weather continued wet and miserable. Clark noted in his journal the abundance of large "Snales without cover," what we now call slugs. During the winter the travelers visited with the Clatsop and other coastal tribes, who sold them roots, berries, and whale blubber, as well as dogs, on which the expedition had been relying to supplement their meat supply. They trapped beaver and otter, fished, hunted elk, and sketched and cataloged the local plants and animals, including different kinds of salmon, sea otter, clams, seaweed, and Oregon grape. Lewis and Clark worked on maps of their journey and polished their journal entries describing wildlife they had encountered. The men explored the nearby headlands and spent much time simply trying to keep themselves, their gear, and their supplies dry during the very wet coastal winter.

"Altho' we have not fared sumptuously this winter and spring at Fort Clatsop, we have lived quite as comfortably as we had any reason to expect we should," wrote Lewis in his journal on March 20, 1806, as the expedition prepared for the homeward journey. The "leafing of the hucklebury riminds us of spring," he wrote on the twenty-second, the day before the group's departure.

Having given the houses and furniture of Fort Clatsop to the Clatsop, the expedition launched eastbound, upriver, on March 23, 1806. Over the next four or five days the party stopped in Chinook, Cathlamet, and Wahkiakum villages, where the Indians gave them dried anchovies, sturgeon, and salmonberries. The party hunted whitetail deer and saw many waterfowl, including a ring-necked duck and sandhill cranes. On April 7, while camped on the Columbia near where Portland, Oregon, is now located, Clark prevailed "on an old Indian to mark the Multnomah R [now called the Willamette] down on the sand" along with the Clackamas River (which Clark spelled "Clarkamos") and Mount Jefferson, which rises in the Cascades to the southeast of Mount Hood.

We "passed several beautifull cascades which fell from a great hight over the stupendious rocks," wrote Lewis in his journal on April 9 as they passed the numerous waterfalls of the western Columbia River Gorge. By the nineteenth they had reached the great falls at Celilo, where Lewis noted that among the Indians gathered "there was great joy . . . in consequence of the arrival of the Salmon."

By the end of April the expedition had reached the country of the Yakama and Wallawalla, east and north of the Columbia River Gorge, where Lewis and Clark saw lizards and rattlesnakes. There the travelers met with a Wallawalla chief named Yellept, with whom they had visited in the fall. Yellept told them that "there was a good road" from the Columbia to the Clearwater, along which they would find "plenty of deer and Antilopes . . . with good water and grass." This route would shorten their journey by "at least 80 miles." Lewis and Clark negotiated the acquisition of horses — with some disgruntlement about the terms of exchange — and canoes with which to transport their gear across the river.

Its progress speeded by the horses and the easier route, on

May 5 the party reached the confluence of the Potlatch and Clearwater Rivers, east of present-day Lewiston, Idaho. Two days' journey east of there, Lewis noted that the "Spurs of the Rocky Mountains which were in view from the high plain today were perfectly covered in snow." The "Indians inform us," wrote Lewis, "that the snow is yet so deep on the mountains that we shall not be able to pass them untill the next full moon or about the first of June." As they continued east, Lewis and Clark made note of ponderosa pine and the good, fertile soil where "the grass and many plants are now upwards of knee high."

On May 14 they reached the east bank of the Clearwater River — in Nez Perce country — near what is now Kamiah, Idaho. There the expedition camped to wait out the melting of the snow in the high country. On hunting parties from that camp the men killed several bears and observed the Columbia ground squirrel, what came to be called Lewis's woodpecker, Clark's nutcracker, western tanager, the short-horned lizard, and the wildflower now known as ragged robin or *Clarkia*.

On June 8 they were still waiting for the mountain snows to melt, which the Indians informed them would not happen "untill the full of the next moon; or about the 1st. of July." Impatient at the thought of waiting any longer, the expedition set out again on June 15, reaching the North Fork of the Clearwater two days later, only to find the way ahead piled deep with snow. But the snow was hard packed and bore their "horses very well." With the help of Indian guides, on June 29 they reached Lolo Hot Springs on the east side of Lolo Pass. The expedition reached Traveler's Rest — what is now Lolo, Montana — on July 1, 1806.

There, the party divided. Lewis and a crew headed north toward what they hoped would be a shortcut to the Upper Missouri by way of the Marias River. Clark and his party — which included Sacagawea and her son — headed east along a southerly route that followed the Yellowstone downstream to the Missouri. On July 4, 1806, Clark and party celebrated the "decleration of Independence" by halting early and partaking "of a Sumptuious Dinner of a fat Saddle of Venison." On the eighth, Clark's party reached the place along the Beaverhead River where they had cached their canoes on the westbound journey. "I found every article safe, except a little damp," wrote Clark. After crossing the Madison and Gallatin Rivers on July 13, Clark dispatched a party of ten men "under the direction of Sergt. Ordway" to take six canoes and provisions from the cache to Lewis's party. Clark's party now numbered about a dozen, including Charbonneau, Sacagawea, and her son, along with forty-nine horses and a colt. "The country in the forks between Gallitins & Maidsens rivers is a butifull leavel plain covered with low grass. . . . I observe Several leading roads which appear to pass a gap of the mountain in an E.N.E. direction about 18 or 20 miles distant," wrote Clark. "The indian woman who has been of great service to me as a pilot through this country recommends a gap in the mountain more south which I shall cross." This was what is now called Bozeman Pass in Montana.

Lewis, meanwhile, traveled northeast along the Blackfoot River toward the Continental Divide. They crossed the Divide on July 7, 1806, at what is now called Lewis and Clark Pass, not far south of the Middle Fork of the Dearborn River. There were immense herds of buffalo. It was mating season for the bison, and Lewis noted in his journal the "tremendious roaring" of the bulls that could be heard for many miles.

Lewis and party then followed what they called the Medicine River — now the Sun River — to the Missouri just upstream from the Great Falls, which they reached on July 11. After accomplishing the portage of the falls, they retrieved some of the gear they had cached on their journey west. One of the men had a frightening encounter with a grizzly on the fifteenth, and mosquitoes continued to cause horrendous discomfort. They then continued north along the Teton River toward the Marias, observing herds of buffalo and numerous wolves. Although it was July 24 when they reached the Marias River, Lewis noted that the air was "extreemly cold." It was windy and rainy, and coyotes visited their camp.

Two days later they made their way through Blackfeet country from what Lewis called "Camp Disappointment," not far from the Two Medicine River — east of what is now Glacier National

Park. On July 26 they saw a party of Blackfeet on horseback. Waving a flag to signal their amicable intent, Lewis and party met and camped with the Indians but remained wary. Early the next morning several of the Blackfeet attempted to steal some of Lewis's party's guns and horses. In the ensuing fight, Lewis shot one of the Blackfeet — the only such incident on the entire expedition. Lewis and men then grabbed their gear and as many horses as they could, threw some of the belongings the Indians had left behind on a burning fire, and fled. They did not stop until two o'clock in the morning, so by the next day they had traveled nearly to the site of Fort Benton. To their great relief, on July 28 Lewis and his men met up with those in their party who had traveled by canoe, and they set off down the Missouri.

"[W]e are all extreemly anxious to reach the entrance of the Yellowstone river where we expect to join Capt. Clark and party," wrote Lewis on August 2. Meanwhile, Clark's party had reached the Yellowstone River near what is now Livingston, Montana, on July 15. The group continued on horseback until finding trees suitable for making canoes. On July 24, having lost several of their horses to Crow Indians, Clark and party launched their boats. In the course of the next week or so, they floated swiftly down the Yellowstone, traveling about 60 miles a day. Not far from the Bighorn River, on July 25, Clark stopped to carve his initials on a rock pillar, which is now called Pompeys Pillar after the nickname by which Clark called Sacagawea's son. Clark's inscription is the only such evidence of the expedition.

On August 7 Lewis's party arrived at the Yellowstone River and discovered that Clark's party had been there about a week before. On August 12, suffering from a bullet wound sustained in a hunting accident — Peter Cruzatte seems to have mistaken him for an elk — Lewis wrote in his journal, "at 1 P.M. I overtook Capt. Clark and party and had the pleasure of finding them all well." Although in pain from his injury, Lewis continued writing long enough to describe the pin cherry tree, a tree he had not seen before.

On August 14 the reunited expedition set out at sunrise down the Missouri toward the Mandan villages where it had spent the winter of 1804. There John Colter was given permission to leave the group to return west to trap. At the Mandan villages the expedition also parted company with Toussaint Charbonneau, Sacagawea, and her son. After several days of meeting with the Mandan chiefs and settling their accounts with their interpreters, Lewis and Clark set off downriver again on August 17.

From the country of the Mandan, Hidatsa, and Arikara, they continued down the Missouri toward Sioux territory. Lewis was recovering steadily from his wound. On August 29 Clark and several men "went out in pursute of Buffalow." There, Clark wrote, "I assended to the high Country and from an eminance I had a view of the plains for a great distance . . . [and] . . . had a view of a greater number of buffalow than I had ever seen before at one time. I must have seen near 20,000 of those animals feeding on this plain."

In a thick morning fog on September 1, after a night of troublesome mosquitoes, the party reached the mouth of the Niobrara River, just south of what is now the South Dakota–Nebraska border. Having had an unfriendly meeting with some Teton Sioux on August 30, the men were relieved that the Indians they met near the Niobrara were the friendly Yankton. That night they camped at the same place they had on September 1, 1804, where they had "met the Yanktons in council at the Calumet Bluffs."

On September 3 the expedition met some American traders on the river. "Our first enquirey was after the President of our country and then our friends and the State of politicks of our country &c. and the State [of] Indian affairs," wrote Clark. Among the news came the report "the Mr.Burr & Genl. Hambleton fought a Duel, the latter was killed." That day the men traveled sixty miles, and the next day they passed the Big Sioux and Floyd Rivers, near present-day Sioux City, Iowa. Making good time downriver, they reached the Platte on September 9. "The Musquetors are yet troublesom," wrote Clark, and "the climate is every day preceptably wormer and air more Sultery than I have experienced for a long time." Over the next few days, they met several parties of Americans making their way upriver, hints of the nation's incipient westward movement.

By September 14 the expedition had reached a spot just downstream from where it camped on July 1, 1804, not far upstream from what is now Kansas City, Missouri. On the seventeenth the men met army acquaintances on the river who, Clark wrote, were "Somewhat astonished to see us return and appeared rejoiced to meet us." This "Gentleman informed us," Clark continued, "that we had been long Since given out [up] by the people of the U S Generaly and almost forgotten," although "the President of the U. States had yet hopes of us." In exchange for a barrel of corn, the army captains gave the expedition some biscuits, chocolate, sugar, and whiskey — items welcomed by the weary travelers.

On Saturday, September 20, they reached La Charette, the small French village just upstream from St. Charles. There the "party requested to be permitted to fire off their Guns which was alowed & they discharged 3 rounds with a harty cheer." Every "person," wrote Clark, "both French and americans seem to express great pleasure at our return, and acknowledged themselves much astonished in seeing us," as "we were supposed to have been lost long since."

On September 21, 1806, with great rejoicing, the party reached St. Charles. Two days later the returning travelers "descended to the Mississippi and down that river to St. Louis at which place we arrived at about 12 oClock." There the Corps of Discovery "received a harty welcom from its inhabitants &c."

The epic journey over, Lewis and Clark began dispatching letters — official and private — to announce their return, unpacking, and storing their belongings, specimens, and papers. On the evening of September 25 they were feted by a dinner and a ball, as they would be from town to town when they traveled to Washington, D.C., to meet with President Jefferson. The last of Clark's entries in the standard editions of the journals notes that September 26, 1806, was "a fine morning we commenced wrighting &c."

CHAPTER 3

Following the Trail Today

As you begin to plan a trip along the Lewis and Clark Trail, I hope you will bear in mind that this book is being written in the spirit of exploration and discovery — not as in charting new country, but as in learning and relishing new experiences. It is my hope that your enjoyment of the places described here will make you curious to learn more and lead you to a concern for and willingness to help protect and restore these places. And whatever your style of preparing for a trip, I recommend flexibility and delight as constant companions.

Where to Go

The Lewis and Clark Trail begins just east of St. Louis, Missouri, and ends at the mouth of the Columbia River, where the Columbia meets the Pacific Ocean on the Oregon and Washington coasts. In 1978 Congress established the Lewis and Clark National Historic Trail, which is now part of the national trails system administered by the National Park Service. In many places a brown and white sign with the silhouette of two figures pointing the way ahead — presumably Lewis and Clark — marks the trail. Lewis and Clark followed a natural path across the country, along rivers and through river valleys and mountain passes. The fundamental contours of this terrain have not changed, so today, highways and paved and developed roads follow or parallel much of the historic trail.

Lewis and Clark's actual river route, however, has been much altered by the damming of the Missouri, Snake, and Columbia Rivers. Dams on these rivers created huge impoundments that inundated much of the original riverbeds, surrounding valleys, and floodplains and changed the rivers' flow. A few free-flowing sections of these rivers and their tributaries remain, some of which are protected under the Wild and Scenic Rivers Act.[1] These — along with many of the impounded reaches of these rivers — can be floated by raft and paddled by canoe or kayak. Some sections of the Lewis and Clark Trail are now designated as hiking and bike trails.

From St. Louis, the trail follows the Missouri River from its confluence with the Mississippi on the Illinois border, upstream through the state of Missouri. It then travels north along the Missouri, where the river forms the borders of Kansas, Nebraska, and Iowa. The trail continues upstream along the Missouri through South and North Dakota and crosses into Montana at the confluence of the Yellowstone River. On their westbound journey, Lewis and Clark followed the Missouri across what is now north central Montana, then south to the river's headwaters, where the Jefferson, Madison, and Gallatin Rivers coincide near what is now the city of Three Forks, Montana.

The trail then turns west and north, skirting the Salmon River before crossing the Continental Divide at Lemhi Pass above the Pahsimeroi Valley. There, realizing the mountains and canyons surrounding the Salmon were too difficult to cross, the expedition headed north through the Bitterroot Valley. At a place they called "Travellers Rest" — now Lolo, Montana — Lewis and Clark headed west along the Lochsa River to the Selway, Clearwater, and Snake Rivers, a route followed by today's Highway 12.

From there the trail continues west from the Snake River cities of Lewiston, Idaho, and Clarkston, Washington. It follows the lower Snake River to its confluence with the Columbia near what are now called the Tri-Cities of Richland, Kennewick, and Pasco,

Washington. The trail then continues west through the Columbia River Basin and river's deep gorge to the Pacific Ocean. It ends on the north side of the Columbia River estuary near the town of Ilwaco, Washington, and across the river at Fort Clatsop near Astoria, Oregon.

On the eastbound journey home, the expedition retraced most of its original route to "Travellers rest." There, the group divided. Captain Clark's party followed a southerly route to Three Forks and then went east along the Yellowstone River to its confluence with the Missouri. There, near Fort Union in western North Dakota, it rejoined Lewis's party, which had gone northeast along the Blackfoot River to the Great Falls of the Missouri, and continued northeast along the Missouri toward the Marias River, as they had come. On the final stretch of the journey back to St. Louis, the travelers took their original route, often camping at the same places they had on the westbound trip.

The Corps of Discovery's entire voyage covered over 8,000 miles and took nearly two and a half years. Contemporary guides to the trail often suggest doing one leg (i.e., St. Louis to the Pacific — rather than the round-trip) of the journey in a typical American two-week vacation. This is entirely possible, but only if you are willing to spend most of your time in a motor vehicle. Because this guidebook is designed to help people get off the main roads, out of their cars, and onto rivers and trails, it suggests that you plan to spend some time traveling well below the speed limit. This also means that you will probably want to choose a particular section — or sections — of the trail to explore.

For purposes of geographic orientation and historical logic, this book is organized regionally, dividing the trail into six sections: **Missouri, Nebraska, and South Dakota,** which takes in the opposite banks of the river in Illinois, Iowa, and Kansas; **North Dakota and eastern Montana; central and western Montana and across Lolo Pass into Idaho,** which includes the Yellowstone country of Clark's return route; **Idaho and eastern Washington;** the **Columbia Basin: central Washington and Oregon;** and the **lower Columbia River to the Pacific.**

Within each of these sections are about ten suggested explorations, hikes, or river trips — in some cases bike trips — that can be done as day trips or as overnight backpack or camping trips. Also included are a number of short hikes or walks. Descriptions of the explorations include approximate round-trip distance, elevation gain if it is a factor, and recommended time of year, as well as information about the landscape and wildlife both as Lewis and Clark saw it and as it is now. It will be for the reader to decide whether the hike is one for the two- and five-year-olds, for a seventy-one-year-old mother who does not like heights, for newcomers to backcountry exploration, or for those with more outdoor experience. Because I hope readers will want to become actively engaged in protecting the landscape they enjoy, I have also included some discussion of the environmental issues facing these places and in some cases mention related conservation efforts.

This guide is designed for independent travel, so commercially guided or organized trips are mentioned primarily in connection with rental of boats, bicycles, or other such equipment. In general, I have refrained from naming individual businesses but instead point readers to the locations where these services can be found. When I have named them, it is by way of orientation rather than to promote a particular business. (Apart from one short trip I took with Sierra Club staff, I received no complimentary, discounted, or subsidized services, equipment, or goods in the writing of this book.) Wherever possible, I refer to public agencies as sources of further information. Once off the freeway or interstate, you will often be traveling in country where amenities such as food, fuel, and indoor accommodations are few and far between, so where relevant, that information is noted as well.

As one guidebook I have read puts it, "No guidebook can alert you to every possible safety hazard or anticipate the abilities . . . of every reader. . . . You assume all risks and . . . full responsibility for your own safety."[2] This is especially true for river trips, where conditions change constantly. And boaters, no matter how good a swimmer you are or how hot and sunny the day, please wear your life jackets at all times. Respect the weather, be sensible about your own stamina and physical abilities (and those of all in your party), stay properly hydrated, leave no trace, and enjoy yourself.

Looking at the Landscape

Despite the changes that have taken place since the early 1800s, many places in the regions explored by Lewis and Clark look — at least at first glance — much as they did 200 years ago. Many others, however, do not. This is particularly true in the grasslands, prairies, and Great Plains. In the American spirit of putting the landscape to work, settlers replaced many of the native plant communities with cultivated crops and with forage grasses to nourish domestic livestock — a process that coincided with the displacement of Native Americans. Agriculture has so thoroughly taken over in the Great Plains and prairies that one has to search to find any substantial extent of native vegetation. Similarly, domestic livestock has so long had access to western grasslands that we have become accustomed to seeing that landscape altered by grazing and unnatural patterns of vegetation. Likewise, logging, fire suppression, tree plantations, and development have changed the natural patterns of forest cover. And when looking at rivers today, we so often see water that has been slowed by dams, wetlands that have been drained, and riverbanks that have been hardened, that we have almost come to assume that is what a river should look like.

As you explore the landscape of the Lewis and Clark Trail, I hope you will develop an eye for differentiating between where the land retains its natural patterns and where it has been altered. Learn the names of wildflowers and plants; get a sense of what grows where. Learn the names of mountains. Take a good look at river stones and the insects that thrive along the water's edge. Spend some time walking cross-country, off trails, and learn to guide yourself with a topographic map and compass. Learn to identify a bird by its song. Learn to identify tracks and scat. When you are watching for wildlife, learn the signs of a community of animals, especially when raptors and predators are present. I like to think of this as getting to know the neighborhood rather than as preparation for a quiz. In an era when preservation of imperiled species and landscapes has become urgent, it seems to me important to know what we have with us. There is no need to keep your nose buried in a field guide while you are out and about, but look carefully and remember what you have seen. You can look it up later or describe it to someone who knows.

When to Go

Deciding where to go along the trail will likely be influenced by when you can travel and how much time you have to spend. Because summer, with its long days and mild nights, is the most reliable time of year for good outdoor weather, many people will choose that season for hiking, camping, and paddling trips. Spring and fall may be good choices for exploring the eastern section of the trail, where summer can be as humid and sultry as Lewis and Clark noted in their journals. Bear in mind that in summer, along many parts of the trail, the mosquitoes (and other insects), as Lewis and Clark noted frequently, can be very "troublesome."

In the mountainous high country of Montana and Idaho, as well as the Oregon and Washington Cascades, snow can fall as early as late August or September and linger well into May and June, so inquire locally when you can about road conditions and river levels. East of the Cascades and west of the Dakotas, wildfires are common in summer, so pay attention to those reports, as well as to fire precautions. Many fires are caused by lightning strikes, but the majority of recent large fires were caused by humans. Afternoon thunderstorms may build anywhere east of the Cascade Mountains in the summer, so always travel prepared for rain. Some places along the trail are ideal for cross-country skiing, so some winter exploring options are noted as well, as are suggestions for seasonal wildlife viewing.

As anyone who spends much time outdoors and in the backcountry knows, wherever you are — whether paddling the Missouri River Breaks or the lower Columbia River, hiking in the Bitterroots or the Dakota grasslands, biking the Katy Trail, or cross-country skiing along the Knife River — it is important to be mindful of the weather and the extent of daylight, and to be ready to tailor your plans accordingly. Fancy gear is no substitute for common sense. The Corps of Discovery carried 100 quills, a pound of sealing wax, one metal sextant, and one compass but no cell phone.

Maps

Thanks to Lewis and Clark — and the many who have come after — there is now a wealth of maps to choose from for plotting a journey along their trail. For travel along major stretches of highway (both interstate and local), state highway maps are extremely helpful. These can be obtained through a state's department of transportation or tourist bureau, and many can be ordered through official state Web sites. Addresses for these and phone numbers are listed here in Appendix C, "Public Agencies, Sources of Maps, and Other Useful Information." Some maps are available on-line. When you are on the road, you may also find state highway maps in national forest and park visitor centers, as well as at local U.S. Forest Service and Bureau of Land Management offices.

For old back roads, major hiking trails, and topographic detail, however, you will need something more informative. There are numerous options. In the western states, where there is a lot of public land, the U.S. Forest Service and Bureau of Land Management publish maps of the areas they administer, many of which coincide with the Lewis and Clark Trail. National forest, national grassland, and Bureau of Land Management maps can be obtained through their local offices and Web sites. For the areas described in this book, contact information for maps is listed along with the individual explorations. The government agency home page information is listed in Appendix C. Individual regional national forest maps are also available at some commercial outlets — generally local outdoor outfitting stores.

The National Park Service offers a brochure with a schematic map of the whole Lewis and Clark Trail and its historic landmarks. This can be ordered through the National Park Service's Lewis and Clark National Historic Trail office in Omaha, Nebraska. Contact information is listed in Appendix C. There is also map information on-line through the maps link at http://www.nps.gov/lecl. This brochure is also available through the National Park Service specialist at the Forest Service's Lewis and Clark Interpretive Center in Great Falls, Montana. The phone number is 406-727-8733; Web site: http://www.fs.fed.us/r1/lewisclark/lcic.htm.

The detailed maps of national parks are also extremely useful. Again, these can be obtained at national park visitor centers (information listed with the explorations here). This series of maps is also available at many commercial outlets, particularly at outdoor gear stores and through some bookstores. It is always best to call ahead to find out if your local merchant has the map you want in stock.

State "recreation maps" are available that highlight national wildlife refuges, state parks, established boat launch sites, campsites, and other such outdoor activity locations. Again, these may be available through outdoor outfitting stores and bookstores that carry maps in their travel departments. Visitor centers at national forests and wildlife refuges, national and state parks, and Bureau of Land Management headquarters often carry these as well.

For those who relish finding their way in the backcountry and are planning to explore relatively small areas, especially for those planning to walk cross-country, 7.5′ (the prime stands for "minute") topographic, or "topo," quad maps — as they have come to be called — are essential. An excellent source for these is the U.S. Geological Survey (the folks who make the maps). See its Web site at http://mapping.usgs.gov and follow the links for the maps that interest you. Or you can call 800-ASK-USGS. Some outdoor outfitting stores and other commercial outlets carry local and regional topo maps, but it is unlikely that you'll find topo maps of Oregon in Vermont.

The most useful all-purpose maps I have found that have full geographic, topographic, and road details are the *Atlas & Gazetteer* series published by DeLorme. Organized by state, these maps are both thorough and manageable. They are easy to find through regular bookstores and many other places where maps are sold, though you may have to special order the volumes for states outside your local region. (And, yes, I bought all of mine retail and have no financial investment in or connection to the company.) A combination of these atlases and Forest Service, Bureau of Land Management, or topo maps is ideal.

Step one in preparing to follow the Lewis and Clark Trail is deciding where along the trail you would like to go. Then you can begin the delicious process of poring over your maps and imagining your journey.

General Preparations

Background Information

Take along a copy of *The Journals of Lewis and Clark*. At the end of the day it is fun to compare your observations with theirs. Take your pick of the one-volume, paperback editions, but do note that individual editors have selected different entries. See "Bibliography and Recommended Reading" for other books about the expedition and its geography that you may want to consult.

Field Guides

Among the pleasures of exploring the country around the Lewis and Clark Trail are the different communities of flora and fauna you will encounter. While it has been two hundred years since Lewis and Clark penned their descriptions of sage grouse, pronghorn, cutthroat trout, ragged robin, and Lewis's monkey flower, seeing them for yourself—particularly for the first time—is exciting. There are many field guides to choose from, and everyone seems to have their favorites, so choose ones that satisfy your level of curiosity and are organized in a way that you find helpful. (A number are listed here under "Bibliography and Recommended Reading.")

Driving

Your primary form of transportation will probably be motor vehicle rather than keelboat or pirogue, so make sure your vehicle and its tires are in reasonably good shape before heading out into unfamiliar territory. Breaking down in the remote reaches of the Charles M. Russell National Wildlife Refuge or on a narrow

Missouri farm road is not most people's idea of a good time. And, remember, cell phones are often useless in such locations.

It may be a long way between fueling stops — and not all towns have gas stations — so fill up when you can. All the travel in this book can be done in a normal passenger car, but do pay attention to signs warning of rocks — they do fall — and be aware of the contour and condition of dirt roads, especially if you are driving a rental car with less clearance than the vehicle you usually drive. When driving in the high country and over mountain passes, you may be surprised by the weather, so carry chains or other traction devices. If a road is too slick or soft from recent rain or snow, or if you encounter unexpected obstacles, ice, snow, mud, or water hazards, be prepared to alter your plans. Even pros can get themselves into hazardous and embarrassing fixes by attempting to ford running streams, mud holes, and snowbanks. If you are traveling on roads that traverse land with gated fences, make sure you leave the gate as you found it, which is probably closed. Easterners and city dwellers will no doubt enjoy the challenge of opening and shutting those barbed wire gates. And since you are a considerate traveler and leave no trace in the outdoors, you will ignore all the macho-gonzo vehicle advertising you see and *stay on existing roads*.

Skills and Equipment

Apart from kayaking, canoeing, or rafting and winter sports, the explorations in this book require no special skills or practice, but they do assume that you are in good enough physical shape to undertake what you have chosen to do. If you are unaccustomed to hiking or backpacking at higher elevations, consider acclimatizing for a day or so before you set out on a strenuous high-altitude backpacking trip. This book also assumes that readers who have experience in the outdoors are familiar with the ethics and practices of no-trace camping. (It means just what it says.) But there is a first time for everyone, so if you are not traveling with someone who knows his or her way around backcountry camping, see the "Bibliography and Recommended Reading" section for expert advice.

As for gear, day hikes, backpacking, car camping, and river trips (daylong or multiday) obviously call for — or accommodate — different equipment. There are, however, some basics. Rain gear, extra clothing to stay dry and/or warm (small, warm hat, gloves), flashlight (bring extra batteries and bulb just in case), first aid kit (know what is in it and how to use it), extra food and water, sunglasses, shade hat and sunscreen, whistle, compass and map, matches or other fire starter, and a knife are some essentials that will help ensure a comfortable and safe round-trip. Remember to take stock of your supplies and check your itinerary for access to food shopping, drinking water, ice, and cooking fuel, particularly if you are on an extended trip. And do yourself a favor and break in the new hiking boots *before* the backpacking trip.

Other useful items to keep in your expedition vehicle include resealable plastic bags — it is worth springing for the ones that actually stay shut — toilet paper, a sponge, garbage bags, larger flashlight, dish towel, work gloves, tarp, some rope, small shovel, extra gallon or two of drinking water, tent, sleeping bag, blanket, cooler for perishable food, and small stove with fuel. Plastic storage boxes with snap-tight lids are a good way to keep your gear organized and ready to go. Comfort needs vary, but something dry to sit on is always nice, as is a pillow if you are car camping. It's a good idea to make a checklist and actually check it — along with the working condition of any equipment like flashlights, tents, mattresses, and stoves — before you leave home. And if you are embarking on outdoor and backcountry adventures for the first time, consider borrowing or renting gear such as tents, sleeping bags, sleeping pads, backpacks, and stoves to see if these are investments you will want to make.

You will undoubtedly have some quiet, or "down," time along the way, so don't forget to bring some reading matter (preferably a paperback and one that isn't too valuable to risk getting damp or beat up). If you are so inclined, a sketchbook can be fun. Binoculars make for much better bird- and wildlife watching, so bring a pair along if you can.

Permits

Whereas Lewis and Clark enlisted the help of tribal members to guide them with safe passage through the territories of various Indian nations and brought gifts of beads, tobacco, fish hooks, and silk ribbon in exchange, present-day travelers need parking permits to leave their vehicles at many trailheads on state park, national forest, national wildlife refuge, National Park Service, and other public lands.

The details of fees and permit requirements change frequently and vary from state to state and areas within a state. Because places to purchase permits are usually located far from trailheads, it is wise to call ahead or to stop at the first ranger station or visitor center you see en route to your hiking destination. Contact information is listed at the back of this book and along with individual explorations. As of this writing, trailhead parking passes are required for most national forests in Oregon and Washington and in some national recreation areas, such as the Sawtooth National Recreation Area in Idaho. National parks usually require a vehicle entrance fee. (Many require payment by cash or check.) If you are planning on visiting several national parks in one year, the yearlong pass may make economic sense because it also covers select historic landmarks and other sites.

A great many state parks charge day-use fees. Most developed campsites, whether on state or federal land, charge a pay-as-you-stay on-site fee. (Bring some checks or cash because most of these campsites have unattended drop boxes where it is not possible to use a credit card.) Some now also have an advance reservation system, so if you are planning to camp in a popular park at a popular vacation time, it is worth calling ahead to assess the situation. When backcountry camping, off-trail hiking, or selecting a riverside campsite or rest stop, be aware of and respect boundaries of public, tribal, and private land.

Caveats

TREADING LIGHTLY: RESPECTING CULTURAL SITES AND ARTIFACTS   I like to think that readers of this book are the kind of travelers and modern-day explorers who know to leave the landscape as they have found it, and that they are able to resist any impulse to disturb artifacts or leave a mark of their passing. Yet simply because there are so many of us, and so many people are expected to visit the Lewis and Clark Trail in the next few years, it is worth mentioning again. Pack *everything* out, even if it means bringing extra plastic bags for your nasty garbage.

Parts of the trail traverse country sacred to Indian tribes and lead to historic and cultural sites that may include artifacts. These *must* be respected and left undisturbed. Tempting as it may be, try not to touch. It is hard to tell an ancient cairn or rock pile from a piece of modern art, so err on the side of caution and leave these exactly as you find them.

Similarly, refrain from picking wildflowers and plants. Many places along the Lewis and Clark Trail are home to rare, threatened, and endangered species that are often difficult to identify or distinguish from their more common relatives and neighbors. Please do not harass or attempt to feed animals of any kind. If you are an angler or hunter, always follow local regulations. Dogs make wonderful hiking and camping companions, but follow any rules about dogs on trails and please make sure they behave as you would like other humans to do. Make sure your pets do not leave messes behind, destroy the landscape or artifacts, or harass other animals (including unfamiliar humans!).

INVASIVE SPECIES   The history of exotic, invasive species, alas, is not a new one in the annals of North America. Early European explorers and settlers often brought plants and animals with them to the New World to replicate the domestic life they had known at home. Other species — like the European rat — came as stowaways. The Europeans also brought diseases, some of which were devastating to the continent's native people.

Some of the Old World species — the rock dove, starling, and song sparrow — quickly naturalized and have become so much a part of the American landscape that it is hard to imagine life without them. Some, like the gypsy moth, were brought with industrious intention — it was hoped gypsy moths could be used to produce silk — but noxious results. The influx of exotic species continues in a similar way today, their speed of travel greatly increased by the pace and frequency of modern transportation. Some invasive species, like the zebra mussel, have arrived on this continent in the ballast water of cargo ships, but they and others easily can be — and are — spread unwittingly by tourists and recreational and business travelers.

There is concern that travelers retracing the Lewis and Clark Trail will, simply out of ignorance, spread invasive species. Aquatic species can stow away in small amounts of water lingering in boats and on boat trailers, fishing tackle, and other watersports gear and equipment. Vegetation — both aquatic and terrestrial — can be carried on shoes, socks, and other clothing, as well as on vehicles, pets, and camping and boating gear. While one does not want to be an alarmist, it is better to err on the side of caution and take the time to clear off burrs, seeds, bits of grass, and leaves and to dry (and when possible wash down) boating equipment when leaving a trailhead or takeout. Think of these measures as companions to leave-no-trace camping and the task will not seem so onerous.

PART II

The Trail

CHAPTER 4

Illinois, Iowa, Missouri, Nebraska, and South Dakota

Camp Wood and Environs of Wood River, Illinois, near St. Louis, Missouri

MONDAY MAY 14TH. 1804

I set out at 4 oClock P.M, in the presence of many of the neighbouring inhabitents, and proceeded on under a jentle brease up the Missourie to the upper Point of the 1st Island 4 Miles and camped. . . . opposite the mouth of a Small Creek called Cold water, a heavy rain this after-noon.

Today, the site of **Camp Wood** (on Illinois Route 3, about 4 miles north of I-270, north of East St. Louis) near the Wood River — which Lewis and Clark called by its French name, Dubois — on the eastern shore of the confluence of the Missouri and Mississippi Rivers, is not a wild or scenic place. Power lines, oil tanks, smoke-stacks, and factories cluster by the highway where a historic marker commemorates the first Lewis and Clark expedition camp-site. The actual site itself has disappeared with migration of the river channel. When I visited there in early 2001, ground was being broken for a new visitor and interpretive center.

To get a sense of what this landscape was like when Captain Clark wrote his opening journal entries, travel a few miles southeast to **Cahokia Mounds State Historic Site** in Collinsville, Illinois, and nearby **Horseshoe Lake State Park.**

Horseshoe Lake State Park is an isolated old oxbow bend of the Mississippi River with a small island reachable by causeway where there is a level, 4-mile bird-watching trail. Many species of waterfowl and woods and grassland birds can be seen here: bluebirds, which are endangered in Illinois, wood ducks, marsh hawks, eastern meadowlarks, green herons, and killdeer among them. The lake is also a stopover for great flocks of white pelicans migrating between their summer habitat in northern Missouri, Iowa, and points north and their winter habitat in Louisiana and Texas. Huge numbers of white pelicans converge at Horseshoe Lake in the fall, in the second half of October, and in late March. These birds are an astounding sight. Hunting is permitted in the park, so it is wise to check on season dates and to wear some safety-orange if walking there in hunting season.

North America's eastern deciduous woodlands and central grasslands coincide in this part of the country to create what is called the Midwest oak savanna. Yet very little of this native pattern of vegetation remains — perhaps no more than 0.02 percent of the estimated historic 30 million acres.[1] But where the woods have been preserved, you will find oak, sugar maple, ferns, and a host of wildflowers.

Horseshoe Lake State Park is off Highway 111 about 2.5 miles north of Highways 55, 70, and 40 between Collinsville and Granite City, Illinois. For more information call 618-931-0280, or see http://www.dnr.state.il.us/lands/landmgt/PARKS/HORSESP.HTM or http://www.dnr.state.il.us and follow the links for state parks.

Cahokia Mounds

Near Camp Wood, while exploring the Mississippi River floodplains, Captain Clark is said to have come across the remains of

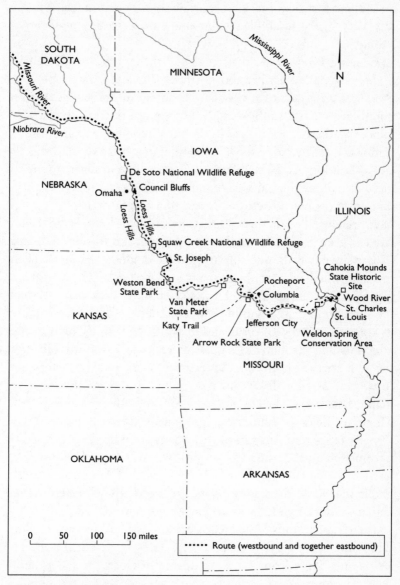

Map 2 The Lower Missouri.

an "Indian fortification" that contained earthen mounds. What he saw very likely resembled what one can see today at Cahokia Mounds.

Cahokia Mounds are the remains of the largest, most extensive prehistoric native civilization north of Mexico. The people who lived here were part of a woodland farming culture that grew corn, pumpkins, squash, sunflowers, and other seed-bearing plants. They hunted, gathered, and fished in the surrounding rivers and forests. Cahokia is estimated to have been larger in A.D. 1250 than was the city of London. At the state historic site are the astonishing series of mounds built by the Cahokia Indians. One of the mounds has a base that covers some 14 acres and rises to a height of 100 feet. Steps have been installed on this mound for visitors to climb. From the top you can get a good sense of this river bottom and woods landscape.

The site has walking trails around the mounds and an excellent museum filled with artifacts from archaeological excavations at Cahokia. The siting of the 2,200-acre park is such that although the surrounding area is suburban, commercial, and industrial, on its trails, the sound of birds and of wind blowing in the branches and whistling through grass takes precedence. A nature trail leads through areas of bottomland forest of American elm, eastern cottonwood, black willow, pin oak, white ash, persimmon, silver maple, hackberry, blackberry, dogwood, and other deciduous trees. There are fields of bluegrass, rose, and hedge rose planted with Osage orange and Russian olive, and seasonal marshes formed by a former channel of the Mississippi River. Watch for meadowlarks, hawks, red-winged blackbirds, bobwhites, and American kestrels, and in the wet areas, snowy egrets, great and little blue herons, and yellow-crowned and black-crowned night herons.

Cahokia Mounds State Historic Site is located west of Collinsville, Ilinois, off I-55, 70, and 255, 8 miles east of St. Louis. The site is open daily from 8 A.M. to dusk; it is closed on federal holidays. The interpretive center is open from 9:00 to 5:00. Admission is free. For more information call 618-346-5160 or see http://www.cahokiamounds.com. The site is administered by the Illinois Historic Preservation Society and has been designated a World Heritage Site by UNESCO.

Up the Missouri to St. Charles and Rocheport along the Katy Trail

JUNE 6TH. WEDNESDAY 1804

Mended our Mast this morning & Set out at 7 oClock under a jentle breese from the S.E. by S passed the large Island, and a Creek Called Split rock Creek [Perche Creek] . . . the water excessively Strong, so much so that we Camped Sooner than the usual time.

JUNE 7TH. THURSDAY 1804

a Short distance above the mouth of [a] Creek, in Several Courious paintings and carving on the projecting rock of Limestone inlade with white red & blue flint, of a verry good quality, the Indians have taken of this flint great quantities. We landed at this Inscription and found it a Den of Rattle Snakes. . . . our Hunters brought in three Bears this evening, and informs that the Countrey thro: which they passed from the last Creek is fine, rich land, & well watered.

From its headwaters in the Rocky Mountains on the east side of the Continental Divide in Montana to its confluence with the Mississippi where the rivers form the border between Missouri and Illinois, the **Missouri River** flows for over 2,300 miles, draining one-sixth of the United States. The Missouri River Basin takes in ten states and is home to about 10 million people and twenty-eight Native American tribes.[2] The Missouri was left behind in the wake of the Ice Age, and melting glaciers carved the river's canyons, bluffs, and great, wide floodplain valley. In its natural state, the Missouri flooded regularly and meandered across its valley. In the process, the Missouri's banks were constantly being eroded and rebuilt. The river's movement continually created new braided channels, oxbow bends, sloughs, backwaters, sandbars, and islands, all of which are important nurturing habitat for aquatic and riparian flora and fauna.

The meandering river created a rich ecosystem with fertile

The Katy Trail. Photo: Rails to Trails Conservancy.

bottomlands, deciduous forests, marshes, and prairies full of wild-flowers. The Missouri River valley was home to a great diversity of wildlife, including wolf, bear, herds of bison, deer, elk, river otter, and great numbers of birds — among them blue heron, egret, curlew, cormorant, bittern, grebe, killdeer, rail, sandpiper, and the interior least tern, bald eagle, and piping plover, which are now listed under the federal Endangered Species Act. The river itself was home to a wealth of fish — including now-endangered pallid sturgeon, along with paddlefish, chub, and gar — and other aquatic species. Many of these species are still present in and around the Missouri; others have disappeared.

Today, 35 percent of the Missouri River is impounded by dams (the largest reservoir system in the country), 32 percent of the river has been channelized,[3] and over 90 percent of its flood-plain has been converted to agriculture.[4] The dams, deepwater reservoirs, levees, stabilized banks, and dikes along the river's main stem and many tributaries have significantly altered the Missouri's ecosystem, imperiling many species of native plants and animals. The lower Missouri River traveled by Lewis and Clark was wide and shallow. Today, the lower river has been dredged, straightened, and narrowed to facilitate commercial navigation. Straightening, narrowing, and dredging the river and hardening its banks have made the river much deeper, swifter, and colder than it was 200 years ago.

High spring flows that used to travel downstream with the great loads of sediment that earned the Missouri the name "Big Muddy" are now trapped in reservoirs behind dams, which also block migration of the river's native fish. Channelization has elim-inated the braids, sandbars, and backwaters and changed the nature of the river's wetlands. This development has eliminated over 350,000 acres of the Missouri's natural floodplain, shortened the river by 72 miles, and caused 127 miles of shoreline habitat to be lost.[5] As currently operated by the Army Corps of Engineers, Missouri River dams release reservoir water in the summer and fall, a flow regime contrary to the river's natural pattern. These changes to their native habitat have caused populations of many Missouri River birds and fish to decline, and many are now listed as state and federal threatened or endangered species.

Local and national conservation groups are now working with government agencies in a slow and difficult process to restore some natural conditions to the Missouri — including managing the dams to mimic a more natural river flow — so as to restore habitat and protect river species. The Sierra Club's Missouri River Basin states chapters are involved in this effort, as is American Rivers through its Missouri River campaign. For more information on these, contact the Sierra Club North Dakota and South Dakota chapters and American Rivers' Nebraska or Washington, D.C., office. Or see http://www.amrivers.org or http://savethemissouri.org. (See Appendix B for regional contact information.)

Along the lower Missouri, if you are traveling west upstream from St. Louis, one of the best ways to see the river is from the **Katy Trail State Park**. The Katy Trail is a walking and biking trail that runs from St. Charles to Clinton, Missouri, on the bed of the old Missouri-Kansas-Texas Railroad (hence the nickname Katy for MK&T). At 225 miles, the Katy Trail is now the country's longest rails-to-trails project and the longest nonmotorized portion of the Lewis and Clark Trail. Without actually getting yourself on the river, the Katy Trail is one of the best places to spend time next to the lower Missouri without sharing the experience with motor vehicles.

The Katy Trail runs right along the river between St. Charles and Booneville, Missouri (trail mileposts 39 to 192). One of the most scenic sections of the trail is between Hartsburg and Rocheport. There high limestone bluffs rise above the riverbanks — and the trail — on the north side of the river. This section of the trail will take you past the Eagle Bluffs Conservation Area near Perche Creek, where Lewis and Clark camped on June 6, 1804, and to "the projecting rock of Limestone" Clark mentioned in his journal entry of June 7, 1804.

The trail is flat and wide, surfaced in crushed limestone, and gains hardly any elevation for most of its length, so it can be tackled by riders of any ability. Trees line the trail, and benches have been placed at convenient intervals for rest stops and river viewing. There are toilets at most trailheads, but no drinking water.

Bicycles can be rented in St. Charles, Rocheport, Columbia (a spur of the trail goes into Columbia), and other trailside towns, but call ahead to check on availability and rental shop hours. Also, if you are concerned about having a bike helmet, panniers, and a comfy seat for an extended trip, inquire in advance about their availability if you are renting. Do the same for availability of child seats, children's bikes, and tandems. It is best to pack water and any meals or snacks you will want on your ride, as commercial establishments directly adjacent to the trail are few. Those that are available are very welcoming to Katy Trail bikers. There is no public camping along the trail, but there are places to camp, with permission, on private land or for a fee. A number of towns along the trail have bed-and-breakfasts that accommodate and welcome bikers, and shuttles can be arranged through some of the bed-and-breakfasts and bike shops to those places not directly connected with the trail.

Spring and fall are the recommended seasons because of the cooler weather and changing foliage.

Recommended Katy Trail Day Trip

Rocheport (milepost 179) to Easley (milepost 162), Wilton (milepost 157), or Hartsburg (milepost 153). Consider Hermann to Rocheport for a two-day trip, stopping for the night in Jefferson City. If riding west beginning in St. Charles, consider exploring the Weldon Spring Conservation Area at milepost 55, where there are hiking trails.

If you begin in Rocheport and are heading toward Hartsburg, ride a couple of extra miles upstream from Rocheport to the MK&T train tunnel, where the trail goes underneath the limestone cliffs that hug the river. If you continue upriver to milepost 175, you can see the Lewis and Clark Cave at Torbettt Spring, above which are the remains of a petroglyph, not far from where Clark sketched one in his journal on June 5, 1804, at a place called "Little Manitou Creek." Today this is called Moniteau Creek, and it runs into the Missouri at Rocheport. *Manitou* is said to be an Indian word for "Great Spirit," these bluffs being sacred to several local tribes.

The trail crosses Perche Creek at milepost 169 near the town of McBaine. Watch for osprey, great blue herons, egrets, plover, cardinals, Canada geese, ravens, and woodchucks. Migrating white

EXPLORING THE LOWER MISSOURI RIVER VALLEY

From the back roads and hiking and bike trails along and near the lower Missouri River, you can see the pleats and bends of wooded hills that rise above the river's wide, flat floodplain. If you look carefully, you can get a good sense of how the Missouri once wandered across the valley. Much of this valley is now planted with orchards growing apples and peaches or with fields of corn, soybeans, and tobacco. Because so much of the valley and floodplain have been converted to agricultural fields and otherwise developed, it is a bit of a challenge to find places where the land looks as it might have 200 years ago. State parks, con-servation areas, wildlife refuges, national forests, and other preserves— although they are often limited in extent—offer the best chance to get a feel for the natural terrain of the lower Missouri.

Bear in mind as you visit these sequestered pockets that many national wildlife refuges were created in tandem with local farming programs. Many of them lease land within their boundaries for farming, and many have been managed to ecourage huntable waterfowl. Thus, while they are generally bucolic and pastoral, and havens for birds and other wildlife, many national wildlife refuges are not wild.

pelicans and sandhill cranes may also be seen near the Eagle Bluffs Conservation area there.

For more information on the Katy Trail, contact the Missouri Department of Natural Resources at 800-334-6946 or the Katy Trail Headquarters at 660-882-8196, or visit http://www. mostateparks.com/katytrail.htm. Also consult *The Katy Trail Guidebook* by Brett Dufur (Pebble Publishing, 1999), available from the publisher at 573-698-3903 in Rocheport, Missouri, or www.pebblepublishing.com.

Arrow Rock State Park and Historic Site

9TH OF JUNE 1804 SATTURDAY

we got fast on a Snag Soon after we Set out which detained us a short time passed the upper Point of the Island, Several Small Chanels running out of the River below a Bluff &

Prarie (Called the Prarie of Arrows) where the river is confined within the width of 300 yds.

The Arrow Rock bluffs have been a well-known Missouri River landmark since before French trappers traveled the river in the late 1600s and the early eighteenth century. The French trappers called them *pierre à fleche*, or "rock of arrows." Arrow Rock State Park and Historic Site are located on Missouri Highway 41 on the west bank of the river in Saline County, about 14 miles north of I-70 and about 6 miles west of Booneville. The park sits on a high bluff overlooking the river, where there are developed campsites, picnic tables, and shelters. There is a short (1.5-mile), primitive hiking trail that leads through the woods from the bluffs; it connects with another trail accessible from the visitor center that passes a spring used by travelers on the Santa Fe Trail. The visitor center and trailhead are a short walk from the main street of Arrow Rock, which is in its entirety a national historic landmark.

PADDLING THE LOWER MISSOURI BY CANOE OR KAYAK

Although it is possible to canoe or kayak the lower Missouri between Booneville and St. Charles, and there are public access points on the river every 20 to 25 miles, river conditions do not make this a particularly popular activity. As noted earlier, in Lewis and Clark's day, the lower Missouri was wide and shallow. Straightening and dredging of the river to accommodate barge traffic, along with the hardening and berming of its banks, have increased its depth considerably. This, in turn, increases the speed of the current—up to 7 miles an hour in the lower river—which can make conditions for paddling difficult.

Two reaches of the lower Missouri have been designated a national recreation river. One lies between Fort Randall Dam and the Niobrara River (which meets the Missouri just south of the South Dakota–Nebraska border), the other between Gavins Point Dam and Ponca, Nebraska. Both can be paddled. But as with farther downstream, the deepened channel and water releases from the dams make for a swift current. The fast water combined with the strong winds that often blow here can create difficult conditions.

Missouri and Osage Indians lived here, and artifacts dating back to 3000 B.C. have been found in the vicinity. The Osage, like other Missouri River tribes, farmed corn, squash, pumpkin, and beans in the fertile bottomlands, fished in the river, and hunted duck, deer, turkey, buffalo, and other game in the woods and surrounding plains.

Lewis and Clark's party made an excursion to the salt licks around Arrow Rock, for which Boone's Lick County — now called Saline County — was named. Salt making was an important local industry in the early 1800s because salt was in demand for curing meat and tanning hides. Hemp was grown here in a lucrative rope-making trade that thrived until the 1850s, when wire took the place of much of the rope used on ships. In the 1820s the prairies around Arrow Rock were among the first of America's grasslands plains to have their sod busted for wheat and corn, changing — most likely forever — the nature of local wildlife and native vegetation.

In 1820 the Osage chief Soldat du Chêne, who was negotiating with the U.S. government on his tribe's behalf, said to the American settlers:

> I see and admire your manner of living, your good warm
> houses, your extensive fields of corn, your gardens, your
> cows, your workhorses, wagons and a thousand machines
> that I know not the use of. I see that you are able to clothe
> yourselves even from weeds and grass. In short, you do almost
> what you choose. You whites possess the power of subduing
> almost every animal to your use. You are surrounded by
> slaves. Everything about you is in chains, and you are slaves
> yourselves. I fear if I should exchange my pursuits for yours,
> I too should become a slave. Talk to my sons, perhaps they
> may be persuaded to adopt your fashions . . . but as for myself
> I was born free, was raised free and wish to die free.[6]

Because of their location on the border between North and South, Arrow Rock and surrounding communities had a particularly difficult time and played a troublesome role during the Civil War and Reconstruction.

A visitor center museum at Arrow Rock tells the history of the area. For information and visitor center hours, call 660-837-3330.

The visitor center is open daily from 10:00 A.M. to 5:00 P.M. in June, July, and August and from 10:00 A.M. to 4:00 P.M. the rest of the year. Or see http://www.mostateparks.com/arrowrock.htm.

Van Meter State Park

15TH JUNE, FRIDAY 1804 —

continued up pass two other small islands and camped on the S.S. nearly opposit the antient Village of the Little Osages . . . the osage were settled at the foot [of] a hill in a butifull Plain which extends back quite to the Osage River . . . next to the river is an ellegant Bottom Plain which extends several miles in length on the river . . . The river, at this place is about one [Clark originally estimated 3] mile wide.

The remains of the Missouri village that Lewis and Clark saw are now encompassed by Van Meter State Park, located just to the southeast of the Missouri River near the tiny town of Miami, Missouri. The park's 983 acres include 114 acres that are designated a natural forest area. Several short hiking trails wind through the woods around the remains of mounds used by the Missouri Indians who lived in the area through the 1700s. Trails skirt the 6 acres of mounds known as the "old fort," circle Lake Wooldridge, and climb a prairie area of Loess Hills known as the Pinnacles and Devil's Backbone. The Pinnacles are rugged, serrated ridges of loess soil, the Devil's Backbone a ridge in the southern part of the Pinnacles. The woods here contain chinquapin, basswood, walnut, oak, and pawpaw. The park's wetlands harbor endangered snails and some rare species of plants. Watch for deer, owls, geese, and snakes. This is a good place to stretch your legs and survey the scenery, but remember that summer is often very humid and buggy here.

The Old Fort Trail (0.8 mile), the Loess Hills Trail (2 miles), and Lakeview Trail (0.7 mile) are accessible from parking areas and are near picnic tables, shelters, and campsites in the park. A visitor center has exhibits depicting the history and natural history of the area.

For more information call Van Meter State Park at 660-886-7537. Summer hours are Monday through Saturday: 10:00 A.M. to 4:00 P.M.; Sunday: 1:00 P.M. to 4:00 P.M. Call ahead for winter hours, or check the Web site at http://www.dnr.state.mo.us. The park is in Miami, Missouri, off Highways 41 and 122, about 12 miles northwest of Marshall, Missouri.

Squaw Creek National Wildlife Refuge: The Loess Hills

JULY 12TH. THURSDAY 1804

after an early Brackfast I with five men in a Perogue assended the River Ne-Ma-haw about three Miles to the Mouth of a Small creek on the Lower Side, here I got out of the Perogue, after going to Several Small Mounds in a leavel plain, I assended a hill on the Lower Side, on this hill Several artificial Mounds were raised. From the top of the highest of those Mounds I had a most extensive view of the Serounding Plains. . . . The bottom land is covered with Grass of about 4 1/2 feet high, and appears leavel as a smoth surfice, . . . on the riseing lands, Small groves of trees are seen, with a number of Grapes and a Wild Cherry.

The Big Nemaha River flows into the Missouri from the west, in what is now Richardson County, Nebraska. Today a view similar to the one Clark described in his journal can be seen by climbing the short Loess Bluff trail (0.5 mile but 200 feet up) — be sure to take this climb if you can because the views are inspiring — and walking the Eagle Pool (1.5 miles, level) trails at the Squaw Creek National Wildlife Refuge near Mound City, Missouri. The loess bluffs were formed by wind-deposited soil following the retreat of the glaciers. On the bluff tops are some of the last remnants of native prairie.

The refuge was established in 1935. Migratory waterfowl flock to its over 7,100 acres of man-made marshes, which were created to partially make up for the loss of natural wetlands that occurred with the deepening and straightening of the Missouri River and development of its banks. Over 300 species of birds stop at the refuge, which is located between two major migratory bird corridors, the Central and Mississippi flyways, as do 31 kinds of mammals and 35 species of reptiles and amphibians.

White pelicans come through in the spring and early fall. Bald eagles arrive in late fall and early winter. Huge flocks of snow geese may be seen here in the fall. Most of these geese nest on the west coast of Hudson Bay and winter along the Gulf coast of Mexico. In the spring also watch for double-crested cormorants, pied-billed grebes, red-tailed hawks, great horned, barred, and eastern screech owls, red-winged and yellow-headed blackbirds, and many kinds of ducks, among a host of other birds.

February through April is the best time to see the greatest variety of migratory waterfowl. Mid-March through May is a good time to see wildflowers and hike the loess hills. Deer fawn and pheasant broods can be seen in June. From mid-August through mid-September, watch for white pelicans and cormorants, which also frequent the refuge in late March. Huge flocks of snow geese arrive in late October and November, followed by bald eagles from mid-November through January.

The refuge is also home to Franklin's ground squirrel, plains pocket gopher, the rare meadow jumping mouse, coyote, red and gray fox, mink, and white-tailed deer, which had disappeared from northwestern Missouri by 1910 and reappeared in the mid-1940s. The Squaw Creek Refuge is also home to the larger of the last two small, known populations of the eastern massasauga, a small species of rattlesnake that lives in the floodplain, wet prairies, marshes, and meadows of northern Missouri. Much of the snake's habitat has been converted to agriculture, reducing massasauga populations so that it is now listed as a Missouri state endangered species and is a candidate for listing under the federal Endangered Species Act. Massasauga migrate in spring and fall, traveling to and from their winter habitat. This is when they are most likely to be encountered by humans. The snakes frequently cross refuge roads and are in danger of being run over by cars, accidents that have contributed significantly to their decline.

Around the visitor center at the refuge are plantings of native

tallgrass prairie wildflowers. Among them are beardtongue, but-
terfly weed, great blue lobelia, little bluestem, purple coneflower,
rattlesnake master, rose verbena, wild petunia, blue wild indigo,
prairie smoke, and queen of the prairie. A number of the plants
and animals seen at the refuge had their first European American
descriptions in the journals of Lewis and Clark.

To tour the entire refuge and reach bird-watching spots, including the Eagle Pool, almost all visitors drive. Some roads may be
closed when wet. The bird-watching is first-rate here, and the loess
bluffs make the refuge a stop well worth making.

The refuge is just over 35 miles northwest of St. Joseph, Missouri,
and 3 miles west of I-29 on Highway 159, at exit 79. Refuge headquarters office hours are Monday through Friday from 7:30 A.M. to
4:00 P.M. For more information contact the Squaw Creek National
Wildlife Refuge, managed by the U.S. Fish and Wildlife Service of
the Department of the Interior, at 660-442-3187.

If you are traveling northwest, upstream along the Missouri from
Kansas City on your way toward St. Joseph, you can also get a sight
of the river from the high bluffs at **Weston Bend State Park**, where
there are 5 miles of wooded hiking trails and a 1-mile paved biking
trail, along with picnic sites and developed campsites. Weston Bend,
like Van Meter State Park, has the feel of midwestern or south central river valley country, whereas at Squaw Creek, the Great Plains
begin to become apparent, as Clark noted on July 15, 1804:

> I had at one part of the Prarie a verry extensive view of al the
> Countrey around up and down the river a Considerable dis-
> tance . . . the hills and under the hills between them & the
> river this plain appeared to extend 20 or 30 miles, those hills
> have but little timber, and the Plain appears to Continue back
> of them.

Weston Bend State Park is 1 mile south of Weston, Missouri, on
Highway 45 (take exit 20 from I-29 onto Highway 273, which
will lead to Highway 45) in a part of Missouri once inhabited by
the Fox, Sac, Iowa, and Kansas, who took advantage of the rich
river bottomlands for farming, hunting, and fishing. In the nineteenth century, white settlers grew hemp and tobacco here, and
tobacco is still a predominant local crop. There is a handful of old

tobacco barns in the park, which runs along a high ridge above the river. Bear in mind if visiting during summer months that the mosquitoes were "so troublesome" to Lewis and Clark's party that they were obliged to don nets. But do brave the bugs, if only long enough to walk out to the platform atop a bluff that gives a good view of the Missouri. For more information call 800-334-6946 or see http://www.mostateparks.com/westonbend.htm.

Continuing upriver into Nebraska and Iowa toward Omaha and Council Bluffs, north of St. Joseph, you will come to the **De Soto National Wildlife Refuge**, which, like Squaw Creek, is a stopping place along the fall migration route for thousands of snow geese. Lewis and Clark's party passed through this stretch of river on August 4 and 5, 1804. On August 4 Clark wrote in his journal:

> here the high Land is Some Distance from the river on both Sides, and at this place the High lands are at least 12 or 15 miles apart, the range of high land on the S.S. appear to contain Some timber that on the L.S. appear to be intirely clear of any thing but what is common in an open Plain, Some scattering timber or wood is to be Seen in the reveens, and where the Creeks pass into the Hill. The points and wet lands contain tall timber back of the willows which is generally situated back of a large Sand bar from the Points.

The next day he noted that,

> In every bend the banks are falling in from the current being thrown against those bends by the Sand points which inlarges and the Soil I believe from unquestionable appearens of the entire Bottom from one hill to the other being the Mud or Ooze of the river at some former Period mixed with Sand and Clay easily melts and Slips into the River.

On August 8 Lewis penned a detailed description of "some hundreds of Pelicans [white pelicans] . . . collected" on a sand bar and noted sighting of "the prairie hen or grouse . . . seen in the praries between the Missouri and the river platte." It was also in this vicinity that Lewis and Clark observed great numbers of geese and their first badger.

There are short (7/8-mile) hiking trails — one at the visitor center and two on the refuge proper — and 12 miles of paved and gravel roads with a self-guided interpretive tour of the birds and wildlife that may be seen. Almost 2,000 of the refuge's over 7,800 acres are farmed and managed to encourage migrating ducks, geese, deer, and pheasants. The refuge was created to help make up for the loss of habitat for wildlife and migratory waterfowl that occurred as the Missouri River's floodplain was converted to agriculture by draining wetlands, the river straightened to enhance navigation, and the banks hardened for flood control. Despite these great changes in the river valley, at the De Soto National Wildlife Refuge you can still see the broad floodplain with the hills rising in the east and west, much as Lewis and Clark described it. When I visited, a dramatic thunderstorm blew in, turning the sky steel blue, with huge clouds that billowed across the whole arc of the horizon and river valley.

The refuge visitor center is open from 9:00 A.M. to 4:30 P.M. daily except Christmas, New Year's Day, Thanksgiving, and Easter. The refuge straddles the Missouri River and the Nebraska–Iowa border. The visitor center is located about seven miles east of Blair, Nebraska off Highway 30. Refuge roads are open from one half hour before sunrise to one half hour after sunset. For further information call 712-642-4121 or see http://midwest.fws.gov/DeSoto.

The Missouri River between Yankton and Ponca

23RD. AUGUST THURSDAY 1804

J. Fields Sent out to hunt Came to the Boat and informed that he had Killed a Buffalow in the plain ahead . . . 2 Elk Swam the river, and was fired at from the boat . . . Several Prarie Wolves Seen to day Saw Elk Standing on the Sand bar. The Wind blew hard and raised the Sands off the bar in Such Clouds that we Could Scercely [see.] . . . in the Plain for half a mile the distance I was out, every Spire of Grass was covered with the Sand or Durt.

Clark wrote the preceding just upriver from what are now Elk Point, South Dakota, and Sioux City, Iowa. Over the next two days the expedition camped near the Vermillion River, which flows from the north, reaching the Missouri at the present-day city

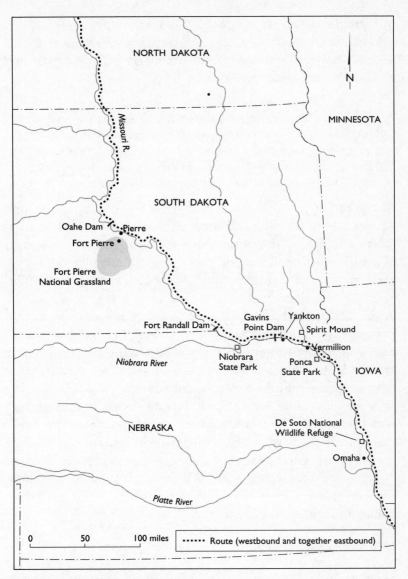

Map 3 Nebraska and South Dakota.

of Vermillion. This is about 6 miles south of a high point of land the Oto, Sioux, and other local Indians described to the explorers as the Mound of Spirits or Spirit Mound. From "the top of this Mound," Clark wrote on August 25,

> we beheld a most butifull landscape; Numerous herds of buffalow were Seen feeding in various directions; the Plain to the North N.W. & N.W. extends without interuption as far as Can be seen . . . Great numbers of Birds are seen in those Plains, Such as black bird, ren, or Praire burd, a kind of larke about the sise of a Partridge with a Short tail &c &c.

You can drive north out of Vermillion, South Dakota, to **Spirit Mound,** about 5.5 to 6 miles north on South Dakota Highway 19, where a landmark sign notes the place. Spirit Mound now rises above cornfields and was for many years on private land. But in 2001 the mound and some surrounding land became part of the South Dakota State Parks system, and work is now under way to create the Spirit Mound Historic Prairie — by restoring native prairie grasses and other plantings — and for an interpretive kiosk and trail to the summit. For more information contact South Dakota State Parks at 605-773-3391 or see http://www.state.sd.us/gfp/sdparks/spiritmound/spiritmound.htm.

A few days after seeing Spirit Mound, Lewis and Clark met with the Yankton Sioux and smoked "the pipe of peace" with several of their chiefs near where Gavins Point Dam now impounds the Missouri. On August 31 Clark noted in his journal that he "took a Vocabulary of the Suoux Language" and described how the Sioux Nation was divided into twenty tribes, listing all of their names and where they lived.

Into the Great Plains

Heading upriver from Council Bluffs past Sioux City, Iowa, a traveler following the Missouri heads west into the Great Plains. Located in the middle of the continent, the grassland plains, wetlands, and river corridors of Nebraska and South Dakota were central to the migration of birds and other mammals across North America. Agriculture and the development of the Missouri River and its wetlands have radically changed those plains where bison, elk, pronghorn, grizzlies, bighorn sheep, black bear, mule, and white-tailed deer made their home, and which nurtured great flocks of migratory waterfowl and shorebirds. By the early twentieth century, much of the prairie wildlife was gone — lost to hunting and the elimination of habitat. Today some 90 percent of South Dakota is devoted to agriculture, as is most of the land in Nebraska.

In the 1950s and 1960s, a series of huge dams inundated nearly all of the Missouri River valley not already flooded by earlier dams. Today about 70 percent of the Missouri is channelized and impounded. In South Dakota and Nebraska, Oahe Dam, Brule Dam, Fort Randall Dam, and Gavins Point Dam have altered this landscape, perhaps forever. Two sections of the lower Missouri that have been designated a national recreation river offer present-day visitors a small glimpse of what the river must have been like. The lower stretch of the Missouri's National Recreation River (designated in 1978), between Gavins Point Dam and Ponca, Nebraska, can be seen from the 892-acre **Ponca State Park**.

The park consists of heavily forested, rolling hills — woods dominated by bur oaks interspersed with elm, basswood, walnut, hackberry, Kentucky coffee tree, and shrubs such as gooseberry, chokecherry, showberry, and wild plum. A huge 320-year-old oak stands in the middle of the park, a landmark known as the "Old Oak Tree." In the spring, from late April to early June, woodland wildflowers, including Canada violet, blue phlox, Dutchman's-breeches, bloodroot, columbine, waterleaf, and white cicely, bloom. On the grassy ridge tops you will find prairie larkspur, purple coneflower, pasque flower, purple prairie clover, shell-leaf penstemon, and yucca, among other prairie plants.

The spring (late April to early May is the peak season) is also a good time to catch sight of migrating and resident songbirds, including warblers, scarlet tanagers, northern orioles, red-breasted grosbeaks, indigo buntings, and ruby-throated hummingbirds. Whippoorwills and barred owls can be seen and heard here, and turkey vultures are seen often in the summer. The fall is a good time to see migrating waterfowl. Bald eagles nest along the river in the winter. White-tailed deer and wild turkeys are common here, and the park reports sightings of small mammals such as red and gray fox, bobcat, raccoon, and opossum.

Ponca State Park has modern cabins, developed campsites, over 17 miles of hiking trails, bike trails, guided horseback rides, a boat ramp, and a swimming pool. Fall deer and pheasant hunting and spring turkey hunting are allowed in the park, as is fishing on the river. The park is open in winter, when the trails may be used for cross-country skiing and snowshoeing. Ponca State Park is 2 miles from Ponca, Nebraska, on S-26E, just off Nebraska Highway 12. For further information call 402-255-2284 or see http://www.ngpc.state.ne.us/parks/ponca.html.

Paddling the Missouri National Recreation River

While not for the first-time or novice paddler, the two national recreation river reaches of the lower Missouri can be canoed or flat-water kayaked. This is not a technically difficult paddle in terms of rapids, but the swift current, changing sandbars, snags, and wind can make it hard to keep on course. Summer weather can change quickly as strong winds, thunderstorms, and occasional tornadoes blow in, so paddlers should keep an eye on conditions and be ready to leave the river when storms threaten. Paddlers should be aware that motorboats and barges also use the river.

One of the more easterly or downstream of these national recreation river reaches runs for 20 miles, from below Gavins Point Dam just west and upstream of Yankton, South Dakota, past Vermillion to Ponca State Park in Nebraska. The other is a 37-mile reach just upstream — designated in 1991 — that begins below Fort Randall Dam and ends at the confluence of the Niobrara and Missouri Rivers, near **Niobrara State Park**. The river here can be 2 miles wide in places and flows through sandstone and chalk bluffs, reminiscent of those described by Lewis and Clark. Releases of water from Gavins Point Dam can make currents and flow unpredictable, so guides warn paddlers to be extremely cautious here and recommend paddling the upstream stretch — from Fort Randall Dam to Niobrara — instead.

If you are experienced and conditions permit, you can obtain access to the downstream reach of the Missouri National Recreation River below Gavins Point Dam on the Nebraska side of the river, opposite the dam just downstream of the Lakeview Golf

Course, off Highway 121. Farms line both sides of the river, but in the fall the changing color of leaves on the shoreline ironwood, cottonwood, black oak, and walnut trees can be inspiring. Continuing downstream past Yankton, with its stockyards and old railroad — now Highway 81 — bridge, you will come to the first pullout about 11 miles past the dam at the Clay County Lakeside Use Area in Vermillion. Downstream of Vermillion the riverbanks are more wooded, and the next — and final — takeout for this reach of river is at Ponca State Park, about 10 miles southeast of Vermillion and 2 miles north of Ponca, Nebraska.

For the upstream or western reach of the national recreation river that flows from Fort Randall Dam to the Niobrara, access is just below Fort Randall Dam on the south side of the river, from either U.S. 181 or South Dakota 46 (through Pickstown, South Dakota). The river access area is a recreation area with a boat ramp and camping and picnic facilities. The next access point is 13.4 miles downstream at Sunshine Bottoms, reachable by partially graveled road from Nebraska Highway 12, a road that can be impassable in wet weather. Continuing 14 miles downriver, you will come to Verdel Landing State Recreation Area, which is reachable from a graveled road off Nebraska Highway 12 (turn north at the Lazy River Acres sign). The final takeout for this trip is 8 miles downstream, about 1 mile downstream of Niobrara State Park in Niobrara, Nebraska, on the south side of the river. This point is also accessible from Nebraska Highway 12, just west of the Standing Bear Bridge, which crosses the Missouri traveling south on South Dakota Highway 37. Because the managed river's conditions make currents and flow difficult, paddling between the Niobrara and Gavins Point Dam through the huge impoundment known as Lewis and Clark Lake is not recommended.

Along the 37-mile stretch of river between Fort Randall Dam and the Niobrara, there are tall limestone cliffs and loess bluffs. The river valley here is 1 to 2 miles wide. Willows and cottonwoods grow along the river, while hardwood trees are found on the upland slopes. Paddlefish, sauger, sturgeon, and walleye can be found in the river here. Eagles winter along the banks, and deer,

ZEBRA MUSSEL ALERT

Since their introduction to the Great Lakes in 1986 in ships' ballast water, zebra mussels have spread to at least twenty states and two Canadian provinces and throughout the Great Lakes and Mississippi Basin. Zebra mussels spread and multiply quickly, threatening native mussel populations. They are also a potential threat to fish. Because zebra mussels are the only freshwater mollusks that can firmly attach themselves to solid objects and grow in clusters, they can easily damage underwater or water delivery pipes, ducts, culverts, screens, and boat engines.

One of the ways zebra mussels can be transported is in water that remains in a boat or on a boat trailer or other boating equipment. There is a serious concern that boats coming from infected waters will transport mussels and their tiny larvae westward into the Missouri and Columbia River systems, which would likely be disastrous. In the Mississippi Basin and Great Lakes, zebra mussels have already damaged industrial and municipal water systems. (Imagine what they could do to the screens that protect fish from dams and irrigation pipes!)

To prevent the spread of zebra mussels and other invasive aquatic species—plants as well as animals—thoroughly scrub and dry your boat and all equipment. If possible, wash your boat with clean water before putting it into the next body of water. With canoes and kayaks this is not difficult, but remember to check inside the boat, where water, sand, and mud can collect—including on rudders and ropes. Remove all visible mussels and plants and dispose of them in a trash bin. Feel the boat's hull and any other parts exposed to water; a rough or gritty surface may mean young zebra mussels are present. Don't forget to clean sponges, pumps, buckets, boots, and footgear worn while paddling, and let them dry thoroughly before their next use. Whenever possible, rinse all gear with clean water. If you are using a trailer, check to make sure water is not collecting in any nooks and crannies. Also check to make sure your boat, vehicle, ropes, straps, and other gear are free of aquatic vegetation before leaving the takeout. Check pets and their gear as well. Take special care to clean and dry your boat and all equipment if you are coming from an area of known zebra mussel populations.

Zebra mussels and other aquatic nuisance species are of such concern that the U.S. Fish and Wildlife Service has begun a program called the 100th Meridian Initiative, aimed at preventing their westward spread. For more information see http://fisheries.fws.gov/FWSMA/Mazebra.htm or http://ANSTaskForce.gov or call 877-786-7267. Or contact the Nebraska Game and Parks Commission at 402-471-5443 and see its Web site at http://www.ngpc.state.ne.us/fish/whatsnew/zebra.html.

fox, and turkey — among other animals — live near the river and in the surrounding woods.

Canoes and kayaks can be rented from outfitters upriver in Yankton, South Dakota.

For more information see the on-line Missouri National Recreational River guide through http://www.nps.gov/mnrr. Or call the National Park Service at 402-667-5530 in Yankton, South Dakota. The Ponca State Park can also help with information on current weather and river conditions. The National Park Service manages the country's national recreational river reaches and designated wild and scenic rivers; information about these can be obtained through its Web site: http://www.nps.gov.

The Niobrara River and Niobrara State Park

SEPTEMBER 4, TUESDAY 1804

Set out early and proceded on [to] the mouth of a Small Creek . . . called Whitelime creek . . . at 1 1/2 miles higher we passed a large Creek . . . called R. au Platte or White Paint . . . between those two Creeks . . . we passed under a Bluff of Red Ceder, at 4 miles 1/2 passed the mouth of the River Qui Courre (rapid river) . . . I went up this river three miles to a Butifull Plain on the upper Side where the Panias [Pawnees] once had a village this River widens above its mouth and is divided by sands and Islands, the current is verry rapid, the river is not navigable for evin Canoes without Great difficulty owing to its Sands.

Lewis and Clark called it the Rapid River or, as the French trappers did, Rivière qui Court or Quicurre — from the French translation of its Lakota name, Niobrara, meaning "running water" or "water that runs." It was here, in the country above the Niobrara, that Lewis and Clark saw their first prairie dogs and pronghorn (in their journals they often refer to pronghorn as "goats") and observed a herd of at least 500 bison.

The Niobrara's headwaters rise in eastern Wyoming. The 100th

Niobrara River. Photo: Will Clay.

meridian crosses the Niobrara about midway along its 300-mile course across northern Nebraska to the Missouri. To the south of the river (roughly south and west of the town of Valentine) are Nebraska's sandhills, underneath which lies part of the Ogallala Aquifer, which extends south into Texas. In 1991, 76 miles of the Niobrara — in three separate sections — were designated a national scenic river to help preserve the river and valley's biological features.

With such a midcontinental location, the Niobrara is home to species of both the American East and West, as well as the North and South. Along its valley is evidence of tallgrass and mixed-grass prairie, eastern deciduous forest, Rocky Mountain pine forest, northern forest, and sandhill prairie. Among the trees in the Niobrara valley are cottonwood, aspen, paper birch, elm, eastern red cedar, and ponderosa pine. On the drier mixed-grass prairie — in an indication of the landscape found to the west — grow yucca and prickly pear.

Eastern species of orioles, flickers, and grosbeaks mingle and mate with their western counterparts here, as do western lazuli and indigo buntings with their eastern cousins. The endangered piping plover and least tern, burrowing owls, sandhill cranes, prairie chickens, sharp-tailed grouse, meadowlarks, whippoor-wills, eastern and western kingbirds, loggerhead shrikes, eastern bluebirds, Townsend's solitaire, wild turkeys, golden eagles, and bald eagles are found along the Niobrara, as, occasionally, is the extremely rare, endangered whooping crane.

The Niobrara valley and surrounding country are home to pronghorn, mule and white-tailed deer, prairie dogs, mink, musk-rat, beaver, bobcat, coyote, red fox, badgers, porcupine, and an isolated subspecies of eastern wood rat (its closest relatives are 400 miles away in Kansas), among other mammals, although the numbers are much reduced from the days when Lewis and Clark observed them here. Great herds of elk once roamed the prairie around the Niobrara. Today the only remaining elk are those in managed herds in the valley's parks, refuges, and preserves. Similarly, the Niobrara valley prairie's remaining bison are those descended from the remnant herd that is protected on the **Fort Niobrara Wildlife Refuge** and on The Nature Conservancy's **Niobrara Valley Preserve**.

Most of the country through which the Niobrara flows is now devoted to agriculture. Consequently, runoff from farms — includ-ing large-scale hog farms — and domestic livestock grazing around the river and its tributary streams have degraded water quality and the condition of the riparian corridor. Residential and recreational development along the river also contributes to the ongoing degra-dation of the river ecosystem. The Niobrara flows primarily through private lands except for where it forms the centerpiece of the Fort Niobrara National Wildlife Refuge, which encompasses the 4,635-acre Fort Niobrara Wilderness, and where it flows through The Nature Conservancy's Niobrara Valley Preserve.

One of the best ways to see the confluence of the Niobrara and the Missouri is from **Niobrara State Park** (1 mile west of Niobrara on Nebraska Highway 12). Between 10 and 14 miles of hiking trails in this pastoral-looking park wind along the bluffs above the river and lead down to the river itself. This is easy hiking along developed trails, but almost the only way — in this vicinity — to get a sense on foot of these two rivers from the point from which Lewis and Clark saw them. Watch for white-tailed deer and wild turkey, which roam the developed campsites, tent sites, and cabins within the park. Guided horseback rides are available in the park, and the trails can be used in winter for cross-country skiing.

Office hours are Memorial Day weekend through Labor Day: 8:00 A.M. to 8:00 P.M. daily; mid-November to mid-April: 8:00 A.M. to 5:00 P.M. Monday through Friday; and 8:00 A.M. to 5:00 P.M. daily the rest of the year. There is a day-use fee for the park. Permits can be purchased at the park office. For more information, call 402-857-3373 or see http://www.ngpc.state.ne.us/parks/niob.html.

To see the protected scenic stretches of the Niobrara and get a fuller sense of what that landscape must have been like 200 years ago, you will have to venture upriver about 132 miles to the over-19,000-acre **Fort Niobrara Wildlife Refuge** and **Fort Niobrara Wilderness** or paddle the river itself between Cornell Bridge and Norden Bridge.

The Fort Niobrara Wildlife Refuge is 4 miles east of Valentine, Nebraska, on Highway 12. There are hiking trails in the refuge, and hiking, horseback riding, and cross-country skiing are allowed in the wilderness area on the north side of the river, although there are no developed trails. No camping is allowed in the wilderness area or in the refuge.

This is sandhill country, where white-tailed and mule deer live along with small numbers of pronghorn, prairie dogs, and other small mammals. In the spring, watch for the amazing courtship

THE PONCA

One of the hiking trails at Niobrara State Park leads to the J. Alan Cramer Interpretive Shelter, which tells the story of the Ponca Indians who lived along this stretch of the Missouri and Niobrara. Lewis and Clark met the Ponca near here in 1804. Descendants of the ancient Mississippi culture, the Ponca are related to the Osage, Kansas, Quapaw, and Omaha. They hunted buffalo in the prairie uplands and farmed the river valleys. By the mid–nineteenth century, white settlers had taken over their croplands, and the white Americans' hunting had taken an enormous toll on the buffalo. The tribe's last successful buffalo hunt was in 1855. In 1858 the Ponca signed a treaty with the U.S. government ceding the United States all but 96,000 acres of their land. The treaty also gave some Ponca lands to the Teton Dakota, with whom the Ponca had long been in competition or at war.

In a misguided attempt to make good on early promises to protect the Ponca from their traditional enemies, the U.S. government authorized $25,000 with which to move the tribe from its Nebraska homeland to Indian Territory in Oklahoma. On a miserable forced march under army escort, the Ponca made the trek of over 500 miles to their new allotted reservation on former Cherokee land, suffering terribly from extreme heat, disease, and despair. In the winter of 1878–79, when Chief Standing Bear's son died, Standing Bear—for whom the bridge at Niobrara is named—and a small party of followers fled the reservation and journeyed north to bury his son on traditional Ponca homeland.

When the government in Washington learned of Standing Bear's escape, it ordered General George Crook to arrest the whole party and return it to Indian Territory. When Standing Bear's arrest became known, two sympathetic lawyers, John L. Webster and A. J. Poppleton, volunteered to take the case and filed a suit charging the government with violation of the writ of habeas corpus. The case raised, for the first time, the issue of Indian citizenship and Indians' entitlement to the full protection afforded citizens by the U.S. Constitution. Although it dodged the full question of citizenship, the case was decided in favor of the Ponca, declaring that an "Indian was a person under the law and therefore entitled to protection of the Constitution and the law of the United States." Standing Bear and his band chose to remain in Nebraska, while other tribal members stayed on in Indian Territory in Oklahoma.

displays of the prairie chicken and sharp-tailed grouse. Bald and golden eagles winter along the river here.

The refuge visitor center is open from 8:00 A.M. to 4:30 P.M. Monday through Friday except on federal holidays. For more information, contact the refuge at 402-376-3789 or see http://www.r6.fws.gov/REFUGES/niobrara/NIOBRARA.HTM.

It is also possible to visit The Nature Conservancy's Niobrara Valley Preserve, along the river south of Norden, Nebraska, and north of Johnstown on the Norden Road. There is a visitor center at the preserve, where a 3-mile North River trail climbs up to the top of the river bluffs, and shorter 0.75-mile and 1.5-mile trails meander on the south side of the river. The Nature Conservancy has been harvesting cedar here, which is encroaching on the prairie, and conducting controlled burns to encourage healthy growth of prairie grasses and forbs (what scientists call wildflowers and which are extremely nutritious plants). The Nature Conservancy also owns land on the south side of the Niobrara downstream from Smith Falls State Park to Norden Bridge. For more information, call the Niobrara Valley Preserve at 402-722-4440.

Paddling the Niobrara

The stretch of the Niobrara that is recommended for paddling (by canoe or kayak) is the reach from Cornell Bridge to Rocky Ford — or shorter segments thereof. There are waterfalls along the river here, the largest of which is the 70-foot-high Smith Falls in Smith Falls State Park. The Niobrara flows swiftly, from 6 to 8 miles an hour, and so is described as a challenging paddle but certainly manageable by competent intermediate paddlers. Water levels stay constant until the lowest water season at the end of the summer, in late August or September. The National Park Service manages the scenic river from its ranger station at Valentine. For information on river conditions, contact the service at 402-376-1901.

There is river access in the Fort Niobrara Wildlife Refuge at Cornell Bridge, 12 miles downstream in Smith Falls State Park, and at Brewer's Bridge and Rocky Ford. One can continue downstream to just before Norden Bridge (a large hole and rapids occur just prior to, and under, the Norden Bridge, so stay left [north] and pull out before the bridge). Because there are more rapids downstream of Rocky Ford, most people leave the river there. From Cornell Bridge to Rocky Ford it is a 20- to 22-mile paddle, which is best done as a full-day trip. A detailed guide to this stretch of river — including where to watch for rapids, holes, and rocks — is available on the Nebraska Canoe Trails Web site at http://www.ngpc. state.ne.us/boating/canoe-nio.html#access. Smith Falls State Park (http://www.ngpc.state.ne.us/parks/smith.html) also has information about river access, or call 402-376-1306.

Canoes and kayaks can be rented in Sparks, Nebraska, about 17 miles east of the Niobrara Wildlife Refuge, or in Valentine. Contact outfitters in these towns about arranging a shuttle. If you are putting in at the refuge, there is a day-use fee, and you will need a sticker for your boat. Smith Falls State Park also requires a vehicle permit. Remember that summer is usually hot and humid in the Midwest and Great Plains, which means it can be buggy on or near the water. Weather can change quickly, so be prepared to get off the river when strong winds, rain, thunder, lightning, or hail threatens, and know that storms tend to build toward the afternoon.

Farm Island and Fort Pierre National Grassland

SEPTEMBER 18TH. TUESDAY 1804

the hunters Killed 10 Deer to day and a Prarie wolf, [coyote] had it all jurked & Skins Stretched. after camping.

I walked on Shore Saw Goats, [pronghorn], Elk, Buffalow, Black tail Deer, & the Common Deer, I Killed a Prarie Wollf, about the Size of a gray fox bushey tail head & ears like a Wolf, Some fur Burrows in the ground and barks like a Small Dog.

What has been taken hertofore for the Fox was those Wolves, and no Foxes has been Seen; The large Wolves [gray wolf] are verry numourous, they are of a light color. Large & has long hair with Coarse fur.

Captain Clark wrote this journal entry as the expedition made its way up the Missouri from the area around what are now Chamberlain and Pierre, South Dakota. The Missouri is now dammed in South Dakota just above Yankton, again by the Fort Randall Dam near Pickstown, and by the Oahe Dam just north of Pierre. These dams, along with Garrison Dam north of Stanton and Washburn, North Dakota, have turned the wandering Missouri into a series of huge, lakelike reservoirs — Lewis and Clark Lake, Lake Francis Case, Lake Sharpe, and Lake Oahe — that flood most of the river in South Dakota.

This eastern prairie, with its fertile river valley wetlands, lakes, and marshes left behind by the great glaciers, became one of the first regions of South Dakota to be converted to cropland. A look at a good topographic map of South Dakota shows the many streams and ponds that riddle its great plains. Traveling through this country today, one sees fields of corn, soybeans, hay, wheat, sunflowers, and sorghum stretching to the horizon in every direction. Because of the extent of private land, it is not easy to find a place to wander extensively, but short walks can be taken at a few state parks and wildlife refuges where one can get a sense of the riverside vegetation — cedar and cottonwood — and the riparian atmosphere Lewis and Clark would have encountered.

The river here was so full of sandbars that Clark wrote on September 30, when they were a short way upstream of what is now the immense impoundment behind Oahe Dam called Lake Oahe, "Sand bars are So noumerous, that it is impossible to describe them, & think it unnecessary to mention them." Although the Missouri's natural floodplain has been inundated and the riverbanks hardened, if you go down to the river just downstream of Pierre, you can imagine how it must have been.

Farm Island

On September 24 Lewis and Clark stopped at an island in the Missouri where they met with chiefs of the Teton Sioux. The meeting was not an altogether cordial one. It took place just after one of the expedition's horses had been stolen by some of the tribe's young men. During the meeting on board one of the pirogues, two of the chiefs became angry, saying they had not received sufficient gifts from the party, and threatened to stop them from continuing through Sioux territory. Establishing a good relationship with the Teton was important to the United States because the tribe controlled so much territory, including areas important to the fur trade. The potentially hostile situation persisted over the next several days but was defused, and the expedition proceeded without harmful incident. But, wrote Clark, "I call this Island bad humured Island as we were in a bad humer."

This island, just offshore from what are now Pierre and Fort Pierre, South Dakota, is Farm Island, which sits in the Missouri just downstream of the Bad River. Farm Island is now a South Dakota state recreation area, with a 500-acre densely wooded "nature area" with several short (a mile or less) hiking trails that can be used in the winter for cross-country skiing. The island is popular for fishing and during hunting season (hunting season is generally from October 1 through April 30) — especially for walleye fishing and Canada goose hunting — so call ahead to find out when to equip yourself with safety-orange or to avoid the hunting altogether if you plan on walking without taking aim at anything. There is good bird-watching here, on a well-used flyway, and if you are lucky you can see flickers, red-backed and black-backed woodpeckers, flycatchers, northern sawhet, great horned and eastern screech owls, ovenbirds, black poll, sora rail, gulls, and chestnut-sided, Tennessee, and black-throated green warblers.

There are developed campgrounds at Farm Island, with boat ramps and a swimming beach, among other recreational facilities. Farm Island Recreation Area is 4 miles east of Pierre, off South Dakota Highway 34. For more information call 605-224-5605 or see http://www.state.sd.us/gfp/fmisland/fmisland.htm. (I cannot resist adding that when I visited Farm Island and stopped to ask directions in Fort Pierre, my informant — who turned out to be a local history buff — pointed toward the river and said, "See, they camped down there near the Pizza Express.")

Fort Pierre National Grassland

As the expedition approached Crow Creek on September 17, 1804, near what is now Oacoma, South Dakota, on the west bank of the Missouri (Chamberlain is across the river here to the east), Captain Lewis described the Great Plains:

> the country breakes of[f] as usual into a fine leavel plain ex-
> tending as far as the eye can reach . . . to the West a high range
> of hills, strech across the country from N. to S. . . . they are not
> very extensive as I could plainly observe their rise and termina-
> tion no rock appeared on them and the sides were covered
> with a virdu[r]e similar to that of the plains this senery already
> rich pleasing and beatiful was still farther hightened by im-
> mence herds of Buffaloe, deer Elk and Antelopes which we saw
> in every direction feeding on the hills and plains. I do not think
> I exagerate when I estimate the number of Buffaloe which
> could be compre[hend]ed at one view to amount to 3000.

"The grasslands of the American West are created by the Rockies and by the coastal mountain ranges of California and the Pacific Northwest. The mountains impose rain shadows downstream of prevailing westerlies, because the rise of warm air along the windward side of the mountains wrings moisture out of passing weather systems. This makes the aridity that makes the treeless plains," explains Richard Manning in *Grassland*.[7] As you approach the Great Plains from the west, this movement of air and moisture is quite apparent and is reflected by the great rolling swoops of the land.

But like nearly all of the United States' native grasslands, almost all of South Dakota's Great Plains are now agricultural fields. The great herds of bison, elk, and pronghorn are gone. The only large tract of public land in central South Dakota is the **Fort Pierre National Grassland**, located a few miles west of the Missouri River, 5 miles south of Pierre. Here you can imagine what it was like before farming and ranching changed the landscape, to look from high arched horizon to horizon and see nothing but undulating swells of blowing grass.

The 116,000-acre grassland — managed by the National Forest Service, part of the Department of Agriculture — is mixed-grass

Pronghorn. Photo: Idaho Department of Fish and Game.

prairie, made up of western wheat and green needlegrass, big and little bluestem, side oats grama, porcupine grass, blue grama, and buffalo grass. There are few woody shrubs or trees, but some cottonwoods, ash, and willow grow in creek drainages, and a few junipers are found on drier hillsides. The grassland provides habitat for pronghorn, white-tailed and mule deer, coyotes, prairie dogs, and sharp-tailed grouse. It is also home to one of the most stable populations of prairie chickens, whose range is now less than 10 percent of what it was historically, left in the country. Here, from early April to about mid-May — depending on weather conditions — sharp-tailed grouse and prairie chickens can be observed performing their remarkable courtship dances on their traditional breeding grounds known as leks.

While the Fort Pierre National Grassland offers an excellent glimpse of what this Dakota Great Plains prairie must have been like at the time of Lewis and Clark, it is not sequestered from agricultural development the way a legislatively protected wilderness area or national park might be. The grassland is interspersed with private rangelands and cultivated fields of wheat, sorghum, and sunflowers. The Forest Service also issues permits for cattle grazing throughout a high percentage of the grassland, primarily from spring to fall — generally May 1 through October 30 — although there is some winter livestock grazing as well. This grazing is done in rotation, so overall no more than a quarter to a third of the grassland is being grazed at one time. In addition to the cattle grazing, there is currently one bison allotment on the grassland. Within the Fort Pierre National Grassland is an 8,725-acre roadless area called Cedar Creek, for which conservationists hope to gain protection under the Wilderness Act.

From September 1 through November 30, off-road vehicle travel is prohibited in the grassland, but it is allowed during the rest of the year. Snowmobiling is permitted. Both highways and unpaved roads traverse the grassland, and the Forest Service cautions visitors that after rains the sticky clay soil — known locally as gumbo — can make driving difficult, if not impossible, on the dirt roads.

There are no established hiking, walking, or biking trails in the grassland, but hikers and mountain bikers can use the area's two-track roads. Camping is permitted anywhere on the grassland, but there are no developed campgrounds with water or rest rooms. The grassland's back roads are used most often in the summer, by ranchers, by people fishing in the area's reservoirs, and by prairie dog shooters. Summer temperatures here often reach between 90 and 100 degrees, and because it is so often dry and hot, the Forest Service discourages open campfires.

There are observation blinds for viewing on the prairie chicken leks during booming season, but visitors must make reservations to use the blinds on specific dates. *Booming* refers to the extraordinary sound of male chest puffing and wing beating that accompanies the prairie chicken and grouse courtship dances. The spring — during prairie chicken and sharp-tailed grouse booming or mating season — and the fall, when temperatures cool a bit, are the recommended times to visit, since summer heat and shadeless terrain can make for uncomfortable hiking, but take precautions not to collide with hunters.

Maps of the grassland are available from the USDA Forest Service, Fort Pierre National Grassland, P.O. Box 417, Pierre,

South Dakota 57501. For further information and current map price call 605-224-5517 or see http://www.fs.fed.us/r2/nebraska/units/fp/ftpierre.html or http://www.fs.fed.us./r2/nebraska/vvc/html.

Homage to Sitting Bull

The Oahe Dam has impounded the Missouri into the immense body of water called Lake Oahe that stretches nearly 200 miles — from Pierre and the confluence of the Bad River, north upstream past the Missouri's confluence with the Cheyenne and Grand Rivers, to beyond the North Dakota border almost all the way to Bismarck. On the west side of the Missouri going north are the Cheyenne River and Standing Rock Reservations. Before construction of the dam began in 1948, Cheyenne River Sioux and other local families farmed the rich Missouri River bottomlands, and many of these families were forced to move when the dam project inundated their farms. Since the dam was completed in 1962, roads on both sides of the river wind through irrigated agricultural fields, mile after mile of corn, sunflowers, soybeans, hay, and wheat. On the east side of the river — off reservation land — there are various recreational access points to Lake Oahe.

Unfortunately, little is left here of the riparian landscape seen by Lewis and Clark. The old riverbank cottonwoods are now submerged under 200 feet of water, and the original river channel is gone. It is, however, interesting to wander some of the back roads and imagine what these Great Plains must have been like before the farms, ranches, and enormous dams. Drive through this country, hike the Fort Pierre National Grassland, and think about the enormous herds of bison that used to thunder across these grassy plains. (You may see some bison that have been reintroduced.) Think also about the many Plains tribes — some of whom followed the bison on nomadic hunts, others of whom hunted on the plains and farmed the fertile river lands along the Missouri and in the wooded areas of the upper Midwest. Among those many tribes were the Arapaho, Assiniboin, Blackfoot, Cheyenne, Comanche, Crow, Gros Ventre, Kiowa, Kiowa-Apache, Sarsi, Teton Sioux, Arikara, Hidatsa, Iowa, Kansas, Mandan, Missouri, Omaha, Osage, Oto,

Pawnee, Ponca, Santee, Sioux, Yankton Sioux, Wichita, Plains Cree, Plains Ojibwa, Shoshone, Caddo, and Quapaw.[8]

An interesting detour for the perspective it offers on the politics and history of the region — although by no means a wild and scenic exploration — is to Sitting Bull's burial site south of Fort Yates off North Dakota Highway 1806, on the Standing Rock Reservation. Sitting Bull, whose Lakota name was Tatanka Iyontanke, was the Teton Sioux leader who helped defeat Lieutenant Colonel George Custer at the Battle of the Little Big Horn in 1876, as the Sioux and other Indian nations resisted the United States' appropriation of their lands and their confinement on reservations. After this battle, Sitting Bull and his followers escaped to Canada. When the United States promised Sitting Bull amnesty in 1881, he returned to American territory where he was imprisoned and then confined to a reservation. Sitting Bull was killed during an attempted arrest at Standing Rock in 1890.

CHAPTER 5

North Dakota
and Eastern Montana

Cross Ranch State Park
and the Garrison Reach of the Missouri

20TH OF OCTOBER SATTURDAY 1804

*I saw an old remains of a village on the Side of a hill which
the old chief with Too ne tels me that nation lived in 2 villages
1 on each Side of the river and the Troublesom Seaux caused
them to move bout 40 miles higher up where they remained a
fiew years & moved to the place they now live.*

*Camped . . . above a Bluff . . . this bank is imediately above
the old Village of the Mandans. The Countrey is fine, the high
hills at a Distance with gradual assents, I kild. 3 Deer The
Timber confined to the bottoms as useal. . . . Great numbers
of Buffalow Elk & Deer, Goats. Our hunters killed 10 Deer
& a Goat to day and wounded a white Bear, I saw several
fresh tracks of those animals which is 3 times as large as a
mans track . . . great numbers of buffalow Swimming the
river.*

Captain Clark wrote this entry in his journal near the site of present-day Fort Abraham Lincoln State Park, just south of Mandan and Bismarck, North Dakota. The park is on the west side of the Missouri and contains a reconstruction of the old "On-a-Slant" Mandan village that Clark describes. The "goats" were pronghorn. The "white Bear" was the expedition's first encounter with a grizzly; grizzlies are lighter than the black bears with which the men were familiar and so were dubbed "white." In late October and early November 1804, the Corps of Discovery camped and met with the Mandan, Hidatsa, and Arikara who lived near the Knife River. As temperatures dropped and snow started to fall, Lewis and Clark's party began building winter quarters, which they called Fort Mandan.

From below Garrison Dam at Pick City (north of Washburn, North Dakota) and the Knife River — which meets the Missouri near Stanton — the Missouri flows freely through what is called the Garrison Reach, now the longest undammed stretch of the river between Garrison Dam and St. Louis. Piping plovers and least terns — both endangered species — live here and nest on river sandbars. Eagles, osprey, Canada geese, and great blue heron fish the river. Pallid sturgeon, fish that have existed since prehistoric times, still swim the Missouri, but their numbers are now so low that they are listed as an endangered species. Whooping cranes, also a federally listed endangered species, may be spotted in the vicinity during their spring and fall migrations, since the Missouri River and its wetlands lie along their primary migration corridor. Garrison, North Dakota, the Audubon National Wildlife Refuge near Lake Sakakawea, and the Long Lake National Wildlife Refuge east of Bismarck, along with North Dakota's northwestern counties, are good places to look for the birds. Spring migration north from the cranes' wintering grounds on the Texas coast is in April. Fall migration south from the birds' nesting grounds in the Northwest Territories is in late October and early November.

The damming of the Missouri has radically altered the river's flow here, eliminating the seasonal flooding that nurtured natural floodplain vegetation and created sandbar habitat for riparian birds like the plover and tern. Great extents of the Missouri's banks have been riprapped here — reinforced and hardened — to curtail erosion. This eliminates wetlands and encourages riverside development, which brings with it additional problems for the riparian ecosystem.

The construction of Garrison Dam began in 1947 and was completed in 1954. The dam flooded over 150,000 acres of Mandan, Hidatsa, and Arikara homelands, including thousands of acres of prime agricultural bottomland, and forced the removal of some 350 families. Not surprisingly, the Pick-Sloan Plan, as the damming project was called, was bitterly protested by the three tribes. Ninety percent of those living on the Fort Berthold Reservation lived within the river valley and were directly affected by the dam. The 178-mile-long impoundment the dam created is called Lake Sakakawea; with 1,340 miles of shoreline, it is the third-largest man-made reservoir in the country. Yet along the Garrison Reach of the Missouri there are still a few places where the river looks as it must have when first seen by Lewis and Clark.

The largest remaining tract of floodplain woodland on the **Garrison Reach** of the Missouri River — about 1,500 acres — is within the **Cross Ranch State Park** and adjacent **Cross Ranch Nature Preserve**, a Nature Conservancy property. Here, in the coulees where streams run, grow cottonwoods, willows, box elder, American elm, green ash, aspen, and bur oak, along with dogwood, red osier, Juneberry, chokecherry, woodbine, wild grape, buffaloberry, buckbrush, wild licorice, sedges, bedstraw, Canada wildrye, field horsetails, and poison ivy. The prairie uplands are covered with wheatgrass, needlegrasses, gramas, and little bluestem and wildflowers such as purple coneflower, prairie lilies, and blazing star. In the southern part of the preserve grow yucca and ball cactus. Some 300 different species of plants have been identified on the preserve.

The park and preserve's prairie areas are home to a great number of birds — about a hundred species — including Say's phoebes, wild turkey, and red-tailed, sharp-shinned, and Swainson's hawks, as well as some rarer species, among them burrowing owls, chestnut-collared longspur, red-tailed hawk, Dakota skipper, western wood pewee, yellow-breasted chat, Baird's sparrow,

Otto skipper, smooth cliffbrake, and Sprague's pipit. There are white-tailed and mule deer here, as well as badger, red fox, bobcat, coyote, raccoon, and other animals, including bison, which were reintroduced to the preserve in 1986.

In the 5,000 to 6,000 acres of the park and preserve, 14 to 15 miles of easy hiking trails wander through the prairie and floodplain forest. Some of the trails can be used in the winter for cross-country skiing. There is camping in the park — both developed and more primitive — as well as access to the river for canoeing and flat-water kayaking. Bear in mind that in the summer the mosquitoes can be fierce, especially after rain, so if you plan on extended hiking, consider spring or fall — September and early October.

Cross Ranch State Park is located 11 miles southeast of Hensler, North Dakota, off North Dakota Highway 200. For more information call the North Dakota Parks and Recreation Department at 701-328-5357 or Cross Ranch State Park at 701-794-3731 or see http://www.state.nd.us/ndparks/Parks/CRSP.htm and follow the links for "Nature" and the Cross Ranch Nature Preserve.

Paddling the Garrison Reach of the Missouri

Although the Missouri is undammed from below the Garrison Dam to Bismarck, the cold, clear water released from the dam has changed a slow-moving, silty, meandering river into one that flows swiftly. These altered conditions may not be ideal for the river's ecology and wildlife, but they make for a paddling season that extends from May until September. This stretch of river does not present technically difficult paddling, but the current can be swift, high winds can make for tough paddling, and there are underwater snags and sandbars to watch for, as well as motorboat traffic, which can be heavy near Bismarck and Mandan.

There are several options for day trips on this stretch of the Missouri. These can be extended into two- to four-day overnights, depending on how fast you paddle and how much hiking and exploring you do onshore. You can put in below the Garrison Dam at the Garrison Dam Downstream Recreation Area and paddle downstream to the confluence with the Knife River near

Stanton, a four- to six-hour trip. From there you can continue on to Washburn or Cross Ranch State Park. The trip from Washburn to Cross Ranch takes two to four hours. Any combination of these segments makes for a good day's paddle.

There is interesting exploring to be done along the Knife River and at Cross Ranch, so a two- to three-day trip would include time to hike some of the trails in those areas. You can also put in at Cross Ranch and paddle an hour or two downstream to the Steckel Boat Landing or Burn Boat Ramp or continue on to the Double Ditch Indian Village, about 15 miles north of Bismarck on the east side of the river.

You can also continue farther downstream to Fort Abraham Lincoln State Park, but the motorboat traffic at the boat ramps near Bismarck can be off-putting for small muscle-powered craft. Some of the prettiest, least-developed parts of the river are the first 12 miles downstream from Garrison Dam to the Knife River and the stretch between Cross Ranch and Double Ditch Indian Village.

If you are planning an overnight, there are islands at the mouth of the Knife River that are public land and make for good primitive camping. Camping is also available at Cross Ranch State Park. Most of the land along the river is private, and camping there is possible only with the owner's permission. There is camping at the Army Corps of Engineers' Garrison Dam Downstream Recreation Area, where there are both electrified and primitive campsites. (Sites on one of the several loops of campsites here are by reservation only through a company called Reservation America. Others are on a first-come, first-served basis with fees payable upon arrival.) Also remember that in summer — the season to paddle — mosquitoes can be thick along the river; if so, a day trip with camping or lodging away from the river may be more enjoyable than spending the evening battling biting bugs.

The Missouri and Knife Rivers here are home to over two dozen species of aquatic mollusks, catfish, walleye, sucker, shiner, garfish, perch, and the endangered pallid sturgeon.

For more information see http://www.state.nd.us/ndparks/Trails/canoeing.htm or call Cross Ranch State Park at 701-794-3731. For river conditions — water levels and releases from Garrison

Dam — contact the U.S. Army Corps of Engineers at 701-255-0015 or 701-654-7411 or see its Web site at http://www.nwd-mr. usace.army.mil/rcc/index.html.

The *Bismarck Tribune* prints the water releases from Garrison Dam daily. For flow information on the Knife River, call Cross Ranch State Park or see the USGS North Dakota Web site home page at http://srv1dndbmk.cr.usgs.gov. Boats can be rented from outfitters near Mandan (canoes only) and in Washburn (canoes and kayaks), which can also help arrange shuttles and offer guided river trips. Cross Ranch State Park also offers canoe rental and transportation. The canoeing pages on the North Dakota state parks Web site list names and phone numbers for outfitters.

For information about ongoing efforts to protect and restore habitat and natural conditions throughout the Garrison Reach of the Missouri, contact American Rivers' "Save the Missouri" campaign at http://www.savethemissouri.org or the Sierra Club's North Dakota chapter by phone or mail (see Appendix B for contact information) or through its Web site at http://www. sierraclub.org/nd.

The Knife River

27TH. OF OCTOBER SATTURDAY 1804, MANDANS. —

came too at the Village . . . situated on an eminance of about 50 feet above the Water in a handsome plain . . . the houses are round and verry large containing several families . . . passed the 2d. Village and camped opsd. The Village of the Weter soon [or Ah wah har ways] which is Siutated . . . above the Knife river.

Thus began the series of journal entries written between October 27, 1804, and March 21, 1805, the winter Lewis and Clark and company spent among the Mandan on the banks of the Knife and Missouri Rivers in what is now central North Dakota. The Knife River flows into the Missouri from the west, and it is here that the landscape begins to change from Great Plains to Rocky Mountain grasslands, prairie, and wetlands — or what remains of them.

Garrison Reach of the Missouri River, with tracks left by beaver dragging willows. Photo: Jonathan Bry.

Although the map of North Dakota indicates little in the way of extended settlement, agriculture, water diversion, and energy development have substantially altered the region's landscape. The Ice Age glaciers that flowed down from the north stopped on what is now the east side of the Missouri River, melting into a huge lake that eventually formed the Missouri. Rivers like the Knife and Yellowstone were blocked by the glacier, which forced their waters to flow east and south. As one walks along the Knife River today at the **Knife River Indian Villages National Historic Site** (managed by the National Park Service) — a place sequestered from the Dakotas' ubiquitous row crops — the ancient flow of water and slope of landscape under an immense sky are much as they must have been two hundred years ago and longer.

The area around the Knife River to the west of the Missouri has been inhabited for some ten thousand years. For about seven hundred years before the coming of Europeans, the Hidatsa and Mandan tribes built large, round earthen homes on the high ground above the river. There they grew sunflowers, beans, corn, and squash. They hunted buffalo, deer, and other game on the vast prairies. At the Knife River Indian Villages site there are remains of Mandan earthen homes — large, round upwellings in the ground, or "circles in the earth," as they were known traditionally — and a reproduction of a Mandan house. The Knife River villages were centers of trade between the various Plains Indian tribes, with people coming from as far away as the Pacific Coast, from north of the Assiniboine River (which flows through Saskatchewan and Manitoba) and the Great Lakes, as well as from the Southwest.

Along the riverbanks here are some of the few remaining Missouri River bottomlands. There are cottonwoods, willow, ash, elder, and elm trees underneath which grow milkweed, grape, fern, strawberry, buffaloberry, chokecherry, Juneberry, and wild licorice, among other grasses and shrubs. Higher up on the prairie terraces grow wheatgrass, big and little bluestem, sedges, grammagrass, and needlegrass. But these have been invaded by a number of nonnative, noxious plants such as leafy spurge, smooth brome, and Canada thistle.

If you are walking the trails here, watch for white-tailed deer, wild turkey, coyotes, badgers, beaver, skunks, ground squirrels, northern pocket gophers, owls, hawks, sharp-tailed grouse, pheasants, bald eagles, and various species of migrating and nesting waterfowl.

As in most of the parks and refuges along the Missouri River and tributaries from the Dakotas east, the hiking here is not difficult. The Knife River Indian Villages Historic Site has about 11 miles of hiking trails, along the river and through the woods, both near the visitor center and a short drive west upstream along the Knife. In the winter, the upstream trails are groomed for cross-country skiing. Although it is not wild or serious backcountry hiking, do spend some time on these trails, which give a good sense of what this landscape was like before development. In the summer, consider a late afternoon or early evening hike; the lowering light makes the wetland riverbank greens stand out in great contrast to the pale yellow prairie grasses, and the North Dakota sunset is impressive. Try to get to the visitor center before it closes; its museum is well worth a visit.

The Knife River itself is generally too shallow to paddle in the summer, but the islands at the confluence with the Missouri are a good camping spot for those paddling the Garrison Reach of the Missouri.

The park is one-half mile north of Stanton, North Dakota, on County Road 37. The visitor center is open all year except for Thanksgiving, Christmas, and New Year's Day. Between September 5 and May 28, hours are from 8:00 A.M. to 4:30 P.M.; from May 29 to September 4, they are 7:30 A.M. to 6:00 P.M. (Dates may vary slightly from year to year.) For more information call the Knife River Indian Villages National Historic Site at 701-745-3309 or see http://www.nps.gov/knri.

Theodore Roosevelt National Park and the Little Missouri River

MONDAY APRIL 15TH. 1805

in a little pond of water fromed by this rivulet where it entered the bottom, I heard the frogs crying for the first time this season. . . . I saw great quantities of gees feeding in the bottoms,

of which I shot one. saw some deer and Elk, but they were
remarkably shy. I also met with great numbers of Grouse or
prairie hens [sharp-tailed grouse] . . . these birds appeared to
be mating; the note of the male, is kuck, kuck, coo, coo
cooo . . . the male also dubbs (drums with his wings)
something like the pheasant, but by no means as loud.

WEDNESDAY APRIL 17TH. 1805.

immense quantities of game in every direction around us as
we passed up the river; consisting of herds of Buffaloe, Elk
and Antelopes with some deer and woolves. tho' we continue
to see many tracks of the bear we have seen but very few of
them, and those are at a great distance generally running from
us. . . . Captain Clark saw a Curlou to-day.

Captain Lewis recorded these journal entries as the party continued north and west along the stretch of the Missouri now inundated by Lake Sakakawea, the impoundment that backs up for
miles behind Garrison Dam. One of the best places to see what the
Missouri's oxbows, prairie benches, badlands, and coulees must
have been like is **Theodore Roosevelt National Park**. The park is
divided into separate North and South Units and lies to the west
of Lewis and Clark's route, on the Little Missouri River. It takes
in grassland benches, extraordinary badland rock formations, and
winding bends of the Little Missouri River.

Bison have been reintroduced to the park and wander freely.
You may get to see them close up, as I did, watching several bison
roll on the grassy ground, sending up clouds of summer dust.
There are pronghorn, mule and white-tailed deer, and elk.
Mountain or bighorn sheep (*Ovis canadensis californiana*) have
also been reintroduced to the park to replace the extinct native
Audubon bighorn — the biggest of the bighorn sheep, which were
found in the badlands of North and South Dakota, the Missouri
Breaks, and other places in the Great Plains.[1] Black-tailed prairie
dogs live in both units of the park, along with snowshoe hare,
jackrabbit, northern pocket gopher, Ord's kangaroo rat, mink,
badger, coyote, and porcupine, among other mammals. Mountain

lion, bobcat, and lynx used to be found in the area but are now rare because of habitat loss. Similarly, the river otters that once lived here are now gone, extirpated by trapping and through loss of habitat, but are beginning to return in some other areas of their range. Efforts are being made to reintroduce black-footed ferrets to the park through a captive breeding program, although the ferrets' success will depend, at least in part, on the health of the prairie dogs on whom they prey.

Prairie dogs — on which well over 100 species prey — are protected within the park boundaries. Outside the park, they are unprotected and have long been regarded as a nuisance to farming and ranching activities and dealt with as such. The park is also home to nearly 190 bird species, including sharp-tailed grouse (like those seen by Lewis and Clark), golden eagles, and sandhill cranes. Bald eagles come through the park during their fall migration.

Both the North and South Units of the park — as well as a third, smaller, unit formed around ranches owned and operated by Theodore Roosevelt — lie within the boundaries of the **Little Missouri National Grassland**. Like the national forests, national grasslands are managed by the U.S. Department of Agriculture for "multiple use," and the Little Missouri Grassland is leased for domestic livestock grazing. There are also many private inholdings — primarily ranches — within the boundaries of the national grassland. At just shy of 70,500 acres in all, Theodore Roosevelt National Park is not large, and from points inside its boundaries, the protected landscapes of the park units stand out in marked contrast to the agriculture beyond.

At over a million acres, the Little Missouri National Grassland is the largest of the national grasslands. It also has the largest livestock-grazing program of any national grassland, with over 40,000 head of cattle grazing the area each year. There is also extensive oil and gas leasing in the grassland, and there are currently over 500 active oil wells within its boundaries. To service the wells and the livestock grazing, some 3,000 miles of roads snake through the grassland, which is home to mule deer, pronghorn, sharp-tailed grouse, prairie falcon, meadowlark, prairie dog towns, reintroduced bighorn sheep, and two rare butterflies, the regal fritillary and tawny crescent, to name but a few of the wildlife species there. In the southern part of the grassland — some 30 miles south of Medora — is the most northeasterly stand of ponderosa pine in North America. Off-road vehicle use has been increasing in the grassland, posing a threat to wildlife and vegetation. Despite the extensive use of the grassland's natural resources, there is an area of over 150,000 acres that remains roadless, which conservation groups and the Three Affiliated Tribes have recommended for congressional designation as legislatively protected wilderness.

Because of all the roads, private inholdings, oil wells, and livestock grazing, it is easier to see the Little Missouri Grassland country from within Theodore Roosevelt National Park, where many miles of hiking trails wander through the backcountry, snaking around coulees, badlands, and high grassy benches and along the river bottoms. Follow some of these paths, and you will quickly see how the grassland landscape here becomes distinctly western. Look for sage, yarrow, yucca, buckwheat, mariposa lily, prairie onion, globe mallow, winter fat, wood's rose, rabbit brush, purple coneflower, prairie rose, blazing star, prickly pear, Indian paintbrush, and a host of other wildflowers, along with juniper, cottonwood, ash, and elm trees.

In the North Unit there are huge round and egg-shaped sandstone rocks (called *cannonball concretions*), striated multicolored cliffs, deep green river banks, and mustard yellow prairie bluffs. Formation of these badlands began some 60 million years ago with the deposition and erosion of ancient sediment and volcanic ash, followed by aeons of shaping by wind, rain, and running water. Some of the cliffs contain layers of lignite coal and bentonite. Some areas, like the northwest corner of the park's South Unit, contain quantities of petrified wood.

The North Unit has a more rugged landscape than the South Unit and is less visited. (It is also my favorite.) Many trails in the North Unit intersect or connect with each other, so it is possible to do either day or short partial day hikes, as well as overnight backpack trips. There are two developed campgrounds in the

North Unit, available on a first-come, first-served basis. Back-country campers must obtain a no-fee permit at the visitor center. If you are hiking or backpacking in the park, remember to bring enough water; using water from backcountry sources is not recommended unless it is boiled first.

A nice hike through some of the badlands coulees in the North Unit follows the Caprock Coulee and Upper Caprock Coulee Trails. They can be hiked together in an easy loop of 4.1 miles. Another possibility is to hike from the Caprock Coulee trailhead to the Oxbow Overlook along the Achenbach Trail — about 3.25 miles each way. Or for a more extensive hike that could include an overnight in the park, consider hiking the whole 16-mile Achenbach Trail, which follows the river and climbs into the hills above. There are two river crossings on this route, so check at the visitor center about water levels before you leave. For a look at a prairie dog town — which can be fascinating — hike about a mile north from the Caprock Coulee trailhead on the Buckhorn Trail.

The North Unit of Theodore Roosevelt National Park is located 15 miles south of Watford City, North Dakota, on North Dakota Highway 85. For more information on the North Unit of the park, call 701-842-2333 or see http://www.nps.gov/thro.

Intrepid long-distance hikers and mountain bikers may want to take the 96-mile **Maah Daah Hey Trail**, which runs from the CCC Campground just outside the North Unit of the Theodore Roosevelt National Park through the Little Missouri Grassland and the South Unit of the park, to the Sully Creek State Park campground south of Medora, North Dakota. The trail crosses prairie and badlands on both public and private land. Camping is permitted on federal public land but not on North Dakota state lands or, obviously, on private land.

The north half of the trail lies east of the Little Missouri River, which it crosses near Theodore Roosevelt's Elkhorn Ranch. The trail then continues south on the west side of the river. Although this trail will probably be used more for long-distance bike trips than for hiking, bicycles are not allowed on the trail in the national park — either ridden or carried — so riders will need to

take another route around the South Unit of the park. As of this
writing, there are plans for a Buffalo Gap Trail open to bicycles
that will skirt the western boundary of the park's South Unit.

Maah Daah Hey is a Mandan word meaning "an area that has
been or will be around for a long time." The trail is not to be
undertaken lightly. There is much steep terrain, and the weather
can be changeable, even in the summer, when in a short period of
time, high temperatures and baking sun can give way to strong
winds, rainstorms, thunder, and even hail.

The trail is managed jointly by the National Park Service, the
U.S. Forest Service, and the North Dakota Parks and Recreation
Department. Trail maps are available from the Forest Service and
Theodore Roosevelt National Park. A schematic map is available
on-line at http://www.nps.gov/thro/tr_mdh.htm. For more information call Theodore Roosevelt National Park (North Unit number as above or South Unit at 701-623-4466), U.S. Forest Service
Medora District at 701-225-5151, or Sully Creek State Park at
701-663-9571. For maps of the Little Missouri National Grassland, contact the U.S. Forest Service Medora Ranger District,
which manages the southern half of the grassland, at 701-225-
5151 (161 21st Street, West, Dickinson, ND 58601), or the
McKenzie Ranger District, which manages the northern half, at
701-842-2393 (1901 S. Main Street, Watford City, ND 58854).
These maps are available only by mail or at the ranger district
offices. For more information on the Little Missouri National
Grassland, see the Forest Service Web site at http://www.fs.fed.us/
r2/nebraska/gpng/litt.html.

A number of conservation groups are involved in efforts to protect the Little Missouri National Grassland and to restore its
wildlife and native vegetation. For information, see the National
Wildlife Federation's Web site at http://www.nwf.org/grasslands/
littlemissouri.html or contact the North Dakota Wildlife Federation at 701-827-5227 or on-line at http://www.ndwf.org; the
Sierra Club's North Dakota office at 701-530-9288; or the
Wilderness Society at http://wilderness.org/newsroom/15most/
little_missouri.htm.

The Confluence of the Yellowstone and the Missouri

THURSDAY APRIL 25TH. 1805.

I ascended the hills from whence I had a most pleasing view of the country, particularly of the wide and fertile vallies formed by the missouri and the yellowstone rivers, which occasionally unmasked by the wood on their borders disclose their meanderings for many miles in their passage through these delightfull tracts of country. . . . the whol face of the country was covered with herds of Buffaloe, Elk & Antelopes; deer are also abundant but keep themselves more concealed in the woodland. the bufflow Elk and Antelopes are so gentle that we pass near them while feeding, without appearing to excite any alarm among them; and when we attract their attention, they frequently approach us more nearly to discover what we are and in some instances pursue us a considerable distance apparently with that in view.

The confluence of the Yellowstone and Missouri Rivers lies just east of the Montana–North Dakota border, about 25 miles southeast of Culbertson, Montana, and 25 miles west of Williston, North Dakota. On their westbound journey, Lewis and Clark continued following the Missouri west and upstream. It was here on the homebound journey that Clark's party, which followed the Yellowstone east from what is now Three Forks, rejoined Lewis's party, which had retraced its original route along the Missouri from the Great Falls. The "Indians inform that the yellowstone river is navigable for perogues and canoes nearly to it's source in the Rocky Mountains," wrote Lewis on April 26, 1805.

Although the confluence is now surrounded by farm fields and there is no backcountry hiking to be done in the immediate vicinity, it is worth a visit because the landscape around the Yellowstone here is still visible much as it must have been 200 years ago. An interesting way to get a sense of the continuity of this scenery is to look at some of the paintings done of this country by Karl Bodmer in the 1830s.

Confluence of the Missouri and Yellowstone Rivers. Photo: Wayne Mumford.

A good place from which to see the confluence is **Fort Union Trading Post**, which has been reconstructed and is maintained as a national historic site. John Jacob Astor's American Fur Trading Company originally built the trading post in 1828. For twenty years or so, a busy and lucrative trade in beaver pelts and buffalo hides was carried on at Fort Union between the Americans and Europeans and the Assiniboin, Blackfeet, Crow, and other tribes of the surrounding regions. By the late 1830s and 1840s, the demand for beaver fur had declined, but with the increasing competition for buffalo hides and growing river commerce, the fort continued to prosper. But in the late 1830s and years following, the outbreaks of smallpox that devastated the Assiniboin, Crow, and Blackfeet tribes, combined with encroaching white settlement throughout the Great Plains, engendered Indian hostility and contributed to the fort's demise. After the Civil War, Fort Union was abandoned in favor of Fort Buford, which was built in 1866, just east of the Yellowstone's confluence with the Missouri, but as a military fort rather than a trading post.

The Fort Union Trading Post is on Montana Highway 327 (or

Charles M. Russell Wildlife Refuge. Photo: Wayne Mumford.

North Dakota Highway 1804) and the Bainville-Snowden Road, which hugs a bit of the Missouri's north shore and follows the railroad, both obviously constructed along the old riverbed trading route. For more information call the Fort Union Trading Post National Historic Site at 701-571-9082 in Williston, North Dakota, or see its Web site at http://www.nps.gov/fous/.

Charles M. Russell National Wildlife Refuge

SUNDAY MAY 26TH. 1805.

In the after part of the day I also walked out and ascended the river hills which I found sufficiently forteiguing. on arriving to the summit [of] one of the highest points in the neighbourhood I thought myself well repaid for my labour; as from this point I beheld the Rocky Mountains for the first time, . . . these points of the Rocky Mountains were covered with snow and the sun shone on it in such a manner as to give me the most plain and satisfactory view. while I viewed these mountains I

felt a secret pleasure in finding myself so near the head of the
heretofore conceived boundless Missouri.

Between Fort Union and the immense earthen Fort Peck Dam,
about 115 straight highway miles west, the Missouri undulates
north and south, looking like a lengthy inchworm on the map.
The river here is narrow until it gapes wide into the enormous —
245,000-acre — reservoir of Fort Peck Lake that extends into the
vast **Charles M. Russell National Wildlife Refuge.** The relatively
sparsely roaded refuge is not easy country to get out into, but it
is well worth making an effort to explore its backcountry away
from the drowned riverbed bays of Fort Peck Lake.

The expedition spent a little over two weeks traveling through
the country now encompassed by the 1.1-million-acre Charles M.
Russell National Wildlife Refuge. What Captain Lewis took to be
the Rockies were actually the Bear Paw Mountains, which lie
about a hundred miles east of the Rockies' main spine. Fort Peck
Dam has radically changed the river, but there is no mistaking the
feeling of elation to be gotten from climbing the shoulders and
benches of the steep canyons, breaks, draws, and coulees of this
Missouri River plains and sagebrush grasslands country. Near the
creeks and river bottom grow willows and cottonwoods, while on
the dry uplands are sage, prickly pear, ponderosa, juniper, and
some Douglas fir.

When Lewis and Clark traveled here, among the many animals
they encountered were grizzlies, "vast quantities of Buffaloe, Elk,
deer . . . Antelope or goats, beaver, geese, ducks, brant and some
swan," porcupines, wolves, prairie dogs, coyotes, bald eagles, and
bighorn sheep. Elk, mule deer, some reintroduced bighorn sheep
(the last of the Audubon bighorn native to the region were killed
near here in 1916),[2] and a few pronghorn still roam the lands
within the refuge, but the buffalo are gone. Prairie dogs and prairie
dog towns are still found on the refuge, but their overall numbers
have been reduced so that the black-footed ferret, one of their principal predators, is gone save for a very small population reintroduced in 1994. The occasional mountain lion and bobcat are seen
on the refuge, but the grizzly bears are gone. The refuge is also

home to golden eagles, ferruginous and Swainson's hawks, northern harriers, and prairie falcons. Waterfowl — herons, geese, ducks, and others — live along the river, while sharp-tailed grouse, pheasants, and some sage grouse live in the uplands' sagebrush steppe.

In the westernmost section of the refuge, well upstream of the reservoir and dam, the Missouri flows in its natural channel, much as it always has. This reach of the Missouri is protected under the Wild and Scenic Rivers Act.

An "auto tour" route follows the only gravel roads in the refuge. All the other roads — save for where Highway 191 crosses the refuge — are clay jeep tracks, which need high-clearance or four-wheel-drive vehicles. These clay roads should be avoided when it rains because they turn to a sticky, slick impassable "gumbo" when wet. There are no established or maintained hiking trails in the refuge, but it is well worth the effort of walking cross-country or following some of the jeep trails — on either day hikes or overnight backpacks — to explore this landscape on foot. Be sure to bring enough water with you, since drinking water is generally unavailable in the refuge.

There are developed camping areas at the James Kipp Recreation Area at the west end of the refuge on the south side of the river, just off Highway 191, and at the Rock Creek boat ramp just beyond the western edge of Fort Peck Lake, as well as at a number of locations around the enormous impoundment that is Fort Peck Lake itself. Unless an area is specified as closed to camping, camping is permitted anywhere on the refuge, and while this guide does not want to encourage off-road driving of any kind, vehicles are allowed to drive up to one hundred yards from an established road to a temporary campsite.

There are livestock grazing allotments in the Charles M. Russell National Wildlife Refuge, but according to the refuge, virtually any area that is off limits to visitors should be fenced, so wandering cattle should not be a problem for hikers and campers. The refuge headquarters are located in Lewistown, Montana — reachable most directly from Highway 191 southwest of the refuge, or from Highway 200. Contact the refuge at 406-538-8706 from 7:30 A.M. to 4:00 P.M. for specific use regulations regarding campfires and for hunting season regulations, or see its Web site at http://www.r6.fws.gov/cmr/. The Web site also has detailed — but not topographic — road maps.

The auto tour route is a good introduction to the refuge and a logical place to scout where you might like to explore further. The tour takes off from Montana Highway 191 south of Zortman in the Little Rocky Mountains just outside the Fort Belknap Indian Reservation, southwest of Malta (which sits at the intersection of Highway 191 and Highway 2, the main road across the northern tier of Montana). The auto tour goes down to the river, where you may see elk browsing under the cottonwoods.

Two good places from which to consider taking off for a cross-country hike are auto tour stops 8 and 9, which are up on high grass and sage benches with some ponderosa pine and prickly pear. The easternmost end of the tour will take you toward the UL Bend Wilderness Area, also a good place to explore — and to look for sage grouse — although that is best accessed from Dry Fork Road, which takes off from Highway 191 south of Zortman and heads east into the refuge. About 25 miles in, Dry Fork Road takes a ninety-degree right-hand turn south and ends about 10 miles later in the UL Bend Wilderness Area. Watch for bighorn sheep at Two Calf Creek or Mickey-Brandon Buttes.

Hiking in the refuge is serious backcountry hiking, so make sure one member of your group is comfortable using topographic maps and a compass. The rugged terrain can have lots of steep ups and downs, but it is not too hard to find a relatively gentle path to navigate along benches and shoulders — especially if you start by following the jeep trails — and avoid any cliff scaling. National Wildlife Refuge (NWR) Road 201 is a good one to use as your main point of navigation, but be sure to explore the upland reaches of the refuge, where some of the most spectacular scenery lies. Away from the roads it is not hard to use your imagination when looking across the swoops of hills and badlands, cliffs, and outcrops shaped by wind and rain into castles and turrets, to picture what this country must have been like when surrounded by a great sea of grass.

For this section of the refuge, you will want topo maps for Bell Ridge East and West, Sagebrush Reservoir, Hanson Flat, Dry

Coulee, Chain Butte, Karsten Coulee, Mickey Butte, Locke Ranch, and Germaine Coulee West. The best size or scale of these maps to use for hiking is the 7.5′ quads of the 1:24,000 scale. To order maps call the U.S. Geological Survey at 888-ASK-USGS. Allow about two weeks or so for order processing and mailing. The refuge will also help you figure out what maps you need for the particular section you are planning to explore. It can also send you a large map of the refuge with the roads, rivers, creeks, camping areas, and boat launches marked — but without topographic detail.

The Missouri Breaks

WEDNESDAY MAY 29TH. 1805

Last night we were all allarmed by a large buffaloe Bull, which swam over from the opposite shore and coming along side of the white perogue, climbed over it to land, he then allarmed ran up the bank in full speed directly towards the fires, and was within 18 inches of the heads of the men who lay sleeping . . . This morning we set out at an early hour . . . at the distance of 2 1/2 Miles passed a handsome river . . . I walked on shore and acended this river about a mile and a half in order to examine it. . . . the water of this River is clearer much than any we have met with great abudance of the . . . Bighorned animals in the high country through with this river passes. Cap. C. who assended the R. much higher than I did has thought proper to call it Judieths River.

THURSDAY MAY 30TH. 1805. —

The hills and river Clifts which we passed today exhibit a most romantic appearance. The bluffs of the river rise to the hight of from 2 to 300 feet and in most places nearly perpendicular; they are formed of remakable white sandstone which is sufficiently soft to give way readily to the impression of water . . . The water in the course of time in decending from those hills and plains on either side of the river has trickled

down the soft sand clifts and woarn it into a thousand gro-
tesque figures, which with the help of a little immagination
and an oblique view, at a distance are made to represent
eligant ranges of lofty freestone buildings, having their
parapets well stocked with statuary . . . As we passed on
it seeemed as if those seens of visionary inchantment would
never have . . . [an] end.

The Missouri River Breaks — deep drainages, creek canyons, coulees, draws, cliffs; all descriptions apply — are a rather mysterious
landscape. They are almost invisible from the farmland fields that
lie on the settled plains above. Travel on most roads through this
region would leave you with almost no sense of the dramatic river
canyon that lies beyond and below. Because so much of the land
above the river is private, the best way to see the **Missouri Breaks**
is from the river itself.

In January 2001, 149 miles of the Upper Missouri River —
already designated a wild and scenic river — and adjacent public
land, from Fort Benton, Montana, downstream to the Charles M.
Russell National Wildlife Refuge, was proclaimed a national monument, giving the area some protection from development that
might destroy its natural or historic features. Most visually
remarkable of these landmarks are the White Cliffs, which were
described so vividly by Captain Lewis and look the same today.

The Missouri Breaks are home to a large herd of elk, to bighorn
sheep, pronghorn, and mule deer. Their sagebrush grasslands are
essential habitat for prairie dogs and are important winter range
for sage grouse. The area around the Judith River contains — in
the words of the national monument proclamation — "one of the
few remaining fully functioning cottonwood gallery forest ecosystems on the Northern Plains." Some of the rock layers along the
Missouri Breaks were laid down during the late Cretaceous era
and contain fossils of ancient plants and animals.

This stretch of river is important spawning habitat for pallid
sturgeon — an endangered species — and home to one of the few
paddlefish populations in the country, along with shovelnose sturgeon, sturgeon chub, blue sucker, and dozens of other fish species.

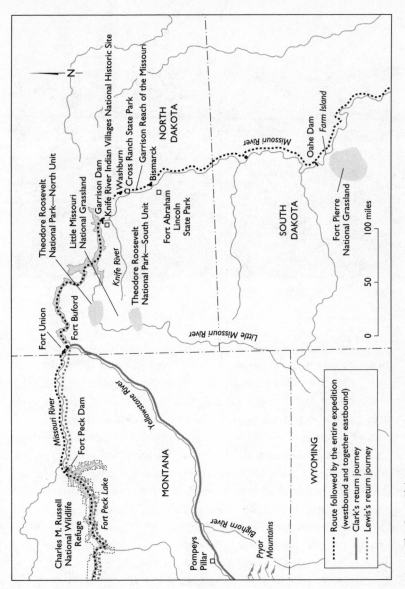

Map 4 *The Great Plains.*

Missouri Breaks. Photo: Wayne Mumford.

Great blue herons, bald and golden eagles, peregrine falcons, mountain plovers, sparrow and ferruginous hawks, and other birds inhabit the shoreline and its cliffs. White pelicans cruise the river corridor and are enchanting to watch as they glide into the water beside your boat as you make your way downriver.

The Missouri River Breaks can be paddled from Fort Benton all the way to Robinson Bridge at James Kipp State Park, which is the last easily accessible, developed river access point inside the Charles M. Russell National Wildlife Refuge — a distance of about 149 river miles. The most dramatically scenic section of the breaks is downstream from Virgelle and Coal Banks Coulee, so many people begin their river trip at Coal Banks Landing and take out at Judith Landing just downstream of the Judith River, a distance of 47 miles. This makes for a comfortable two- or three-day trip, depending on weather, wind, and how much hiking you do along the way. The whole 149 miles can be done in five to seven days, and the stretch from Fort Benton to Loma Bridge in a day.

The length of a day's paddle will also be determined by where you camp. Most of the public land along the breaks is indeed cliffs, and there is limited public land suitable for camping. The paddling is easy, flat water with a few riffles, but when the wind begins to blow upriver, the river whips up quickly to frothy white-caps and stiff waves. When this happens, it is best simply to get off the river because the wind often heralds rain or a thunderstorm. Thunderstorms can come up quickly, so keep an eye out and be prepared to get off the river if a storm does develop.

Recommended Two- or Three-Day Paddle: Coal Banks to Judith Landing

There is easy access to the river and a place at which to leave vehi-cles at Coal Banks Landing, just upstream of Virgelle. If coming from Great Falls (allow 1.5 hours), take Highway 87 north 12 miles past the town of Loma and look for the turnoff just past milepost 66, where a sign says Missouri River Canoe Co. and there is a Bureau of Land Management (BLM) sign for Coal Banks Landing. If coming from Havre, take Highway 87 south 7 miles past Big Sandy to the turnoff for Virgelle (allow an hour). From either turnoff it is 8 gravel miles to Virgelle and Coal Banks Landing. There is no permit or fee required to launch, but you are asked to check in and register with the ranger on duty. Coal Banks Landing is at river mile 41. The "wild" section of the river's des-ignated wild and scenic reach begins at river mile 51.5.

Depending on what time of day you set out, how fast you are paddling, and, perhaps most important, the weather, a good place to camp the first night is at Eagle Creek on the west side of the river at river mile 56. Eagle Creek is across from LaBarge Rock, which you may recognize from Karl Bodmer's paintings. Lewis and Clark's party camped here on May 31, 1805. There is a grove of cottonwoods here by the river, but remember that in high winds these can be hazardous, so check for dead and falling limbs before setting up camp. Eagle Creek is on private land, but the Bureau of Land Management has a scenic use easement arrangement with the landowner to allow public access. Otherwise, the next best place to camp is the campsite on the south side of the river near river mile 63 just before Hole in the Wall, or try the north side near mile 61. For those who launch late in the day, just before mile 47 on the north side is a possible campsite as well.

If you are taking your time and hiking to explore side canyons along the way, you may want to spend the second night at the Slaughter River campsite on the north side of the river at mile 77. This was Lewis and Clark's campsite on May 30, 1805. Before camping or coming ashore to hike, check your river map to make sure you are on public land. Judith Landing is just past river mile 88.

Because winds can come up in the night, make sure your boat is securely tethered and away from the water. Take note of Lewis's May 31, 1805, journal entry describing the "mud so tenacious that [the men] . . . are unable to wear their mockersons." The riverbank mud is as slippery and sticky as it was two hundred years ago, and its grasp strong enough to destroy late-twentieth-century river sandals. When hiking above the river, keep an eye out for rattlesnakes.

Potable drinking water is available at Coal Banks Landing, Hole in the Wall, and Judith Landing, but otherwise remember to bring enough water. Unless boiled or filtered — and even then I would think twice — Missouri River water is not safe for drinking.

One other cautionary note: the Missouri Breaks may have a wild and scenic river designation and status as a national monument, but they are intermingled with state and private lands. The Missouri Breaks are therefore open to domestic livestock grazing under the Bureau of Land Management's "multiple use" mandate, and the river corridor is often full of cattle and their leavings. A look at a landownership map will show how much private land there is adjacent to and interspersed with the public. Much of this land is used for livestock grazing. Cattle come down the draws and creeks from the higher country, especially in hot weather, at all hours of the day and night. They wade the banks and cool themselves under the cottonwood trees and even cross the river in shallow spots. The BLM signs tell visitors to "Leave no trace," but clearly they have forgotten to instruct bovine visitors in this ethic. When I paddled here in the summer of 2000, cattle and their leavings were all over the public stretches of the riverbank, including

NOXIOUS WEEDS

As in all of Montana—and the rest of the West—travelers here should be aware of the problems presented by noxious weeds and other nonnative plants that compete with native vegetation, often with severely detrimental consequences to indigenous plant communities and wildlife habitat. Noxious weeds are estimated to be spreading at a rate of between 4,000 and 5,000 acres a day on BLM lands throughout the West, primarily due to livestock grazing.[3] It helps to learn what these invasive plants look like and to avoid picking or transporting them. This means checking shoes, socks, pant legs, pets, vehicles, and gear to make sure these pesky plants and their seeds are not hitching a ride. For more information on noxious weeds in Montana, see http://www.mtweed.org.

campsites. Despite the cows, given the extensive alteration most of the Missouri River has undergone since the days of Lewis and Clark, paddling the Upper Missouri Breaks is an expedition well worth making.

Whether you begin at Fort Benton or Coal Banks and take out at Judith Landing or Robinson Bridge, you will want both maps 1 and 2 and maps 3 and 4 of the Upper Missouri National Wild and Scenic River published by the Department of the Interior (sections 1 and 2 come on one map, sections 3 and 4 on a second). These are available through the Bureau of Land Management's Lewistown Field Office at 406-538-7461 or by writing to P.O. Box 1160, Lewistown, MT 59457. For additional information, see the BLM's Upper Missouri River Breaks National Monument Web site at http://www.mt.blm.gov/ldo/um/. Canoes and touring kayaks can be rented, and shuttles arranged with outfitters in Fort Benton or in Virgelle at the helpful Virgelle Mercantile, which also sells maps.

The Yellowstone River and Pompeys Pillar

JULY 15TH. 1806

I proceeded on down the river on an old buffalow road . . . below the mountains Shield River discharges itself into the Rochejhone . . . it heads in those Snowey Mountains to the

NW with Howards Creek, it contains some Timber Such as Cotton & willow in it's bottoms, and Great numbers of beaver . . . the river also abounds in those animals as far as I have Seen . . . I saw two black bear on the side of the mountains this morning. Several gangs of Elk from 100 to 200 in a gangue of the river, great numbers of Antelopes.

JULY 25, 1806

after Satisfying my Self Sufficiently in this delightfull prospect of the extensive Country around, and the emence herds of Buffalow, Elk and wolves on which it abounded, I decended and proceeded on a fiew miles, Saw a gang of about 40 Big horn . . .

Captain Clark wrote these entries in his journal on the expedition's eastbound journey, often calling the Yellowstone by a version of its French name, *roche*, meaning "rock" and *jaune*, meaning "yellow," after the pale stone bluffs near the river's mouth. The first entry above was written near what is now Livingston, Montana, the second near Pompeys Pillar, northeast of Billings. "For me to mention to give an estimate of the different Species of Wild animals on this river particularly Buffalow, Elk, Antelopes & Wolves would be incredible," Clark wrote of this landscape.

It is along the Yellowstone that the only physical evidence of the Lewis and Clark expedition remains. This is Captain William Clark's inscription on the 150-foot sandstone outcrop known as Pompeys Pillar. The "remarkable rock," as Clark described it, is covered in petroglyphs and other markings of early travelers and inhabitants of the region, including the Crow, who call the pillar the "Mountain Lions Lodge." Captain Clark called the rock Pompeys Tower, after the son born to Sacagawea and the expedition's interpreter, Toussaint Charbonneau, while the expedition camped at Fort Mandan in the winter of 1805. In January 2000, President Clinton proclaimed Pompeys Pillar, and an area of about 50 surrounding miles, a national monument.

The **Yellowstone River** rises in the mountains of northwestern Wyoming. It flows dramatically through Yellowstone National

Park, and altogether for some 670 undammed — though not undiverted or undeveloped — miles to the Missouri, making it the longest essentially free-flowing river in the continental United States. The Yellowstone flows through protected wilderness and parks, agricultural country, and heavily settled residential communities. It descends from the Teton, Beartooth, Absaroka, and Gallatin Mountains and moves north and east into drier prairie country until it meets the Missouri on the Montana–North Dakota border.

Because it is not dammed, the Yellowstone is free to create side channels and sandbars, and to carry sediment and gravel naturally, providing good and varied habitat for fish and other wildlife. Upriver, the Yellowstone is known for its cold-water trout fishing. Downstream the river widens and becomes warmer, creating floodplain habitat that is home to great numbers of waterfowl and migrating songbirds — an environment that nurtures deer, elk, pronghorn, and other mammals.

The Yellowstone is not without problems, however. In many places the river's banks have been hardened or restricted by levees in an attempt to control the floodplain in ways that facilitate riverside development. Many engineered diversions along the river channel water into irrigation systems, which consequently alter the habitat crucial to native fish such as sturgeon and paddlefish. Agricultural runoff and erosion of banks from heavy streamside livestock grazing have also degraded river conditions. Upriver, stocking of nonnative trout threatens the native cutthroat trout, which are a cornerstone of the riparian corridor's food chain.

Paddling the Yellowstone

A great way to get a sense of the Yellowstone is to paddle the river by canoe or touring kayak, or to float it by rowing or paddle raft. When the river is running high, currents can be swift throughout its largely flat-water flow, and under any conditions the Yellowstone is not thought of as a sluggish river. Do inquire locally about river conditions before setting out. Many novices paddle this river in the company of those more skilled, but it is not recommended for an entire party of rank beginners. And most people may actually end up rafting the river, especially when flows are high early in the season.

Some upstream sections of the river are heavily used in the summer, and the river's two whitewater reaches — between Gardiner and Corwin Springs and through Yankee Jim Canyon — are popular for raft trips. The section of the river that flows through Paradise Valley around Livingston is the most popular, and there is an annual July float from Livingston to Billings. Those who like having rivers to themselves might want to avoid that time. But the Yellowstone is a long river, and stretches downstream from Billings get less recreational traffic and offer a way to experience the nature of the river corridor — especially if you ignore the railroad and highway that run close to the river for much of its length.

To paddle your way to Pompeys Pillar, consider putting in at Gritty Stone (8 miles to Pompeys Pillar) or Voyager's Rest (5 miles to Pompeys Pillar). For a longer paddle, continue on to Captain Clark (26 miles) or to the confluence with the Bighorn River at Manuel Lisa (38 miles). Wherever you go, stay alert for snags, changes in current, and water entering the river from tributaries or irrigation devices.

To see a more remote, prairie section of the Yellowstone that is less used than the reaches of the river that flow through Paradise Valley near Livingston and Gardiner, consider floating the 50 miles from Terry to Glendive. If you want to rent a canoe or kayak, your best bet is to do so in Livingston (try the friendly and helpful folks at Rubber Ducky River Services, who run shuttles and rent both canoes and kayaks for independent trips) or Bozeman, but do call ahead to make reservations. Both communities have listings of outfitters on their chamber of commerce Web sites, and numerous companies offer guided trips on the Yellowstone. White-water rafting trips are the most popular of these offerings.

No permits are necessary for a small, private party to float or paddle the Yellowstone. A fishing access guide that shows boat ramp locations is available (free of charge) through the Billings office of the Montana Department of Fish, Wildlife and Parks (http://fwp.state.mt.us) at 406-247-2940. The BLM publishes the "Floaters Guide to the Yellowstone" for the upper reaches of the river above Billings and Park City, as well as a series of recreation guide maps (about four dollars each), which include landownership and river access points for the whole length of the river. These are available from the BLM office in Billings at 406-896-5000.

For information on a campaign to protect and restore the Yellowstone, see the Greater Yellowstone Coalition's "Saving the Yellowstone River" program via its Web site at http://www.greateryellowstone.org or call its office at 406-586-1593 in Bozeman, Montana.

Hiking the Pryor Mountains

Due south of Billings and the main stem of the Yellowstone are the Pryor Mountains, a range that rises to the west of the Bighorns and the Bighorn River. This is southern Rocky Mountain country. The elevation is high — between about 4,000 and 8,500 feet — and there are steep canyons, limestone outcrops, dramatic buttes and mesas, Great Basin high desert country, high subalpine meadows, and forest.

The Pryors' unusual variation in topography makes them a region with a great diversity of vegetation, including some species of plants found nowhere else in the world. The Pryors contain some of the most northeasterly of Douglas fir forests and the most northern stands of mountain mahogany. Elk, mule deer, bighorn sheep, black bears, mountain lions, and bobcats make their home here, as do golden eagles, peregrine falcons, and over 200 other bird species. Crooked Creek, which flows through a limestone canyon, provides important habitat for Yellowstone cutthroat trout, native brook trout, and rainbow trout. Wild and remote, the Pryors are relatively undisturbed, but increasing use by off-road vehicle enthusiasts is beginning to erode fragile soil, spread weeds, and disturb wildlife habitat.

As one of my informants has said, any description of the Pryors "would be incomplete without a mention of rattlesnakes." Yes, they do live here, but don't let that put you off. Generally, and unless provoked, rattlesnakes prefer to hide and flee than attack. But keep an eye out, especially in the cooler weather of spring and fall, when you may happen upon snakes denning, or curled in hollows to keep warm. If you see a rattlesnake, give it room, do not under any circumstances harass it, and continue on your way.[4]

The Pryors encompass a large wild horse range managed by the BLM, where there are indeed wild horses. The northwestern part of the area around Lost Water Creek Canyon is part of the Custer National Forest, while the country between the east flank of the mountains and the Bighorn River is in the Bighorn Canyon National Recreation Area, managed by the National Park Service. The Crow consider the Pryor Mountains sacred. To the north and east of the public lands is the Crow Indian Reservation, about 45,000 acres of which are closed to nontribal members in order to protect cultural sites.

There are few roads into the Pryors, and there are no established trails apart from jeep roads. In the rain shadow of the Absaroka-Beartooth range, the Pryors get little rainfall, and temperatures can be high in summer. Still, there are some relatively accessible ways to explore this rugged terrain. The easiest access to the Pryors from the north is from Highway 310 coming south from Bridger. At 2.5 miles south of Bridger, turn east (or left) onto Pryor Mountain Road. The road runs along Sage Creek before entering Custer National Forest, where it becomes Forest Road (FR) 3085. Take this road to its junction with FR 849, which will be the left-hand fork. From here there are several options for day hikes. Among them are to hike the jeep road, FR 3092 along Commissary Ridge above Crooked Creek — about 4 miles in, for an 8-mile round-trip hike. Or you can take FR 849 out to its end, Dry Head Vista, and hike for a couple of miles or so to the southeast there along the rim.

There are no fees or permits for parking in the national forest, but developed campgrounds do require a fee, payable on a first-come, first-served basis. For more information about the Custer National Forest contact the Forest Service at 406-657-6200 or see http://www.fs.fed.us/r1/custer/.

Just to the east of the Pryors themselves is the Bighorn Canyon National Recreation Area. Its recreational management is organized around the impoundment lake behind Yellowtail Dam at Fort Smith, Montana, which backs up the Bighorn River into Bighorn Lake, extending for over 60 miles in both Montana and Wyoming.

Beartooths and Absarokas

The Beartooth and Absaroka Mountains range across the Montana-Wyoming border to the northeast of Yellowstone National Park — south of the Yellowstone River about midway between Billings and Livingston, Montana. The area ranges in elevation from nearly 7,000 to 11,500 feet, with snow-covered peaks rising above. The volcanic Absarokas lie to the west, the granitic Beartooths to the east. Much of this area is encompassed by the 943,626-acre Absaroka-Beartooth Wilderness. Some 23,383 acres of the wilderness are in Wyoming, the remainder in Montana. These high granite mountains, alpine meadows, great swoops of tundra, and countless lakes, streams, and tarns are home to bighorn sheep, mountain goats, moose, marmots, elk, deer, and black and grizzly bears, among other mammals. Much of the region hovers around the tree line, which occurs at around 9,000 feet. On the high slopes grow Douglas fir, Engelmann spruce, subalpine fir, and whitebark pine. The grassy sage meadows are covered in wildflowers — among them lupine, penstemon, shooting stars, heather, lilies, gentian, larkspur, paintbrush, and columbine.

The summer season here is short, limited to July and August, which — along with September — are also the best, most possible times to visit the Beartooths. Because of the high, mountainous terrain, the weather is changeable, and storms blow in nearly daily, bringing heavy rain, thunder, lightning, and often hail. The high elevation can make for strenuous hiking, especially for those unaccustomed to the altitude, so bear that in mind and acclimate yourself accordingly. Since the hiking season in the Beartooths and Absarokas is short, chances are you will see other visitors when you are out. But this is exhilaratingly beautiful and expansive country that readily absorbs its visitors.

The campgrounds and trailheads in the wilderness area are accessible from the portion of Highway 212 known as the Beartooth National Scenic Byway, which runs between Red Lodge and Cooke City, Montana, and may be one of the more dramatically scenic roads in the country. The highway is usually open from Memorial Day until the end of September or middle of October, depending on weather. To check on road conditions across the state, call the Montana State Highway Department at 800-226-ROAD. Or contact the Forest Service Red Lodge District Office for information about conditions in the wilderness and forest area: 406-446-2103.

Even if you are backpacking and plan on backcountry camping, stopping at the Beartooth Lake campground is a good way to orient yourself. Given the changeable weather and the high elevation, however, you may want to consider setting up a base camp and doing long day hikes to better enjoy the walking, instead of lugging a 40-pound pack on trails that can be slick with mud and entail many stream crossings.

Recommended Day Hikes

A pair of trails — numbers 619 and 621 — takes off from the Beartooth Lake campground on the east side of Beartooth Lake. Both head north along the east side of a creek and then head west after skirting two lakes, climb up onto grassy, wildflower-strewn meadow ridges, and wander through stands of pine. There are several wide stream crossings at the beginning of the trail, so be prepared to brave some icy water. You can pick up a trail that runs north-south back to Beartooth Lake and do the day's hike as an approximately 8-mile loop or retrace your steps at any point along the way.

Another wonderful day hike takes off from the trailhead below the Clay Butte Fire Lookout and heads north above Beartooth Butte. This Granite Lake trailhead is a few miles west of the Beartooth Campground off Highway 212. Park off the road before the switchbacks that climb up to the lookout and find the trailhead toward the east end of the area carved out for parking. This trail begins at nearly 9,600 feet, so pace yourself for the elevation, which climbs to about 10,000 along the way. The trail crosses wide, grassy wildflower meadows and climbs up onto tarn and boulder-strewn tundra, where the buttes often have snow throughout the summer. You can follow the trail's west fork to Granite Lake and beyond or head east above Beartooth Butte. If you have organized yourself with a shuttle, you can follow the trail back to the west side of Beartooth Lake. If not, wander as far as the day and your stamina allow and then retrace your path to the Clay Butte trailhead. It is between 3 and 4 miles to Granite Lake, which makes for a loop hike of about 7 or 8 miles back to Beartooth Lake.

Both of these hikes take you up to wonderful lake basins strewn with chunks of quartz, tufts of heather, and year-round snow. The views of the mountains are extraordinary, and the tundra, alpine meadows, and lakes are exquisite. Remember that early summer brings mosquitoes, that storms can roll in at any time, and that you are in grizzly country. Two maps you will want to have are the Absaroka-Beartooth Wilderness Map and the North Half Shoshone National Forest Map. For conditions check with the Beartooth Ranger District of the Custer National Forest at 406-446-2103.

CHAPTER 6

Central and Western Montana and across Lolo Pass into Idaho

The Great Falls Area and Ulm Pishkun

THURSDAY JUNE 13TH. 1805.

I had proceded on this course about two mile with Goodrich at some distance behind me whin my ears were saluted with the agreeable sound of a fall of water and advancing a little further I saw the spray arrise above the plain like a collumn of smoke which would frequently dispear again in an instant caused I presume by the wind which blew pretty hard from the S.W. I did not however loose my direction to this point which soon began to make a roaring too tremendous to be mistaken for any cause short of the great falls of the Missouri. . . . I hurryed down the hill which was about 200 feet high and difficult of access, to gaze on this sublimely grand specticle. . . . Immediately at the cascade the river is about 300 yrds. wide; about ninty or a hundred yards of this next the Lard. Bluff is a smoth even sheet of water falling over

*a precipice of at least eighty feet the remaining part of about
200 yards on my right formes the grandest sight I ever beheld . . . the irregular and somewhat projecting rocks below
receives the water in it's passage down and brakes it into a
perfect white foam which assumes a thousand forms in a
moment sometimes flying up in jets of sparkling foam . . .
from the reflection of the sun on the sprey or mist which
arises from these falls there is a beatifull rainbow produced
which adds not a little to the beauty of this majestically grand
scenery.*

Captain Lewis lamented the inadequacy of his written description
and wished he had with him a "camera obscura" to better capture
the details of this wondrous sight. Here the expedition caught its
first cutthroat trout, which now bears the scientific name of
Oncorhynchus clarki. Upstream from the Great Falls were
Crooked Falls, Rainbow Falls, Colter Falls, and Black Eagle Falls,
all of which had to be portaged — an undertaking that took nearly
a month. There were buffalo, grizzly and black bears, pronghorn,
deer, and rattlesnakes. The men saw a Western meadowlark here
and had to step carefully lest the prickly pear thorns pierce their
"mockersons."

The portage over the steep terrain was arduous. Canoes had to
be taken out of the river and dried before they were carried or
placed on wheeled carts and pulled. The wind was often strong
and gusty, so much so, wrote Lewis on June 25, 1805, that some
of the men "hoisted a sail on the canoe and it had driven her
along on the truck wheels. This is really sailing on dry land." On
July 15, the portage completed, the expedition was waterborne
once more. Prickly pear and sunflowers were blooming, and
golden currants and serviceberries ripe in profusion.

Today, the **Great Falls of the Missouri** are trapped behind Ryan
Dam. Crooked Falls, Rainbow Falls, and Black Eagle Falls are all
dammed, and Colter Falls is submerged by the impoundment
behind Black Eagle Dam. The Forest Service runs an extensive
Lewis and Clark Interpretive Center located on the river just
upstream of Black Eagle Dam, where a walking path follows the

WESTSLOPE CUTTHROAT TROUT

The cutthroat trout caught by Lewis and Clark's expedition were westslope cutthroat trout (*Oncorhynchus clarki lewisi*), a subspecies of cutthroat trout that colonized the inland Pacific Northwest during the last period of glaciation. The westslope cutthroat trout was once found from the upper Missouri River Basin on the east side of the Continental Divide in Montana west into Idaho, Oregon, and Washington. Today, as a result of habitat degradation and competition from introduced nonnative fish and hatchery populations, many runs of westslope cutthroat trout have disappeared, and the remaining populations are declining at what scientists call an alarming rate. In 1997 conservationists petitioned the U.S. Fish and Wildlife Service to list the westslope cutthroat trout under the Endangered Species Act. In the spring of 2000, the U.S. Fish and Wildlife Service said that such a listing was not warranted, but the fish have again been proposed for protective listing under the ESA. Though they are scarce, if you are lucky, you may see cutthroat trout in the streams and lakes high in the mountains, as some friends and I did in Glacier National Park. It is in the upper Missouri River Basin—the only place east of the Continental Divide where westslope cutthroat trout still exist—that the cutthroat are especially imperiled.

east bank of the river for about 7 or 8 miles. There are native plantings of silver sage, blanket flower, and balsamroot around the interpretive center, and cottonwoods shade part of the riverside path, but twentieth-century development dominates the landscape. A General Mills plant, an auto body shop, a municipal golf course, a power plant, and various other establishments of industry and commerce line the Missouri around Great Falls.

The Lewis and Clark Interpretive Center is located on the northeast side of Great Falls at Giant Springs Heritage State Park. The center is open from 9:00 A.M. to 6:00 P.M. daily from Memorial Day weekend through September 30; and from 9:00 A.M. to 5:00 P.M. Tuesday through Saturday, and from 12:00 to 5:00 P.M. on Sunday, from October 1 through Memorial Day weekend. For more information call 406-727-8733 or see the center's Web site at http://www.fs.fed.us/r1/lewisclark/lcic.htm.

To reach the Great Falls themselves, you must drive east out of Great Falls on Highway 87 toward Havre and turn right at

Ulm Pishkun. Photo: Wayne Mumford.

Morony and Ryan Dam Road, a narrow two-lane that runs through barley and wheat fields and across railroad tracks before turning steeply downhill following the sloping great curves of coulees to the river. There is an old-fashioned state park at the bottom of the falls where they tumble through the dam, and it is easy to see what these huge falls must have been like before the dam was built in 1915. Although this is definitely not a strenuous wilderness excursion, it is worth a detour to get a sense of the lay of the land, to see how it is now used, and to see what is left of the falls. The falls themselves resemble the Great Falls of the Yellowstone, with their cascades crashing over the ochre and orange rocks.

Not far upstream from where the expedition relaunched its boats after the portage around the Great Falls is the town of Ulm, where the lower Smith River joins the Missouri. Just north of town is **Ulm Pishkun State Park,** located at the site of a remarkable ancient buffalo jump that was used to hunt buffalo by running them off the high cliffs. Many tribes used Ulm Pishkun — thought to be one of the highest buffalo jumps in Montana — the Blackfeet, Salish, Gros Ventre, Sioux, Shoshones, Kootenai, Crow, and Assiniboin among them. Its last known use was in 1500. A short but impressive drive from the park's visitor center is the buffalo jump itself, located on a butte that rises high above the plains below. A series of short walking trails (about a mile in all) circle the cliffs and the tabletop of the rise, where prickly pear dot the grass, and which is home to an extensive black-tailed prairie dog town. To the southwest is the immense landform called Square Butte, and from atop Ulm Pishkun it is easy — if one ignores the wheat fields that stretch out for miles in every direction — to imagine what this country was like two hundred years ago. The prairie dogs are enchanting to watch, especially if you happen to be there late in the day, when the light angles low and orange across the plains and the prairie dogs emerge from their burrows to face the setting sun. Stand and watch the prairie dogs and scramble gently along the encircling cliffs, and you will have a sense of the immensity and enormous history of this landscape.

As one of the interpretive signs says:

> Before you, the Missouri River swerves east toward the Mississippi. Behind you lies the Rocky Mountain Front Range, still bearing remnants of the Old North Trail, a trade route used for 12,000 years.
>
> Between the Highwood Mountains to the east and the starkly noble Square Butte on the southwestern horizon, bison gathered by the tens of thousands to feast on seasonal grasses. Where bison gathered so did Plains Indians, celebrating and hunting. A buffalo jump was an event of great excitement and thanksgiving.
>
> The spirit of thankfulness still permeates this place. Many native and non-native people find Ulm Pishkun very powerful. Please respect this sacred site and all the creatures who belong here.

To reach Ulm Pishkun State Park, take I-15 10 miles south of Great Falls to the Ulm exit and then follow signs to the park 6 miles northwest on county roads. For further information call the park at 406-866-2217. Limited information is available through the state parks link on the Montana Department of Fish, Wildlife and Parks Web site: http://fwp.state.mt.us/.

Gates of the Mountains Wilderness

If you would like to stretch your legs and explore more extensively, venture farther south, upstream along the Missouri from Ulm to the Gates of the Mountains Wilderness Area. The 28,562-acre wilderness area lies to the east of the river, where it is impounded behind Holter Dam and Hauser Dam. You can reach the area by crossing Wolf Creek Bridge at the north end of Holter Lake, but the better roads leading to the established trailheads are reached by crossing the Missouri at York Bridge via Highway 280 northeast of Helena. From Highway 280 you can continue east to the Hanging Valley National Recreation Trail or head north on the York-Nelson Road, then east at Beaver Creek Road to the Refrigerator Canyon Trail. Drive carefully on Beaver Creek Road, which twists and turns and is frequented by logging trucks.

On both of these trails, you will probably want to do an out-and-back sort of hike, retracing your steps, unless you have arranged for someone to pick you up at what you choose to be your ultimate destination. If you hike the Refrigerator Canyon Trail all the way to the Missouri, you can catch one of the Gates of the Mountains tour boats as a ferry. For information and tour boat schedules, call Gates of the Mountain Boat Tour at 406-458-5241. Refrigerator Canyon Trail climbs about 2,500 feet altogether. Refrigerator Canyon's narrow corridor is about 3 miles up the trail. This could be your destination for a day hike. If you continue on, you will climb out onto a series of meadows, before a steep downhill to the river about 16 or so miles from the trailhead.

The Gates of the Mountains Wilderness Area is administered by the Helena National Forest. For more information contact the Forest Service office in Helena at 406-449-5201 or see its Web site at http://www.fs.fed.us/r1/helena/.

Glacier National Park

To get out into the backcountry and roadless expanses, you will have to venture off the actual Lewis and Clark Trail a bit. The spectacular scenery of **Glacier National Park**, the **Bob Marshall**

Wilderness, Cabinet Mountains, and **Yaak Valley,** not to mention the opportunity to immerse yourself in the wild, makes these detours well worth the effort. The areas and explorations are arranged here in a generally east-to-west fashion, to gather in one section places near the Lewis and Clark Trail for both their outbound and return journeys.

While a great many acres of this northern Rocky Mountain country are protected in Glacier National Park and the Bob Marshall, Great Bear, and Scapegoat Wilderness Areas, the ecological integrity of much adjacent public land — particularly the lower-elevation plains at the foot of the mountains to the south and east of Glacier — is threatened by logging, mining, and oil and gas exploration and extraction. The area provides important habitat and a migration corridor for many animals, including wolves, grizzly bears, moose, wolverine, bighorn sheep, and elk. Preserving the wildness of this landscape is essential to the long-term survival of these and many other native species of flora and fauna.

Before ascending the Missouri to its Great Falls, Lewis and Clark scouted part of what they named the **Marias River.** The Marias flows into the Missouri from the north, but Lewis and Clark thought there was a chance this stream might be the main stem of the Missouri. The Marias meets the Missouri at Loma, about 10 miles east of Fort Benton, after descending from the massive mountains that give rise to **Two Medicine River** high in the snows of what is now the eastern edge of Glacier National Park. Lewis and Clark did not know it, but what is now called Marias Pass on the Continental Divide, just outside Glacier National Park and the Blackfeet Indian Reservation, is a much shorter route between the Missouri and Columbia River watersheds. The Burlington Northern Railroad took advantage of this fact, and its rails now snake along the deep gorge of the Flathead River here and climb the divide at Summit before heading east toward Browning and Cut Bank.

There are countless wonderful hikes to take in Glacier National Park. Anywhere you go, you will traverse amazing scenery with the possibility of wildlife sightings — including grizzly bears, bighorn sheep, moose, mule deer, elk, black bears, mountain lions, and mountain goats. Because the elevation is high, snow lingers into June or beyond, and it can fall again in August and September, so be sure to check conditions with park rangers before setting out. Also take seriously the information about hiking in grizzly country. This is especially true if you are camping and picnicking or if you will be passing through berry-rich terrain at a time of year when mother bears may be out with their cubs. Here is a sampling of a few hikes. No doubt you will discover others.

On the west side of the park — which you will probably enter from West Glacier — a lovely, easy half-day hike is along the trail to **Avalanche Lake.** The trail follows Avalanche Creek, which tumbles in rapids of turquoise blue and white snowmelt, up to Avalanche Lake at the foot of Sperry Glacier. It is 2 miles to the lake, and you will gain about 500 feet in elevation. You may see cutthroat trout in the lake, and deer are likely to be browsing nearby.

For a longer, more altitudinous day hike, take the trail to **Sperry Chalet.** The trailhead is across the road from Lake McDonald Lodge. The first part of the trail switchbacks through the woods along Sprague Creek before emerging into the open of small waterfalls and tumbling streams with views of Gunsight Mountain. The trail is 6.4 miles each way and gains 3,432 feet in elevation.

Farther inside the park, about 24 miles from the Apgar Visitor Center (not far from the West Glacier entrance) along the Going-to-the-Sun Road, you will come to the Logan Pass Visitor Center. Park here and cross the road to the **Highline Trail** trailhead. This is a wonderful trail that clings to the side of the mountain known as the Garden Wall, which trickles with snowmelt and for much of the summer is festooned with wildflowers, including Lewis's monkey flower. Watch for mountain goats, bighorn sheep, and marmots — and keep an eye out for grizzlies. The trail climbs about 6 miles to the **Granite Park Chalet.** From there, if you have arranged a shuttle or can catch one of the buses that sometimes run through the park back to Logan Pass, you can descend about 3.5 miles through the woods on a bit of trail known as the Loop. Otherwise, you can retrace your steps and possibly take a detour up the edge of the Grinnell Glacier near a rock ridge called the Salamander. Or you can climb the spur trail that leads north from

Granite Park on the trail to Many Glacier to the lookout at Swiftcurrent Mountain.

If you are backpacking, the Sperry Chalet and Highline Trails connect with a network of trails to make for two-day and longer overnight trips. Permits are required for overnight backpacking and are issued for specific backcountry campgrounds. Because of grizzly bear activity, the park asks that people use designated campgrounds only and be scrupulous about packing out any food and trash, whether or not it belongs to you. As a safety precaution, before setting out, be sure to check with rangers about any recent grizzly sightings or activity. This is no joke. Bears here have hurt people, and bears, being intelligent animals, will return to a location where they have found food before.

There are campgrounds at Granite Park Chalet and at Sperry Chalet.

More people visit the west side of the park than the east, but the **Two Medicine Lake** section of the park is, if possible, even more impressive than the west. You can reach Two Medicine either from East Glacier or via the Going-to-the-Sun Road. (The Going-to-the-Sun Road is occasionally closed by snow or roadwork, so check before you set out.) The mountains seem more massive around Two Medicine, and the country wilder and more remote. Here you get a distinct sense of the north. Hudson Bay Divide is not far away.

A number of hiking trails take off from near the Two Medicine campground. From here you can circumnavigate Two Medicine Lake heading west on a spur trail to Upper Two Medicine Lake or to No Name Lake on the way to Dawson Pass — a loop of 6 to 7 miles. Or you can head north from Two Medicine Lake on a trail that puts Rising Wolf Mountain to your west and hike up to Oldman and Pitamakan Lakes at Pitamakan Pass. From there you can make a loop and head back to Two Medicine via Dawson Pass, for a strenuous hike that gains almost 3,000 feet in elevation and is probably best done as an overnight of about 18 miles. Or you can do a portion of this as a long day hike. These trails can be combined with others to make for overnight or multiple-day backpack trips. There are campgrounds at Upper Two Medicine Lake, No

Name Lake, Cobalt Lake, and Oldman Lake and elsewhere within a day's hike of Two Medicine. There can be bugs by the lakes in June or July — depending on when the snow has melted — so bring something to ward them off. Bring enough water if it is a dry season or if you are hiking later in the summer because water sources may have dried up by August. And, again, remember this is grizzly country, so heed the park's advice and warnings.

The backcountry of Glacier National Park is rugged, and weather can change at any moment, so always hike prepared for wet, chilly, or cold weather. The hat and gloves that seemed silly in the morning sunshine may be a lifesaver later in the afternoon. If you want to stay in the park and are not backpacking, you may want to find a campsite before you hit the trail, or if you are feeling flush (or the weather is really wet), see if you can stay in a cabin attached to one of the lodges in the park.

MOUNTAIN GOAT

A great place to watch for mountain goats is the aptly named Walton Goat Lick Overlook off Highway 2 about halfway between West Glacier and Summit. Bring binoculars for a good sight of these agile, apparently gravity-defying creatures.

For more information call Glacier National Park at 406-888-7800 or see http://www.nps.gov/glac.

The Bridgers and the Gallatin Range

JULY 25TH. THURSDAY 1805

we proceeded on a fiew miles to the three forks of the Missouri those three forks are nearly of a Size, the North fork appears to have the most water and must be Considered as the one best calculated for us to ascend.

So wrote Captain Clark as the expedition approached the Jefferson, Madison, and Gallatin Rivers, which form the headwaters of the Missouri. By then the men were exhausted, and as Lewis wrote on July 24, "our trio of pests still invade and obstruct us on all occasions, these are the Musquetoes eye knats and prickley pear,

equal to any three curses that ever poor Egypt laiborured under."
A year later, on the homeward journey, Clark's party again passed
this spot on its way east along the Yellowstone, skirting the area
near what are now Bozeman, Livingston, and Billings, Montana.

The Gallatin Range lies to the east of the Gallatin River, west
of the Yellowstone River, and to the south of where the railroad
and I-90 follow a creek valley east toward the Yellowstone. The
Bridgers range to the north, east of the Missouri. The Gallatin
rises in the country that now forms the northwestern corner of
Yellowstone National Park, flows north through the Gallatin
National Forest, and meets the Missouri at Three Forks. The
Gallatin National Forest is now home to some of Montana's
largest herds of elk and moose and provides important habitat
for elk, bighorn sheep, grizzly bear, a wolverine, lynx, and goshawk. The Gallatin and its tributaries are also home to some of
the last wild populations of Yellowstone and westslope cutthroat
trout.

One place from which to explore the Gallatin National Forest
is the trails that lead into the Spanish Peaks area of the Lee Metcalf
Wilderness. You can approach the Spanish Peaks from the east—
from trailheads off Highway 191 south of Bozeman—or from the
roads that lead in from the west off Highway 287 east and south
of Ennis. One of the more popular trailheads is the one at the
Spanish Creek Ranger Station off Spanish Creek Road about 25
miles south of Bozeman on 191. From there it is about a 6-mile
hike that gains about 3,000 feet to the lake basin. The network of
trails makes it ideal for an overnight or multiple-day backpack.

Another great hike is up along Hyalite Creek past a series of
waterfalls up to Hyalite Lake at the foot of Hyalite Peak, which
towers at over 10,000 feet in the heart of the Gallatin Range. The
hike is about 5.5 miles and gains between 1,500 and 2,000 feet in
elevation, so it is a good day hike. To find the trailhead, take
Highway 345 south out of Bozeman and turn left (east) on South
19th Road, then right (south) on Forest Road 62, which goes
down Hyalite Canyon to Hyalite Reservoir. Follow this around
the reservoir. The trailhead is at the end of the road, about 12
miles in.

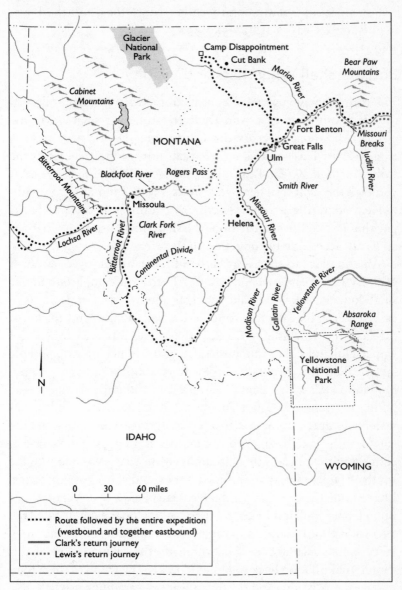

Map 5 The Rocky Mountains.

For more information and weather conditions, call the Bozeman Ranger District at 406-587-6920

Bob Marshall Wilderness and Vicinity

The route Lewis's party took on its homeward journey followed the Blackfoot River east from Traveler's Rest near what is now the city of Missoula, to cross the Continental Divide near today's Rogers Pass. This route skirts what has now been protected as the **Bob Marshall**, Great Bear, and Scapegoat Wilderness Areas. If you pick the right trail here, you can still walk for many days without encountering a road. There are countless hikes and backpacking possibilities in the Bob Marshall. Here are a few that are an easily accessible introduction to the area.

A good place to start is at **Holland Lake**, about 20 miles north of Seely Lake, east of Highway 83. There is a campground (and small lodge) at Holland Lake that gets a lot of use, but it can serve as a first-stop base camp. From there a trail skirts the north side of the lake before climbing up into the wilderness area by way of Upper Holland Lake, Sapphire Lake, and a bunch of little pothole lakes called the Necklace Lakes. It is about 6 miles to Upper Holland Lake, with a gain in elevation of about 4,000 feet, so the hiking is strenuous. The trail starts off in the woods and passes waterfalls and tumbling streams before emerging out onto the ridges of the lake basin. You can do this as a long day hike or else connect with the trails that circumnavigate Shaw Mountain to the south or Holland Peak to the north for extended backpacking trips. I have done the day hike to the Necklace Lakes by taking trail 35 up to Upper Holland Lake and then picking up the connector Trail 110 to Sapphire Lake and going north on Trail 110 to the small lakes before heading back downhill on the continuation of this trail to make a loop back to Holland Lake. The views of the mountains — the Missions and the Swan Range — are impressive.

This is a popular way into the Bob Marshall for hikers and horse and llama packers, so be prepared for some trail traffic at the lower elevations. But this is big country, and hiking parties quickly get absorbed into the landscape. And this is bear country, so behave accordingly. Be prepared to adapt your plans to the weather (it can snow in June or August), and remember to come prepared to deal with the mosquitoes, which, as Lewis and Clark often wrote, can be "exceedingly troublesome." For information on current conditions call the Swan Lake Ranger District at 406-837-5081.

Another easy way into the north edge of the Bob Marshall and western edge of the Great Bear Wilderness is from the **Jewel Basin**, a beautiful lake basin high on the slopes of Mount Aeneas, Three Eagles Mountain, and Tongue Mountain, northeast of Flathead Lake. To reach the Jewel Basin, take Highway 83 about 20 miles north of Swan Lake. Take the right at Echo Lake Road to Echo Park, where there will be a right turn and a sign for the Jewel Basin. This becomes Forest Road 5392, which climbs about 7 miles up to the trailhead.

From there a network of trails leads around the lake basin, making for numerous day hike and backpacking possibilities. For the sake of the view — ignore the radio antenna — it is well worth hiking up to Mount Aeneas and making a loop trail down through the Picnic Lakes, possibly adding on a stop at Black Lake, depending on how you feel. Or hike past Birch Lake on up to Crater Lake and retrace your steps for a day hike, or continue on to Big Hawk Lake for an overnight. Depending on when the season's snows retreat, wildflowers can still be spectacular here well into August, with a profusion of paintbrush, lupine, columbine, bear grass, penstemon, larkspur, and lilies.

Some of the lakes here are home to westslope and Yellowstone cutthroat trout. Watch for mountain goats, mule deer, elk, marmots, bobcats, and mountain lions. If you are really lucky, you may see a wolverine. The elevation is high enough that you will see subalpine fir and Engelmann spruce, as well as western larch, whitebark pine, and other conifers. Altogether there are some 35 miles of trail in the basin, for hikers only; no horses are allowed. This is bear country, so behave accordingly. And, flatlanders, remember that you will be starting your hike at over 4,000 feet. For more information, and to check on conditions, call the Swan Lake Ranger District at 406-837-5081.

Those who wish to explore the Bob Marshall from a starting point close to the Lewis and Clark Trail may want to hike in from the **Morrell Falls** Trail or via **Monture Creek**. Morrell Falls is

about 10 miles north of Seely Lake off Highway 83. Just north of
the town of Seely Lake, take Forest Road 477, then Forest Road
135 to Forest Road 136, following the signs for the Morrell Falls
National Recreation Trail. The hike to the falls is about 2.5 miles
each way, and the falls are quite large and powerful. (Beware of
mosquitoes by the nearby lakes in early summer.) From there, connecting trails will lead into the Bob Marshall, where you have
your pick of extended backpacking possibilities. To hike along
Monture Creek, take Forest Road 107, which becomes Forest
Road 89, north from Highway 200 near the town of Ovando, to
the trailhead at Monture Creek. Trail 27 follows the creek due
north and connects with a series of other trails for extended
overnight trips. Or walk as far as you like for a retrace-your-steps
day hike. On its homeward journey, Lewis's party camped near
here on July 5, 1806. For more information call the Seely Lake
Ranger District at 406-677-2233.

Cabinet Mountains and Yaak Valley

To the west of the Bob Marshall Wilderness, Glacier National
Park, and Flathead Lake are the Cabinet Mountains and the Yaak
Valley. The Cabinet Mountains run generally north and south,
south of the Kootenai River. The Yaak River flows into the
Kootenai from the north. This northwest corner of Montana is
home to the state's only rainforest, and among its old-growth forest are some of the country's oldest western red cedars, some dating back five hundred years. With relatively low elevation and
high precipitation — it often rains about a hundred inches a year
here — the Cabinet-Yaak is one of the most biologically diverse
areas in this part of the country. This lushly forested region is one
of the few places in the continental United States where none of
the native species has become extinct. The area is an important
migration corridor for grizzly bear and gray wolves, and essential
habitat for wolverine, fisher, lynx, common loon, mountain lion,
elk, sturgeon, westslope cutthroat trout, and torrent sculpin. The
Yaak was home to the last population of woodland caribou in the
lower forty-eight states; the last official sighting of caribou there
was in 1987, with several unconfirmed reports in the 1990s.[1] The

ancient trees give shelter to pileated woodpeckers, pine martens, golden and bald eagles, northern goshawks, harlequin ducks, boreal, great gray, and flammulated owls, and peregrine falcons. The wet woods harbor a profusion of plants, flowers, mosses, ferns, and small amphibians. Many of the Yaak's plants and animals are now imperiled and classified as threatened, endangered, or sensitive species.

The Yaak Valley encompasses about 471,000 acres, of which 150,000 are roadless. Some 97 percent of the Yaak Valley is national forest, but not one acre is protected as wilderness. Consequently, the Yaak is constantly being logged and is also at risk from potential mining activity. A 94,000-acre portion of the higher elevation of the Cabinet Mountains is protected as wilderness, but that leaves a great expanse of biologically rich forest open to logging and other development. For eloquent descriptions of the Yaak and an impassioned plea for its permanent protection, read the work of Rick Bass, particularly "The Book of Yaak."

A good point from which to hike into the Cabinet-Yaak is a couple of trailheads near Libby. One possible route is the short but steep hike into Leigh Lake. About 8 miles south of Libby on Highway 2, turn off onto Forest Road 278. Take this about 2.5 miles to Forest Road 867, which you will follow to the trailhead. The trail climbs about 1,000 feet in 1.5 miles, so be prepared. Snowshoe Peak towers over the lake from the west. At over 8,700 feet, it is the highest mountain in the Cabinet Range. Leigh Lake sits at just over 5,000 feet above sea level, and snow often persists here until midsummer.

Another, longer, hike that begins near Libby is to Cedar Lakes — there are two, one upper and one lower. You can do this as a long, 12-mile day hike or extend it to a 16-mile or longer overnight, remembering that you will be gaining over 4,000 feet in elevation on your way to the lakes. To reach the trailhead for what is known as the Scenery Mountain Lookout Trail — and the trail certainly is scenic — drive about 5 miles northwest of Libby on Highway 2 to Forest Road 402, also called Cedar Creek Road which you will take to the trailhead. There you will find Trail 141, which heads up to the Cedar Lakes.

There is also the option of taking the trail that will fork to your right (or north) to climb up to the lookout on Scenery Mountain. This is spectacular country in the heart of the massive Cabinet Mountains, with a view down to the Kootenai River and Kootenai Falls. When you look at the river, bear in mind that the only remaining known spawning grounds and rearing habitat for young Kootenai River white sturgeon are in the 11-mile stretch of the Kootenai below Libby Dam, not far from where you will see the river. This is serious huckleberry country, so if you know how to identify them, then feast away — but, remember, the berries are also beloved by bears.

For more information and to check weather conditions, call the Libby Ranger District at 406-293-8861. Snow does linger well into the summer here, so call ahead. This is grizzly territory, so behave accordingly.

A good way to explore the Yaak River country is to hike into the lakes that pepper the area around Mount Henry, about 30 miles north of Libby. To reach the trailheads here, take Pipe Creek Road (also called Highway 567) north out of Libby to Vinal Creek Road, where a whole network of trails climbs up into the lakes. The elevation gain is not much more than 500 feet, and you can do a 10- to 12-mile day hike or extend the trip into an overnight or multiple-day backpack trip. Be prepared for mosquitoes near the water, especially close to snowmelt time. This is really pretty country. Watch for deer, moose, and black bear.

For more information and to check weather and road conditions, call the Three Rivers Ranger District at 406-295-4693.

The Bitterroots and West to Lolo Pass

SEPTEMBER 12TH THURSDAY 1805.

The road through this hilley Countrey is verry bad passing over hills & thro' Steep hollows, over falling timber &c.&c. continued on & passed Some most intolerable road on the Sides of the Steep Stoney mountains.

SEPTEMBER 14TH 1805

a verry high Steep mountain for 9 miles to a large fork from
the left which appears to head in the Snow toped mountains
. . . Encamped opposite a Small Island at the mouth of a
branch on the right side of the river which is . . . Swift and
stoney, here we were compelled to kill a Colt for our men
& Selves to eat for want of meat & we named the South
fork Colt Killed Creek, and this river we Call Flat head
River . . . the flat head name is Koos koos ke [now called
the Clearwater].

SEPTEMBER 15TH. 1805

Several horses Sliped and roled down Steep hills which hurt
them very much the one which Carried my desk & Small
trunk Turned over & roled down a mountain for 40 yards &
lodged against a tree . . . after two hours delay we proceeded
on up the mountain Steep & ruged as usial . . . From this
mountain I could observe high ruged mountains in every
direction as far as I could see.

Though modes of transportation have changed markedly since
Captain Clark described the journey across the Bitterroots, the
terrain itself—apart from roads and logging—has not. The
Bitterroot Mountains form much of the border between Montana
and Idaho, rising 9,000 to 10,000 feet above the river valleys
formed when the last glaciers receded, probably less than 10,000
years ago. Across the valley to the east rise the Sapphire Mountains. To the west rise the steep mountains of the Clearwater,
Sawtooth, Lemhi, Pahsimeroi, and Wallowa Ranges, whose glacial peaks feed the streams running west to the Pacific. There are
subalpine lake basins, steep forested canyons, waterfalls, rushing
streams, lush mountain meadows, and rugged rocky peaks that
often remain snow covered year-round. Large herds of elk and
mule deer live in the Bitterroots, where moose, black bear, bobcats, cougar, beaver, river otter, and the occasional wolverine also
make their home. Eagles and osprey fish the rivers. It was here that

Lewis and Clark noted their first sighting of Steller's jays and blue, spruce, and ruffed grouse. Lynx, grizzly, and fishers used to live here, but they are now almost certainly gone, though wolves are beginning to return. The Bitterroots' rivers — the Bitterroot, Lochsa, Blackfoot, Clark Fork, and countless tributary creeks among them — are vital habitat for native salmon, steelhead, and cutthroat and bull trout. The area also harbors many rare and endemic plants and plant communities. Depending on elevation, the forested slopes are covered with cedar, Douglas fir, larch, ponderosa and lodgepole pines, and subalpine fir.

Much of the Bitterroot Range falls within the Lolo National Forest and Bitterroot National Forest, and a portion of the mountains and surrounds fall within the protection of the 1.3-million-acre Selway-Bitterroot Wilderness, which straddles the Montana-Idaho border not far from where Lewis and Clark crossed the mountains toward the rivers that would lead them to the main stem of the Columbia. The area is an important wildlife migration corridor. With substantial roadless areas to the north and south of the Selway-Bitterroot Wilderness — including the Great Burn, which is known as a "hot spot" of biodiversity — the area could remain a wildlife corridor if conservation measures are undertaken to protect these places. The Bitterroot and surrounding forests have long been under stress from continual and extensive logging, and more recently from recreation, particularly heavy snowmobile use.

There are any number of wonderful hikes — day trips and backpacking overnights — to be taken in the Bitterroots, both from the east side of the range and to the west, above Lolo Pass near the Lochsa River. By following forest roads off Highway 12, the main road that parallels the Lochsa (a route long followed by the Nez Perce, who traveled between the Rocky Mountains and the salmon waters of the Snake, Columbia, and Clearwater River systems, and hence referred to as the Niimiipuu Trail, Niimiipuu being the tribal language name for the Nez Perce), one can trace the path Lewis and Clark took through these mountains and hike to some of their campsites. As of this writing, these places are not overly visited, and because of the fragile nature of the landscape, it would be ideal if they remained so. There is, however, concern about an influx of visitors around the bicentennial of the Lewis and Clark expedition, so some restrictions on use will be imposed in at least one area that is sacred to the Nez Perce.

A great day hike with wonderful views is the trail to the lookout on **St. Mary's Peak** by way of a trail accessible from just south of Stevensville, Montana. To reach the trailhead, take St. Mary's Road, which, if you are traveling south on Highway 93, will be on your right less than 1.5 miles south of the Stevensville junction. There is a sign for St. Mary's Peak, and the road is also called Forest Road 739. Follow the switchbacks of Forest Road 739 until the road ends and follow the trail up from there. It is between 3 and 4 miles uphill from about 7,000 feet to the lookout, and those who enjoy cross-country trekking can make their way down to a wonderful little pothole lake. If you take this hike in late summer or early fall, look for aspen leaves that have begun to turn golden yellow or marmalade orange. This trail is a good introduction to the Bitterroots, but it is popular, so go early in the day if you can.

Another good day hike, which can be extended to an overnight if you hike the whole length of the canyon or climb the side trail (number 303) to High Lake, is the **Blodgett Canyon** trail, which follows Blodgett Creek upstream from the east side of the mountains going west from Hamilton, Montana. To find the trailhead, from Highway 93 at Hamilton, take Bowman Road to Ricketts Road (a left turn) to Blodgett View Drive or Blodgett Camp Road to the trailhead of Trail 19. The trail goes through the forest, where steep canyon walls rise up on either side, and gains not much more than 1,000 feet in elevation above 6,000 feet for its entire length. About 6 miles up the canyon is Trail 303, which climbs over 1,000 feet to High Lake. (This side trail is steep and not always well maintained.) About another mile up the canyon is the Selway-Bitterroot Wilderness boundary. And if you continue on another 6 or 7 miles to the top of the canyon, where there is another lake, the ridge west of the lake is the Montana-Idaho border. Near High Lake and on the steeper sections of the trail, watch for mountain goats, and keep an eye out for deer, elk, and moose.

Lochsa River. Photo: Wayne Mumford.

For information on weather conditions call the Stevensville Ranger District of the Bitterroot National Forest at 406-777-5461.

The Lochsa

Above the Lochsa on the west side of the Bitterroot Valley, in the country that Lewis and Clark's expedition traversed on its way to the Snake River, many trails lead from the river corridor up toward the mountain ridges. These forests are also riddled with a spaghetti maze of logging roads and a distressing number of clear-cuts. Although probably not a sight you want to bring home snapshots of, it is worth looking at some of the clear-cuts to see what they entail and get a visual sense of their impact on the forests and their wildlife.

If you are following the Lewis and Clark Trail—which followed the Nez Perce, or Niimiipuu, Trail—along the Lochsa by way of Highway 12, you will probably want to stop at the **Bernard De Voto Memorial Grove** of massive cedars, fir, and spruce, about 10 miles west of Lolo Pass. This is not a hiking spot but a short stroll among ancient trees that tower over the Lochsa at the foot of Crooked Fork. Similarly, it is worth making the stop for the short walk around the **Colgate Licks** high above the road about 12 miles west of the Powell Ranger Station. This is one of several warm or hot springs along the Lochsa, and the water is indeed warm—but don't think about immersing yourself here because the water is only inches deep.

To explore this country from the vantage point from which Lewis and Clark saw it on their way west, take one of the many trails that follow the creeks that flow into the Lochsa. A lovely one is the trail that follows **White Sands Creek** upstream. To get there, take Forest Road 369 on the south side of the Lochsa about 2 miles west of the De Voto Grove. The road will turn to the east. Drive no more than a mile, crossing a bridge over the creek. The trailhead is less than half a mile beyond that. The trail follows the west bank of the creek up toward Colt Creek Cabin, climbing gently. Take time to wander along the creek bank as well, admiring the round river rocks and watching for otter. Anglers will find this creek tempting, but be sure you have a valid fishing license with you. This is a lovely hike to take in the fall, when the leaves are starting to turn. Take this as a day hike or continue along the trail, which goes for over a dozen miles, to connect with others that lead up to the ridges near Hidden Peak and Elk Summit.

To hike some of Lewis and Clark's actual trail above the Lochsa, take Forest Road 569, which you will find not far from the Powell Ranger Station, to Forest Road 500 about 5 dirt road miles north of Highway 12. It is possible to pull over and find the foot path at any number of places along Forest Road 500, but some particularly scenic parts to walk are near the places called **Indian Post Office**, the **Sinque Hole Camp**, and **Smoking Place**. You are high up into the forest ridges, between 6,500 and 7,000 feet, and the views — yes, some with clear-cuts — at the open spots can extend east across the Bitterroots for many miles. *These are important and sacred cultural sites for the Nez Perce, so please respect them, do not disturb any cairns or other artifacts, and tread carefully.* In fact, to protect this area from overuse, beginning in 2002 the Forest Service will be issuing permits, by lottery, for a limited number of vehicles to drive these roads between July and October. For more information call the Clearwater National Forest office in Orofino, Idaho, at 208-476-8245 or see its Web site at http://www.fs.fed.us/r1/clearwater.

But there is a whole network of trails in addition to these that lead off to the north of Forest Road 500, which continues west for many miles, making a loop back toward Highway 12. In the fall hunters use the forest roads, so try not to look like deer, elk, or bear as you hike. And make sure your vehicle is prepared for driving unimproved roads.

In the spring and early summer, when the water is high, the Lochsa is a popular river for white-water rafting. A number of local outfitters — many based in the Missoula vicinity — guide trips here. The water is icy cold and the current strong, so unless you have substantial experience, this is probably not a river you will want to attempt to float without guidance. By late summer the water level drops considerably, and the Lochsa seems an altogether different river in August than it does in May, when waves of snowmelt come crashing over the rocks.

The best way to map your exploration of the country along the Lochsa is with the help of the Forest Service's Clearwater National Forest Map, or with topographic quads if you are so inclined. The Clearwater National Forest Map can be obtained through the Forest Service, so check with any of the local ranger stations, including the Powell Ranger Station, located at milepost 162 on Highway 12 on the Idaho side of Lolo Pass. For more information call the ranger station at 208-942-3113. The office is open Monday through Friday, 7:30 A.M. to 4:00 P.M., Pacific time.

Spending time on foot in this landscape will give you a good sense of what it must have been like to traverse this country before the days of motorized transport, as well as how this land has been used and what needs to be protected. Look carefully at a map, and you will see that a number of roadless areas converge near here, creating an important potential for the conservation and recovery of wildlife corridors.

CHAPTER 7

Idaho and Eastern Washington

Lemhi Pass, the Pahsimeroi Valley, and the Salmon River

MONDAY AUGUST 12TH. 1805.

after refreshing ourselves we proceeded on to the top of the dividing ridge [the Continental Divide at Lemhi Pass] from which I discovered immence ranges of high mountains still to the West of us with their tops partially covered with snow. I now decended the mountain about 3/4 of a mile which I found much steeper than on the opposite side, to a handsome bold runing Creek of cold Clear water. Here I first tasted the water of the great Columbia river [actually, Agency Creek, which flows into the Lemhi River].

TUESDAY AUGUST 13TH. 1805.

We set out very early on the Indian road which still led us through an open broken country in a westerly direction. . . . we had proceeded about four miles through a wavy plain parallel to the valley or river bottom when at the distance of about a mile we saw two women, a man and some dogs on an eminence immediately before us.

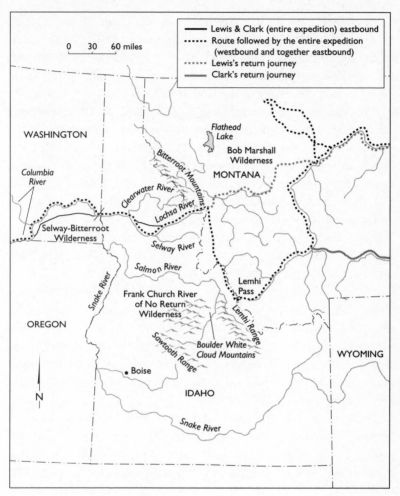

Map legend:
— Lewis & Clark (entire expedition) eastbound
······ Route followed by the entire expedition
    (westbound and together eastbound)
······ Lewis's return journey
— Clark's return journey

0   30   60 miles

WASHINGTON

Columbia River

Flathead Lake

Bob Marshall Wilderness

MONTANA

Bitterroot Mountains

Clearwater River

Lochsa River

Selway-Bitterroot Wilderness

Selway River

Salmon River

Snake River

Frank Church River of No Return Wilderness

Lemhi Pass

Lemhi Range

OREGON

Sawtooth Range

Boulder White Cloud Mountains

WYOMING

Boise

N

IDAHO

Snake River

Map 6 Across the Continental Divide.

Where Lewis and Clark and company found themselves in mid-August 1805 was not actually at the shores of the Columbia River but at the Lemhi River — near the upper Salmon River — in what is now eastern Idaho along the Montana border and the Continental Divide. The Lemhi Mountains, the longest range in Idaho, run north from the Snake River plain near the lava beds and volcanic rock that surround the Idaho National Engineering and Environmental Laboratory, to just south of the present-day town of Salmon. With many peaks in the range rising close to 11,000 feet, some of the highest mountains in Idaho are here, including Diamond Peak, which at over 12,000 feet is the third-tallest mountain in Idaho. Idaho's tallest mountain, Borah Peak, is just across the valley in the Lost River Range.

The Lemhis are surrounded by large, broad, high desert valleys. To the east is the Lemhi Valley, to the west, the Pahsimeroi, to the southeast, the Lost River Valley, and to the southwest, the Birch Creek Valley. These valleys have been inhabited for at least 10,000 years and have been the site of many archaeological discoveries. This is Lemhi-Shoshone country, the homeland of Sacagawea, guide and interpreter to Lewis and Clark.

The Pahsimeroi and Lemhi country is visually striking for its stark, massive aridity. The Lemhis lie in a rain shadow. The moisture that comes from the Pacific falls primarily to the west, leaving these high-elevation valleys generally dry but watered by the streams that flow out of the surrounding mountains. The Lemhis are quite different from the jagged, snow-covered peaks of the Sawtooths or Bitterroots. They tower in a palette of bronze and russet browns, a geologic legacy of volcanic activity that took place some 25 to 50 million years ago. Some of these mountains are as much as 20 miles in girth.

There are at least 500,000 acres of roadless land in the Lemhis, none of which is currently protected as wilderness. Except for grizzly bears, all of the animals native to the region — including black bear, bobcat, cougar, bighorn sheep, mountain goat, elk, mule deer, coyote, and moose — are still present. The valleys around the Lemhis are now home to most of Idaho's pronghorn, and reintroduced wolves are beginning to settle the region. Alas for the landscape, the most ubiquitous animals you are likely to see in these valleys today — and in the higher-elevation backcountry as well — are cattle that have degraded the integrity of stream banks, meadows, and springs.

The U.S. Forest Service, which oversees the Salmon and Challis National Forests in the north part of the range and the Targhee National Forest in the south, manages most of the Lemhi Mountains. Many of the surrounding valleys are also public land,

Lemhi Pass. Photo: Wayne Mumford.

managed by the Bureau of Land Management. There is logging and livestock grazing in the forests, and livestock grazing and farming in the valleys.[1] Logging and livestock grazing occur on both public and private land. This grazing has degraded riparian areas and wet meadows, and off-road vehicles have begun to take an erosive toll on the dry slopes of the Lemhis — a situation that could be remedied with wilderness designation and more protective management of the area.

When setting out to explore the Lemhis, remember this is high country, where snow lingers well into the spring, leaving dirt roads soft as it recedes. So the best time of year to really explore this country is full summer, from July through September. The weather here is also very changeable, so in summer be prepared for cold, heat, wind, and thunderstorms, but remember that snow is possible even in early July or late August.

Enthusiasts following the Lewis and Clark Trail faithfully — and coming from the east — will want to approach the Lemhis as Lewis and Clark did, by way of Lemhi Pass. The pass can be reached by way of Highway 324, which heads west from I-15 just north of the Clark Canyon Reservoir, at the Clark Canyon Dam on the Beaverhead River, to the southwest of Dillon, Montana. Take Highway 324 west and then south of the town of Grant, and then pick up Road 300, which will take you west along Trail Creek, then across the Continental Divide at Lemhi Pass, heading toward the town of Tendoy.

There are few established hiking trails in the Lemhis, and many of the trails involve fording creeks that can become impassable in high water, so inquire about conditions before you set out. Alternatively, be prepared with a plan B in case your original destination is unreachable. Also remember that the way most hikers will find their way into these rugged mountains will be by the same creek beds that miners used, so don't be dismayed to see remains of gravel pit activity.

A fairly accessible day hike that has a great view of Diamond Peak is up **Bunting Canyon** along **Badger Creek** in the southern part of the Lemhis. The best way to orient yourself to find Badger Creek is from the town of Howe, which is at the junction of Roads 22 and 33 at the southern end of the Lost River Valley, about 60 miles northwest of Idaho Falls. From Howe head northwest on a country road that travels up the middle of the valley. About 25 miles north of Howe, to your right you will find Forest Road 148, which follows Badger Creek. Drive more or less to the end of the road, depending on conditions, and find the trail that follows the creek, which branches to your right (the east). This is Bunting Canyon. The trail climbs about 3 to 4 miles up the rugged forested canyon surrounded by peaks that rise 11,000 feet or more. You will be hiking at about 7,500 feet, so those unaccustomed to such altitude may need to catch their breath.

For information on road and weather conditions — you may also want to ask whether cattle are grazing up the canyon — call the Lost River Ranger District of the Challis National Forest in Mackay, Idaho, at 208-588-2224.

Farther north you can hike in the **Frank Church River of No Return Wilderness**, which encompasses most of the Salmon River drainage. At nearly 2.4 million acres, this is now the largest wilderness area in the United States outside of Alaska. The hiking

WOLVES

The gray wolves (*Canis lupus*) that now make their home in central Idaho are descendants of those reintroduced to the area in 1995 and 1996 as part of a recovery program managed by the Nez Perce tribe, along with the U.S. Fish and Wildlife Service, the National Park Service, and the U.S. Department of Agriculture's Wildlife Services. Evidence of gray wolves has been found in Idaho dating back to the end of the last Ice Age, but these predators had been effectively extirpated from the state by the 1940s. The wolves are now doing well (despite local political opposition to their presence), breeding, establishing new packs, and dispersing across the landscape, moving west into Oregon and Washington. For more information on Idaho's wolves, contact the Wolf Research and Education Center in Winchester, Idaho, at 208-924-6960, or see its Web site at http://www.wolfcenter.org.

and backpacking possibilities here are endless, but one hike that takes you into the wilderness west of the north end of the Lemhis is in the **Hat Creek Lake Basin** from **Upper Iron Lake,** north of the town of Challis.

To reach the trailhead, drive north from Challis on Highway 93 until you come to Iron Creek and Forest Road 045, which is a left turn going west. Follow signs to Iron Lake Campground. Another approach to Iron Lake is from Williams Creek Road (also called Forest Road 021), which heads west from Highway 93 about 5 miles south of Salmon, and Forest Road 020, or Ridge Road, which approaches the lake from the north. The latter approach puts you on better-maintained roads than the first. From the trailhead at Iron Lake a trail of about 4 miles follows the ridgeline to Hat Lakes, all up around 9,000 feet. Look for cutthroat trout in the lakes. And as you travel through the area, keep an eye out for a sight of Borah Peak, Idaho's highest mountain, which rises to 12,662 feet in the Lost River Range. For more information, call the Cobalt Ranger District of the Salmon National Forest in Salmon, Idaho, at 208-756-2240.

The **Salmon River,** both the main stem and the Middle Fork, is much beloved by river runners. Both forks plunge through steep canyons that create Class IV rapids — and some even more challenging, depending on water levels — so these are trips for experienced rafters and paddlers. Most people who run these rivers do so piloted by guides. Many outfitters float the main and the Middle Fork of the Salmon, so if this is on your wish list of things to do, check your favorite sources for information and plan ahead.

The Boulder Mountains, White Clouds, and Sawtooths

In the southern part of the Salmon River drainage are the astonishing peaks of the **Boulder, White Cloud,** and **Sawtooth Mountains,** a seemingly endless expanse of mountains with peaks towering over 9,000, 10,000 and 11,000 feet. Together these mountains — along with the Pioneer Mountains — are sometimes referred to as the "Salmon River Mountains" because this is where the headwaters of that great river rise. The Boulder and White Clouds alone encompass an area of about 800 square miles of unprotected wildlands — the largest contiguous unprotected national forest land in the West. These mountains are home to black bears, bighorn sheep, cougars, moose, pronghorn, elk, deer, mountain goats, wolverine, and wolves. The rivers and streams here are critical habitat for imperiled salmon, steelhead, and trout. In late spring and early summer, look for sandhill cranes in the meadows here.

Unfortunately, the Boulder and White Cloud Mountains are threatened by gold and other metals mining, an extremely invasive activity that causes long-lasting damage to fragile streams and the mountain landscape. There is also active logging in the forests, subdivision-type development in the Stanley Basin, and increasing use of the area by off-road vehicles, all of which damage mountain slopes, displace wildlife, and shatter the natural quiet. Conservation groups have proposed wilderness protection for all undeveloped areas of federal land here — protection that would preserve the integrity of the region's rich wildlife habitats.

This is spectacular country, with no end of hiking and backpacking possibilities. It is high country, however, so it is often not possible to get onto dirt roads until June or July because they remain soft for some time after the snow recedes.

SOCKEYE SALMON

While you are at Redfish Lake, stop and consider the fact that the lake was named for the multitude of sockeye salmon that used to spawn there—turning the lake red with the shimmer of their scales—and that these salmon made their way from this high mountain lake to the Pacific Ocean and back, a journey of some 900 miles each way. In 1990, because of the proliferation of dams throughout the Snake and Columbia River basin and the degradation of habitat caused by logging, livestock grazing, and other development that followed decades of overfishing in the early days of European American settlement, only one Snake River sockeye returned to Redfish Lake. Those now surviving are in a captive breeding program. Snake River sockeye have now entirely disappeared from most of their historic range. This, alas, is part of the legacy of Lewis and Clark but a condition that, with a great deal of hard work, could still be reversed.

It is important to know that the Pacific Northwest salmon—which include the salmon of the Snake River and its tributaries—are not merely a traveling fish phenomenon or a dining delicacy. Salmon are an integral part of the region's entire ecosystem. Salmon transport nutrients from the ocean to inland streams, and from the mountains to the sea. Biologists have recently discovered that the nutrients found in salmon actually help to nurture the growth of the region's enormous trees—trees that are equally essential to the ecosystem's health. Bears are part of this cycle. Bears eat salmon and then deposit their nutrient-rich leavings on the forest floor.[2] Clean, cold, free-flowing water; trees to shade streams and nourish them with woody debris that fosters instream habitat for fish; fish that help return nutrients to the soil by way of creatures that eat them—these are just a few of the ways that salmon help maintain a healthy ecological balance. And this balance is as important to humans as it is to other living things.

A wonderful hike to take once the road is dry is to **Sawtooth Lake** along Iron Creek west of Stanley, Idaho. The Sawtooth Lake trailhead is at the end of Iron Creek Road, or Forest Road 619 off Highway 21. There is a sign for Sawtooth Lake about 2.5 miles west of Stanley. The trailhead is a little over 3 miles down the road. The hike up to Sawtooth Lake, which is about 4 miles and climbs about 1,700 feet, goes by another lovely lake, Alpine Lake. The trail leads into the **Sawtooth Wilderness Area**, and there are other trails leading off in various directions that can be taken to extend a day hike into an overnight or several-day backpacking trip. There are fir and lodgepole pine and wonderful subalpine meadows. Be prepared to ford Iron Creek if the water is still high. Also remember that the weather here up above 8,000 and 9,000 feet is extremely variable; snow squalls can whip through at any time.

Another good hike to take, as an introduction to the Boulder and White Cloud Mountains, is to Fourth of July Lake in the Sawtooth National Forest. To reach the trailhead, take Fourth of July Lake Road, which heads east from Highway 75, about 15 miles south of Stanley or 47 miles north of Ketchum. Fourth of July Road, a bumpy dirt road, climbs up from the valley floor into a pine and aspen forest. The trailhead is 10 miles up the road, at 8,800 feet in elevation. Given the altitude, it is best to wait until the Fourth of July or so to reach the trail (and that is when alpine and subalpine wildflowers will be blooming). The trail to the lake, which sits in a partially wooded bowl at 9,365 feet, is 1.6 miles and follows a stream. From Fourth of July Lake you can continue on a mile or so west to Washington Lake or climb another 555 feet up to Ants Basin Divide, on a series of switchbacks that take off from the left fork in the trail from Fourth of July Lake. The views from there are spectacular. For those who like rock scrambling, it is possible to climb up the ridge to the top of 10,300-foot Mount Blackman. As always, in the high country — especially when on exposed ridges — keep an eye on the weather for approaching storms.

Sawtooth Lake is in the Sawtooth National Recreation Area, for which trailhead parking permits are required. These can be obtained at any Forest Service ranger station or visitor center. The Golden Eagle Passport (the annual pass for national parks) will cover the fee for the permit, but you will still need to get the tag to display in your vehicle's windshield. For more information call the Sawtooth National Recreation Visitor Center (it is open seven days a week and is located 8 miles north of Ketchum, Idaho; other ranger station hours vary) at 208-727-5000 or 208-727-5013. Permit regulations — and prices — seem to vary constantly, so call ahead to find out what permits are required and where to obtain them.

If you are in the Sawtooths in late spring, when the back roads are not yet passable, consider driving in to **Redfish Lake** off

Highway 75 south of Stanley and following one of the trails that lead up above the lake from there. Redfish Lake is not far from where Lewis recorded his first taste of Pacific salmon on August 15, 1805. The road to Redfish Lake is paved, but I have been there in May and found it under a foot or more of snow. There is a large parking area at the trailhead on the north side of the lake. From there you can climb quickly into the Sawtooth Wilderness Area, hiking along creeks and ridgelines to tiny mountain lakes through sage interspersed with balsamroot, lupine, paintbrush, and other wildflowers.

Selway-Bitterroot Wilderness

After crossing the Continental Divide at Lemhi Pass, Lewis and Clark's expedition made its way through the steep mountainous country above the Salmon River. Given the river's swift and rocky course, Lewis and Clark declared the Salmon unnavigable, an obvious decision given their gear and craft. They then headed north up the Bitterroot Valley before turning west along the Lochsa River, after crossing the Continental Divide again at Lost Trail Pass. They followed a high route above the Lochsa and reached the Clearwater River on September 14, 1805. The confluence of the Lochsa, Selway, and Clearwater Rivers is near what is now Lowell, Idaho. The Clearwater and Selway Rivers flow through what are now the Clearwater and Nez Perce National Forests, within which lies the Selway-Bitterroot Wilderness.

Here — as in adjacent unprotected areas of the steep, forested slopes above the Lochsa known as the Lochsa Face — is important habitat for elk, deer, grizzly bear, mountain lion, lynx, goshawk, and gray wolves. The fast-moving cold-water streams provide essential habitat for salmon, steelhead, and westslope cutthroat trout. This habitat is especially important given all the river flow that was lost after construction of the many dams throughout the Snake River Basin, including Dworshak Dam on the North Fork of the Clearwater.

An easy way into the wilderness is by way of the trails that begin at the **Wilderness Gateway** campground located off Highway 12 about 20 miles east of Lowell, Idaho. The main campground and trailheads are just east of the Lochsa Historical Ranger Station. On the south side of the river, a well-marked trailhead will lead you up a series of switchbacks onto the slopes. There you can follow the Idaho State Centennial Trail, which takes you to a lake basin some 12 miles up. Or you can take a left-forking branch of the trail that follows Boulder Creek toward Stanley Hot Springs. Day hikers will probably want to hike no more than 5 to 6 miles in before retracing their steps back to the river. Backpackers have numerous possibilities. One would be to hike up along Boulder Creek to the lake near Stanley Butte and return by the Centennial Trail. It is steep, rugged country, so pace yourself. And watch for mountain lions; I saw one here.

For more information call the Clearwater National Forest at 208-476-8425 or 208-476-3775 or see its Web site at http://www.fs.fed.us/r1/clearwater/.

The Clearwater River and Mallard-Larkins Pioneer Area

MONDAY (WEDNESY.) 25TH OF SEPTEMBER 1805 —

I Set out early with the Chief and 2 young men to hunt Some trees Calculated to build Canoes, as we had previously deturmined to proceed on by water I was furnished with a horse and we proceeded on down the river . . . Passed down on the N side of the river to a fork from the North . . . we halted about an hour, one of the young men took his guig and killed 6 fine Salmon two of them we roasted and we eate . . . I Saw fine timber for Canoes.

The river from which the young men plucked the salmon was the Clearwater. The spot Captain Clark described here was the confluence of its north and middle forks. Dworshak Dam now blocks the North Fork of the Clearwater upstream of this point, but up toward the North Fork's headwaters is a primitive area called the **Mallard-Larkins Pioneer Area,** which lies within the Clearwater and St. Joe National Forests. This area is important habitat for mountain goats, wolves, elk, cutthroat and bull trout, and other wildlife. It has become especially important for wildlife because many of the surrounding slopes and valleys were heavily logged, particularly in the 1960s. The area was first proposed for wilderness designation in the 1960s, and while it has received the special moniker of "pioneer" area, it lacks the full protections of congressionally legislated wilderness.

If you have been traveling along the Lochsa from the east, you will have noticed that the country has begun to change from steep, forested slopes to the rounded grassy hills typical of Snake River country — geology and topography typical of the central Columbia River Basin. But the peaks of the Mallard-Larkins area, which are just to the northeast of where this marked change begins, are full of sharp ridges, peaks, and tiny pothole lakes like those in the Bitterroot country.

To reach the Mallard-Larkins take Highway 12 to Greer, Idaho, about 14 miles northwest of Kamiah, and turn east on Highway 11 toward Weippe. Continue on Highway 11 past Weippe, to Pierce and on to Headquarters. From the town of Headquarters take Forest Road 247, also called Beaver Creek Road, to the junction of Forest Road 700 to Forest Road 705, which follows **Isabella Creek** — about 20 or so miles from Headquarters. (If you take the east fork at the junction you will be at the Aquarius Campground.) The trailhead is about 3 miles up this road. From there you can hike to a grove of ancient cedar trees known as the **Heritage Grove**, about 2 miles up the creek, and then head west across the creek to hike up Elmer Creek to Larkins Lake near Larkins Peak, about another 5 miles. Alternatively, you can follow Forest Road 700 where it crosses west over Isabella Creek and drive the switchbacks up to a trailhead that will take you more directly up to Larkins Lake and Larkins Peak (about 6,600 feet) by way of Grassy Point (about 6,200 feet) and Goat Ridge, also a hike of about 7 miles. The views are wonderful.

There are Douglas fir, grand fir, white pine, wildflowers, and huckleberries. It can be hot here in the summer, and be prepared for mosquitoes near the lakes. The best general map to use for this area is the Forest Service's map of the Clearwater National Forest.

For more information call the Clearwater National Forest at 208-476-8425 or 208-476-3775 or see its Web site at http://www.fs. fed.us/r1/clearwater/.

The Snake River and Hells Canyon

OCTOBER 10TH WEDNESDAY (THURSDAY)

passed 2 Islands and two bad rapids at 3 miles lower passed a Creek on the Lard. with wide cotton willow bottoms . . . we arrived at the heade of a verry bad riffle at which place we landed near 8 Lodges of Indians . . . at five miles lower and Sixty miles below the forks arrived at a large southerly fork which is the one we were one with the Snake or So-So-nee nations. . . . This South fork or Lewis's River which has two forks which fall into it . . . on this fork a little above its mouth resides a Chief who as the Indian say has more horses than he can count and further sayeth that Louises River is navagable about 60 miles up with many rapids at which places the Indians have fishing.

The creek was Lapwai Creek, which flows into the Snake River about 7 or 8 miles east — or upstream — from what is now Lewiston, Idaho. What Captain Clark called Lewis's River is the Snake River. The Snake rises in the mountains of Wyoming and flows over 1,000 miles, west across Idaho and then north through the deep gorge of Hells Canyon — the deepest in North America — to where it joins the Columbia River in Washington's sagebrush steppe. The Hells Canyon region has been the homeland of the Nez Perce for centuries — or as the Nez Perce might say, since time immemorial. Archaeological remnants indicate that humans have inhabited the area for at least 7,100 years.

Located in the center of the Columbia River Basin, Hells Canyon is an important point of dispersal and a migration corridor for plants and animals throughout the Northwest. Its dramatic changes in elevation foster a wide diversity of flora and fauna, including some species that live nowhere else. There is desert with cactus and bunchgrass. There are grassy slopes dotted with firs and pines, and alpine peaks with spruce, fir, and pine. Grizzly bears still live here, and wolves wander through. Among the animals that live here are bald and golden eagles, great gray owls, osprey, seven species of hawks, prairie falcons, American kestrels, a great variety of songbirds, bighorn sheep, elk (in the largest free-roaming herd in North America), mule deer, mountain lions, coyotes, bobcats, black bears, many kinds of bats, mountain goats, rattlesnakes, lynx, and wolverine.

Some 650,000 acres of this region have been included in the Hells Canyon National Recreation Area, which straddles the Idaho-Oregon border and is managed by the Forest Service. About a third of this area has been protected as the Hells Canyon Wilderness, but the remainder is threatened by logging, livestock grazing, and motorized recreation — by off-road vehicles on land and jet boats on the river.

About 70 miles of the Snake River that flows through Hells Canyon has been designated a wild and scenic river and looks much the way it always has. But in the past century, dams on the Snake River have utterly altered the river's flow. Among these are four large dams on the lower Snake River — from just downstream of Lewiston to just above the confluence of the Snake and the Columbia — built in the 1960s and 1970s. Together the dams have turned rivers once full of roaring rapids into a slackwater navigation corridor that badly degrades conditions for anadromous fish. In the upper reach of Hells Canyon, the Hells Canyon Complex of three large dams completely blocks fish passage and disrupts the downstream ecology of the undammed section of the river. Both the private dams of the Hells Canyon Complex and the federal dams on the lower Snake are the subject of intense scrutiny by scientists and conservationists who believe that restoring free flows to the Snake is vital to recovering the wild runs of salmon and steelhead that the dams have decimated.

Despite the threats and changes, this is spectacular and dramatic country. Jagged, snow-covered peaks tower to the east, notably the Seven Devils Range. To the west of the river are the higher and equally rugged glacial Wallowa Mountains. Great

grassy benches of canyon plunge and curve as the contours of the
land descend toward the Snake and its tributary streams. Look for
paintbrush, lupine, mariposa lily, lazuli buntings, squeaking and
chattering pikas, and balsamroot. Near mountain streams look for
bright monkey flower, gentian, penstemon, and figwort.

There are many maintained trails in the Hells Canyon National
Recreation Area and the adjacent Eagle Cap Wilderness in the
Wallowa Mountains. Included among these trails is a portion of
the historic Niimiipuu Trail, the path followed by the Nez Perce
on their flight to avoid the pursuing U.S. Army in 1877. Once you
have spent some time exploring this remarkable landscape, it is
easy to see why this country is beloved by and sacred to the Nez
Perce.

When Lewis and Clark traveled here, the Nez Perce tribe was
one of the "more numerous and powerful in the Northwest,"
writes historian Alvin Josephy. Their central homelands were in
the Salmon, Clearwater, and Snake River country, where the states
of Idaho, Washington and Oregon now coincide, but to hunt and
gather the Nez Perce traveled east to the Bitterroots and west to
the Blue Mountains.[3]

To get a sense of the alpine terrain here, follow the trails that
lead to the lake basin of the **Seven Devils**, which are accessible
from the Heavens Gate Scenic National Recreation Trail, or from
the Hells Canyon Wilderness trailhead, about 15 or 6 miles,
respectively, southwest of Riggins, Idaho. To reach the trailhead,
take Forest Road 517 about a quarter mile south of Riggins off
Highway 95, and take the left fork about 4 miles in, continuing
on for a total of 17 miles to the Seven Devils campground and lake
basin trailheads. Another mile in is the Heaven's Peak lookout,
which has a wonderful view of the Snake River canyon and surrounding mountains. There are numerous day hike and backpack
possibilities here. When planning your outing, remember that you
will be gaining about 7,000 feet in altitude, gaining and losing
many hundreds of feet within a matter of miles.

On the Oregon side of Hells Canyon, a wonderful wilderness
hike is the one up to **Bonny Lakes** from the Wagon Road trailhead
off the Wallowa Mountain Loop Road, also called the Hells

Snake River Canyon. Photo: Wayne Mumford.

Canyon Scenic Byway. To reach the trailhead, take the Imnaha Highway about 8 miles east out of Joseph, Oregon, and then turn south on the Wallowa Mountain Loop Road. The well-marked trailhead, with ample parking, is about 10 miles south of this junction. Here you have a choice of trails. Trail 1828 climbs about 4.7 miles to where it meets trail 1819, which you will follow a little over a mile to trail 1802, which will take you to Bonny Lakes on its way to Aneroid Lake. (If you have arranged a shuttle and are backpacking, there are great trails down from Aneroid Lake to a trailhead above Wallowa Lake, near the town of Joseph.) Bonny Lakes are about 8 miles from the trailhead, so this is a long day hike but well worth the effort. While you are in the vicinity, hike — or drive — along the Imnaha River, which flows through beautiful canyons on its way to the Snake.

One of my favorite views of the country above the Snake River and Hells Canyon Area is from **Joseph Canyon**, which extends east toward the Snake from Highway 3, which runs north from Enterprise, Oregon, to Lewiston, Idaho. About 30 miles north of Enterprise is the Joseph Canyon Viewpoint. Stop and look; the

view is spectacular. Joseph Canyon is said to be the birthplace of
Chief Joseph, the renowned Nez Perce chief who led his people
through the war of 1877.[4]

Continue on from the viewpoint, pull off the road east at any of
the many turnoffs, and walk cross-country out on the canyon shoulders. If you plan to do this kind of cross-country, off-trail hiking,
make sure you are on public land. In most states, private land will
be posted as such, but check a map with landownership to be sure.
(A good map to use for this purpose is the U.S. Forest Service map
of the Wallowa-Whitman National Forest.) There is logging here in
the Wallowa National Forest, so do not be surprised to encounter
active operations or many stumps. But the grassy benches are beautiful, and walking where there are no trails is a wonderful way to
get a sense of what it must have been like to explore this country
200 years ago. Look for mariposa lily and brodiaea.

For more information about the Hells Canyon National
Recreation Area, call the Forest Service at 208-628-3916 (Riggins,
Idaho) or 541-426-4978 (Enterprise, Oregon) or 509-758-0616
(Clarkston, Washington), or see its Web site at http://www.tcfn.org/
tctour/parks/HellsCanyonNRA.html. The Forest Service in Enterprise should also be able to answer questions about the Wallowas
and Eagle Cap Wilderness. For the conservationist perspective on
Hells Canyon and information on current conservation campaigns,
see the Hells Canyon Preservation Council Web site at http://www
.hellscanyon.org or call its office in La Grande, Oregon, at 541-963-
3950. Occasionally the council offers river trips through Hells
Canyon to benefit the organization.

The wild and scenic portion of the **Snake River** also makes for
a great white-water trip, but since there are serious Class III and
IV rapids at the beginning of the reach, most people will float this
with an experienced guide — whether on a private or a commercial
trip. This is a popular float trip that can also be paddled by kayak
or canoe (though some may want to portage the first two large
rapids). The designated wild reach of the river extends for 31
miles below Hells Canyon Dam, just about to Pittsburgh Landing,
and the designated scenic reach continues for 36.5 miles beyond
that. The highest flows are in April and May and generally drop
throughout the summer, but as releases are controlled from the

dams, it is wise to check on current water and flow levels. To do so call Idaho Power at 800-422-3143. Reservations are required for those floating the river from the Friday before Memorial Day through September 10. You probably would also prefer to be on the river — or near it — when jet boats are not. Thanks to work on the part of conservationists, during the summer, use of these noisy motorboats is limited on this portion of the Snake. For more information on river conditions, boating permits, and jet boat restrictions, call the Forest Service at 509-758-0616; for reservations call 509-758-1957. Also see the National Park Service Web site at http://www.nps.gov/rivers/Snake.html.

The Palouse

OCTOBER 16TH. WEDNESDAY 1805

a cool morning, deturmined to run the rapids, put our Indian guide in front our Small Canoe next and the other four following each other, the canoes all passed over safe except the rear Canoe which run fast on a rock at the lower part of the Rapids, with the early assistance of the other Canoes & the Indians, who was extreanmly ellert every thing was taken out and the Canoe got off without any enjorie further than the articles [with] which it was loaded [getting] all wet. . . .
In every direction from the junction of those rivers the countrey is one continued plain low and rises from the water gradually, except a range of high Countery which runs from S.W. & N.E. and is on the opposit Side about 2 miles distant from the Collumbia and keeping its derection S.W. untill it joins a S.W. range of mountains.

Lewis and Clark had reached the confluence of the Snake and Columbia Rivers, where they were met by a great number of Wanapum, Yakama, and Wallawalla who had gathered there to catch and to dry fall-run salmon. Today, the confluence of these two great rivers is the site of cottonwood plantations, a pulp mill, a not very wild national wildlife refuge, and the commercial outskirts of the cities of Kennewick and Pasco, Washington.

Sage grouse. Photo: Idaho Department of Fish and Game.

To the north and east of where the Snake and Columbia meet are the great rolling grass hills and coulees of the Palouse. The Palouse has an exceptionally deep layer of rich soil laid down aeons ago in the wake of ancient volcanoes and sculpted by the retreat of glaciers. When white settlers began arriving in the mid–nineteenth century, they used this soil for dryland farming — farming that continues today — beginning a steady process of altering the natural patterns of vegetation so that agriculture has now nearly entirely eclipsed the native grasslands and intermingled sagebrush steppe. The agricultural produce of the Columbia Basin is important business both regionally and nationally but has taken a great toll on the basin's ecology.

Construction of the four lower Snake River dams in the 1960s and 1970s further altered this landscape, flooding large portions of the original river canyon, turning rapids to slackwater, and inundating tribal fishing sites. The four lower Snake River dams completed the heavily subsidized navigation corridor, which extends from the mouth of the Columbia to Lewiston, Idaho. These four dams generate hydropower (well under 10 percent of

SAGE GROUSE

It was in this country above the Snake River that Lewis and Clark first described the sage grouse (*Centrocercus urophasianus*), which they called the "Cock of the Plains." An indicator species for the sagebrush steppe, sage grouse have inhabited the western United States and southern Canada since the Pleistocene epoch. Nineteenth-century settlers and travelers reported huge flocks of sage grouse that darkened the sky. Sage grouse and sagebrush country are inseparable.

The historic range of sage grouse closely conformed to the distribution of short and tall sagebrush in what became sixteen western states and three Canadian provinces. But since 1900 sage grouse populations have shrunk, and they no longer occur in Arizona, British Columbia, Kansas, Nebraska, New Mexico, or Oklahoma. Sage grouse populations have declined as much as 45 to 80 percent over the past twenty years as a result of habitat destruction, degradation, and fragmentation. About 99 percent of Idaho's Snake River plain has now been converted to agriculture, and about 90 percent of similar sagebrush steppe country of Oregon and Washington is now gone. The total sage grouse population, now estimated at 140,000 individuals, represents only about 8 percent of historic numbers. Very few are left in Washington.

Like the prairie chicken, the sage grouse has an extraordinary courtship ritual that takes place in early spring on leks—mating grounds—to which a population of birds returns year after year. The males puff their chests, drum their wings, spar with each other, and emit unforgettable sounds of "poinking," cooing, and swishing—all in hopes of attracting a female. Tribes of the region, the Wasco, Warm Springs, and Paiute among them, incorporated elements of this ritual into their own songs and ceremonial dances.

Efforts are now under way among conservation groups to secure legal protection for the sage grouse. For the latest information on sage grouse and sagebrush steppe protection, see http://www.sagegrouse.org, a site maintained by the conservation group American Lands Alliance and its partners. For some eloquent words on the sagebrush steppe and sage grouse, read the opening chapters of Rachel Carson's *Silent Spring*.

what the region uses) and make it easier for a limited number of large farms to pump river water for irrigation. The dams store no drinking water and perform no flood control. They block free passage for migrating anadromous fish, eliminating spawning and rearing grounds and changing water chemistry, contributing mightily to the decline of the Snake River's wild salmon runs.

Twelve species of Columbia and Snake River salmon are now listed under the Endangered Species Act as threatened or endangered, and the Snake River's coho salmon are now extinct. If current trends in this decline are not reversed, scientists fear that the Snake River's spring chinook salmon could become extinct within the next twenty-five years.[5]

For more information on the plight of wild Snake River salmon and efforts to save and restore them, contact the Save Our Wild Salmon coalition at 503-230-0421 (its other office numbers are listed here in Appendix B) and see its Web site at http://www. wildsalmon.org. For detailed information about numbers of fish passing through the dams and for maps of the Snake and Columbia River dams, see the Fish Passage Center's Web site at http://www.fpc.org.

This is the bad news. The good news is that the Palouse is still beautiful country. The dramatic hills, with their sharply notched draws and great open vistas of sky, can be astonishing. From certain vantage points, on a clear day the view extends nearly to the Blue Mountains and the Cascades. You can see storms blowing in from many miles away, and the rainbows can be fantastic.

Because this is nearly all private land, it is not easy to strike out on foot today to explore this country. One interesting bit of public land from which to do so — if you can get there — is the **Juniper Dunes Wilderness,** an unusual area of actual sand dunes about 5 or 6 miles northwest of the Snake River, a little over 10 miles north of Pasco, Washington, west of the Pasco-Kalhotus Road north of Highway 12. In the dunes grow old juniper trees, desert wildflowers, and shrubs that harbor desert wildlife such as kangaroo rats, porcupines, rattlesnakes, and coyotes. Unfortunately, as of this writing, there is no legal public access to the Juniper Dunes Wilderness Area; it is surrounded by private land, and permission is needed from the landowner to cross that property. This situation may change, so check with the Bureau of Land Management's Spokane, Washington, office for further information: 509-536-1200.

Another place from which to get a view of the country around the Snake River to the east of the Palouse is the high buttes near Danger Point in the **Wenaha-Tucannon Wilderness** in the Blue Mountains and Umatilla National Forest, south of Dayton, Washington. The pine and fir forest here is home to white-tailed and mule deer, elk, bighorn sheep, black bears, cougars, coyotes, and pine martens. The Wenaha and Tucannon Rivers and their tributary streams are important habitat for chinook salmon and steelhead. This is steep, rugged country, and snow can begin in September and linger well into June, so call ahead for road and weather conditions.

To reach the trailhead that leads to a series of trails along the ridges near Oregon Butte, take Eckler Mountain Road east out of Dayton (it can be reached by taking Fourth Avenue south and is also called County Road 9124). This becomes Skyline Drive, then Forest Road 46; you will stay on it between 25 and 30 miles to Godman Camp, where you will take Forest Road 4608 east to the end of the road, where the trailhead is. From there you can hike up 3.5 miles to 6,401-foot-high Oregon Butte and perhaps continue along the ridgeline to Danger Point. There is a whole network of trails here, so the trip can easily be extended to a backpacking expedition. Be aware that this is popular country for fall hunting trips, so check with the Forest Service for hunting season dates, and consider some safety-orange accoutrements if you are hiking among hunters. There is also a winter ski area nearby. For more information call the Forest Service Region 6 office in Portland, Oregon, at 503-808-2971.

The Hanford Reach of the Columbia River

The 51-mile-long Hanford Reach of the Columbia River — located just downstream of Priest Rapids Dam and upstream of its confluence with the Snake — is the last free-flowing nontidal stretch of the Columbia in the United States. It is here that approximately 80 percent of upper Columbia Basin fall chinook salmon now spawn, making protection of the Hanford Reach vital to recovery of Columbia River salmon.

In the summer of 2000, the Hanford Reach of the Columbia and 195,000 surrounding acres of grasslands and sagebrush-steppe were proclaimed the Hanford Reach National Monument. The monument is important habitat for sage grouse, white pelicans, sandhill cranes, bald eagles, peregrine falcons, trumpeter swans, and other sensitive bird species, as well as for the endangered pygmy rabbit. Pygmy rabbits have ears only 2 inches long, and there are so few of these tiny rabbits left in Washington that they have all been gathered for a captive breeding program.

Archaeological sites over 10,000 years old have been found here, as have mastodon and rhinoceros fossils. Curiously, the Hanford Reach and immediately surrounding land have been sequestered from the agricultural development that has claimed much of this region, thanks to their proximity to the adjacent Department of Energy's Hanford Nuclear Reservation — the country's most contaminated nuclear waste site. And it should be noted that although the Hanford Reach is considered free-flowing, its water levels are influenced by Priest Rapids and other dams farther upstream on the Columbia, and the fate of the salmon that spawn and are born here depends on how well they fare passing through, or in transport or passage around the four large dams on the lower Columbia.

For information about the Hanford Nuclear Reservation see the Department of Energy's Web site at http://www.hanford.gov; for the environmental watchdog perspective see http://www.hanfordwatch.org.

Paddling the Hanford Reach

The best — and nearly only — way to really see this landscape is by paddling the **Hanford Reach** from Vernita Bridge through Coyote Rapids to the White Bluffs (19 miles) and then to Ringold (19 miles farther downstream). You will float over salmon and steelhead spawning grounds and past mule deer, coyotes, beaver, California quail, ring-necked pheasants, great blue herons, egrets, white pelicans, and a host of other waterfowl. The White Bluffs — fossil-filled cliffs up to 600 feet high — are home to cliff swallows, great horned owls, red-tailed hawks, falcons, and other raptors. (You will also pass some of Hanford's oldest nuclear reactors — not a pretty sight.) Although this is not a technically difficult paddle, strong winds, high water, and river currents can make for dangerous conditions. For a paddling guide see http://www.hanfordreach.org/extras/tour.htm. For further information on the area contact the U.S. Fish and Wildlife Service at 509-371-1801.

CHAPTER 8

The Columbia Basin and Columbia River Gorge

Central Washington and Oregon

The Deschutes River and The Dalles

OCTOBER 19TH. SATURDAY 1805

I assended a high clift about 200 feet above the water from the top of which is a leavel plain extending up the river and off for a great extent, at this place the countrey becomes low on each Side of the river, and affords a pros[pect] of the river and countrey below for great extent both to the right and left; from this place I descovered a high mountain of emence hight covered with Snow, this must be one of the mountains laid down by Vancouver, as seen from the mouth of the Columbia River, from the course which it bears which is West I take it to be Mt.St.Helens, destant about 120 miles a range of moutnains in the Derection crossing a conical mountain S.W. toped with snow.

This journal entry was written from the mouth of the Umatilla River. The mountain Captain Clark described was not Mount St.

Helens but Mount Adams. (Since its eruption in 1980, however, Mount St. Helens is markedly less conical than Mount Adams.) While the landscape itself is otherwise essentially unchanged, if Lewis and Clark surveyed this stretch of the Columbia River today, they would find the flow of its water much altered.

Just upstream on the Columbia from the mouth of the Umatilla River is McNary Dam. Built in 1953, it is one of the four large federal dams on the lower Columbia that—along with those on the lower Snake—create the flat-water navigational corridor that facilitates barging of goods and produce from Lewiston, Idaho, to the ports of Portland, Oregon, and Vancouver, Longview, and Kalama, Washington. Between the Umatilla and the John Day River—about 70 miles downstream—the current of the Columbia has been stilled by the John Day Dam (built in 1968), which sits a few miles west of where the John Day River empties into the Columbia. A few large farms, mainly on the Washington side of the river—including some of the region's largest potato growers, who produce spuds for the fast-food industry—pump irrigation water from the reservoirs behind these dams. These lower Columbia River dams generate electricity that is fed into the western power grid managed by the Bonneville Power Administration, but they store no drinking water and were not designed for flood control.

The construction of the four lower Columbia River dams began in 1938 with Bonneville Dam, the farthest downstream. The damming and subsequent flooding of rapids, side channels, and natural riverbanks effectively took from the Columbia River tribes their traditional fishing sites. It also greatly reduced the number of salmon able to migrate up and down the Columbia's main stem. Twelve species of Columbia and Snake River salmon are now listed as threatened or endangered under the Endangered Species Act. Over the past thirty years, numbers of wild Snake River salmon have fallen by almost 90 percent. And since the last of the lower Snake dams was built in 1975, all runs of Snake River salmon have been listed under the Endangered Species Act.

While radically altered ecologically and physically, the Columbia River from where it is joined by the Snake to the Pacific Ocean

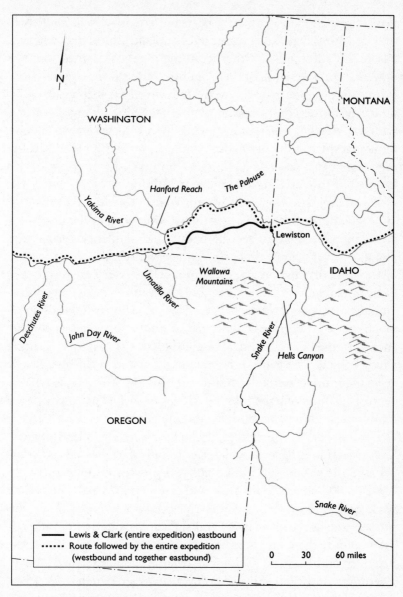

Map 7 The Columbia River Basin.

flows through extraordinarily beautiful country. Near the Umatilla and John Day Rivers are high grassland slopes and volcanic basalt cliff scablands. Farther west, the riverbed deepens into the dramatic forested cliffs of the Columbia River Gorge, remarkable for its multitude of plunging waterfalls. Even a casual visitor may notice how the color scheme of the landscape changes — along with the weather — from mustard yellows to deep greens, as one moves west from the dry Columbia Basin plateau to Hood River, the crest of the Cascade Mountains, and the rainy curtain of the Pacific Northwest's coastal temperate rainforest.

If you are exploring the Columbia Basin for the first time and approaching from the east, you may want to take Highway 12 along the Columbia to see the basalt cliffs and rock formations along the river near Wallula Gap and at Hat Rock State Park (east of Umatilla off Highway 730). Although the river here now bears little resemblance to the currents Lewis and Clark's expedition would have encountered, it is well worth a look. While scenic, much of the land directly along the Columbia between its confluence with the Snake and the Deschutes River is developed or privately owned. There are some state parks and areas of river beach access, but none are really suitable for hiking. You can, however, venture inland along the John Day River or strike out on your own on public land in some of the adjacent canyons.

For more accessible hiking, try an easy 4 to 4.5 miles along the lower **Deschutes River** — which Lewis and Clark passed on October 22, 1805 — on the trails that lead upstream along the river from the Deschutes State Park and Recreation Area. This is not backcountry wilderness, since railroad tracks run along the canyon above the river here, and the campground is developed. Try to ignore these intrusions and concentrate instead on the rushing river and the arid Columbia Basin grasslands rising above. There is a good view of the river if you choose the high route when the trail forks. Either route will give you a good feeling for the lay of the land. There is sage among the grass of the lava- and basalt-strewn canyon. Cottonwoods, sumac, and willow cluster by the river, and cold water rushes over the river-smoothed rocks.

To reach the trailhead take Exit 97 for Deschutes Park from I-84 and follow the signs to Deschutes State Park. The trailhead is at the south end of the farthest parking area. Follow the river for about a mile and a quarter, and then choose the low or high trail, the latter of which leads up to an overlook and allows you to make a nice loop trail. A separate mountain bike trail also follows the river here for about 16 miles. It can be very hot here in midsummer, so this is a good place to go in the cooler weather of spring and fall.

Just downstream of the Deschutes, which takes its name from the French for river rapids or waterfalls, was **Celilo Falls**, the immense rapids and falls of the Columbia that were a great tribal fishing site — one of the most important of the Columbia River system — until the falls were inundated by construction of The Dalles Dam in 1957. Called Wyam, which means "Sound of Water upon the Rocks" or "Echo of Falling Water," by the Wyampum who lived near the falls for over 12,000 years, this is thought to be one of the longest continuously inhabited communities in North America, writes Elizabeth Woody, whose grandfather fished at Celilo.[1] For countless generations people came from across the river, both up- and downriver, to gather at Celilo to catch salmon, cook and dry fish, trade, exchange news, visit with family and friends, and celebrate. The first spring salmon caught is a sacred event, honored by the entire community with a feast of salmon, game, roots, and berries. The tradition continues today despite the damming of the river and decline of the salmon. "Our culture, tradition and ceremonies all center around the river and salmon. I cannot overstate its cultural importance," one Pacific coast tribal leader told me. The loss of Celilo to those whose ancestors fished at Wyam is incalculable, but if we act decisively — and in time — restoration of the Columbia's salmon runs may still be possible.

An interesting vantage point from which to view the site of Celilo Falls from the Washington side of the river is **Horsethief Lake State Park**, which perches on the volcanic cliffs off Highway 14, a couple miles east of the junction with Highway 197. Most of the park — located at the site of a former Wishram village (the historic plaque commemorating the Indian village is posted on a rest room door) — is a well-watered lawn, shade trees, and picnic table sort of place, but if you drive east of the park proper less than a mile, on your right you will see a brown and white sign indicating where you can pull off to hike a trail along the bluff. It is a detour worth making, since this is one of the only places with pedestrian access to this stretch of riverside cliffs, and there is a great view of Mount Hood directly south across the river. Don't drive too fast coming out of the park or you will miss the turnoff. Highway 14 is narrow and curving and gets fast-moving truck traffic, so drive carefully. And when hiking the brushy areas near the cliffs, watch out for poison oak and for ticks.

Horsethief State Park also offers guided tours of the pictographs and petroglyphs that decorate the cliffs here. Among these images is the famous pair of eyes known as *Tsagaglalal,* or "She Who Watches." Tours start at 10:00 A.M. on Friday and Saturday from April to October, and reservations are required. For reservations, call the Horsethief State Park office at 509-767-1159. The park recommends making reservations at least two to three days in advance. There is an answering machine, but to confirm a reservation, you must actually speak to a park ranger. For more information also see the park's Web site through the list of parks at http://www.parks.wa.gov/alpha.asp.

West of The Dalles on the Oregon side of the Columbia, a lovely place from which to view the river and see how the land changes from the rainforest and peaks of the Cascades to the rolling hills and sagebrush steppe of the interior Columbia Basin, is the **Tom McCall Preserve** at **Rowena Crest** near Mosier, Oregon. Easy, level trails here meander down toward the river. There is also a steep trail that gains over 1,000 feet in a little over 1.5 miles and leads up to a ridge with terrific views. In the spring and early summer the wildflowers here — lupine, balsamroot, cornflowers, and brodiaea among them — are spectacular.

To reach the preserve take Exit 69, the Mosier exit, off I-84 and follow the signs to Rowena Crest. There is a large parking area, and trails lead clearly either down around the flats and some wetlands closer to the river or up the steep hill above. The flat trails are an excellent place for those who may not enjoy or be able to do hilly walks in the Columbia River Gorge.

The Pacific Crest Trail

OCTOBER 29TH. TUESDAY 1805

at 4 miles lower we observed a small river falling in with great
rapidity on the stard. side below which is a village of 11 houses,
here we landed to smoke a pipe with the natives . . . The inhab-
itants of the village are friendly and chearfull; those people
inform us that . . . ten nations live on this river and its waters,
on buries, and what game they can kill with their Bows &
arrows . . . The Countrey on each side begins to be thicker tim-
bered with Pine & low white Oake verry rockey and broken.

OCTOBER 31ST THURSDAY 1805

a remarkable high detached rock Stands in a bottom on the
Stard. Side near the lower point of this Island on the Stard.
Side about 800 feet high and 400 paces around, we call the
Beaten [Beacon] rock . . . [a] Great Shute or falls is about 1/2
a mile, with the water of this great river compressed within
the space of 150 paces in which there is great numbers of both
large and Small rocks, water passing with great velocity form-
ing [foaming] & boiling in a most horriable manner, with a
fall of about 20 feet.

The rocky and hilly country described in these journal entries
marked the beginning of the Cascade Range. Those who hike up
above Rowena Crest will see some of these oaks. **Beacon Rock**
now has a flight of stairs that curve up around it so that the curious can walk up to its top. Beacon Rock can be reached from
Highway 14 about 10 miles west of Stevenson, Washington.

The great chutes, or falls, of which Captain Clark wrote were
the cascades that used to tumble at Cascade Locks before the
lower Columbia dams were built. There is now a bridge across the
Columbia at Cascade Locks, poetically named the Bridge of the
Gods, reflecting the local tribal legends and geologic history.
Geologists think this may be the site of an ancient natural stone
bridge, probably created by the Bonneville landslide, which is esti-

mated to have occurred sometime between 1550 and 1750.[2] Some local tribal legends recount damming of the river with fire and rocks by the jealous mountain brothers Wy'East (Mount Hood) and Klickitat or Pah-toe (Mount Adams) as they sparred over winning the beautiful Loo-wit (Mount St. Helens). The view down the Columbia Gorge from here is impressive.

Those looking for a serious expedition can embark on the **Pacific Crest Trail** from Cascade Locks and head north into Washington, or south around the west side of Mount Hood. If you are going to begin hiking the Pacific Crest Trail (or PCT, as it is often called) here, I recommend hiking south because you more quickly enter actual protected wilderness around Mount Hood, whereas there is heavy logging around much of the area above the river in Washington. There are many ways to hike this stretch of the Pacific Crest Trail. It can be hiked from the Columbia River Gorge to Mount Hood, begun on Mount Hood at Barlow Pass or up at Timberline Lodge at the base of Mount Hood's summit — or combined with any number of connecting trails in the Columbia Gorge. (See the section on Mount Hood for more information.)

To reach the trailhead at Cascade Locks, take Exit 44 off I-84 and follow the signs to the Bridge of the Gods. There is parking just off the road leading to the bridge tollbooth. It is about 55 miles from Cascade Locks to Barlow Pass on the east side of Mount Hood, so get yourself a copy of the Oregon Northern Portion of the Forest Service's Pacific Crest National Scenic Trail map and start planning. This is hilly, forest walking, and once on Mount Hood you will want to make sure you are always prepared for wet and chilly weather, no matter what the season. Also remember that in summer and early fall — the dry season — water sources may have dried up, so fill up whenever you can. On any of these long multiday hikes, you will probably want to arrange a shuttle from your final destination to your point of departure, so figure that into your plans.

One loop combining the PCT with Columbia Gorge trails that would make a good two- to three-day trip would involve taking the Pacific Crest Trail south to where it connects with Trail 434 heading west to meet Eagle Creek Trail 440 and taking the Eagle Creek trail north back to its trailhead just off I-84 at Exit 41 near the Columbia. For more information and maps call the Nature of

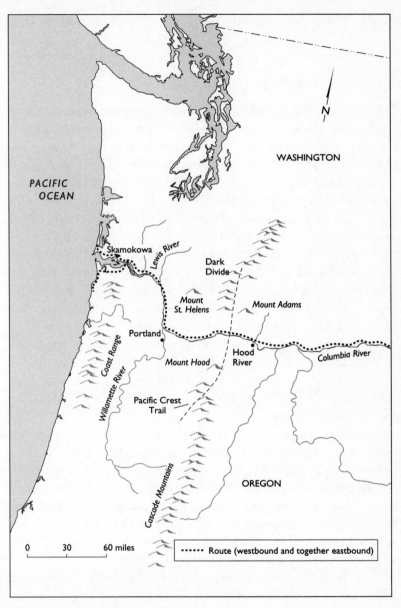

Map 8 The Lower Columbia River.

the Northwest Information Center in Portland, Oregon, at 503-872-2750.

The Columbia River Gorge

There are dozens of hiking possibilities in the Columbia River Gorge. On the Oregon side of the Columbia, most of these hikes gain elevation quickly as they switchback up the cliffs that form the gorge, with its dramatic, plunging waterfalls. In spring and early summer the trails are lined with larkspur, wild iris, rose, tiger lilies, lupine, balsamroot, paintbrush, and other bright wildflowers. In all, at least 800 species of native wildflowers are found in the Columbia Gorge, some 15 of which live nowhere else. The rare Larch Mountain salamander and western pond turtle still live here, as do peregrine falcons, bald eagles, and cougars, but the coho salmon are gone, as are the condors, wolves, and grizzly bears. Much of the Columbia River Gorge is protected under the Columbia River Gorge National Scenic Area Act, but many conservationists feel stronger enforcement of the act and stronger protections are needed to preserve it from development pressures.

For more information about Columbia River Gorge wildflowers, see the Forest Service's Web site at http://www.fs.fed.us/r6/columbia/wildflowers.htm.

Trails in the Columbia River Gorge can be hiked when fall and winter rains have abated sufficiently so that slippery mud is not a problem, and snow has receded at the higher elevations — but acclimated northwesterners will head out in weather others might shun. Those visiting the Columbia River Gorge for the first time will want to take the slow road, the old scenic Highway 30, which passes numerous waterfalls (many of which have hiking trails adjacent), rather than the speedier I-84.

A favorite hike here is one that follows **Eagle Creek** south and upstream past a series of dramatic waterfalls. This hike gains only about 1,200 feet in 6 miles, occasionally clinging to the side of the creek canyon walls, sometimes passing through tall, old fir trees and crossing the creek on high wooden bridges. If you hike 6 miles in, you will come to Tunnel Falls — an enormous, plunging waterfall with a tunnel bored into the rock wall behind it that you can walk through. Many people make this their destination, but if you are ambitious and want to turn this into a backpacking trip, the Eagle Creek Trail connects with others leading either to the Pacific Crest Trail or the trail that loops around Tanner Butte. You will want to organize a shuttle if you do anything other than retrace your steps down Eagle Creek because you probably will not want to hike the connecting mileage on roads.

To reach the Eagle Creek trailhead, take Exit 41 (it is signed for a fish hatchery) from I-84, but you have to do this approaching from the west traveling eastbound because there is no westbound Exit 41. If you are coming from the east (heading toward Portland), take the Bonneville Dam exit (Exit 40) and backtrack. Follow the road along the creek inland from the hatchery. There is a large, paved parking area. This is a popular hike, so start early on a weekend or go on a weekday. And because it is less exposed than some other hikes in the Columbia River Gorge, it is an ideal one for misty or drizzly weather.

If you want to park at established trailheads in national forests in Oregon and Washington—and you probably will if hiking there—you will need a trail pass parking permit. These are obtainable at ranger stations, the Nature of the Northwest Information Center in Portland, Oregon, and some other outlets, including the Multnomah Falls gift shop. With the exception of the Multnomah Falls shop, most of these are far from trailheads and often closed on weekends, so you will want to get a permit before you reach the trailhead. For more information—the permit regulations are in flux—and maps, call the Nature of the Northwest Information Center in Portland, Oregon, at 503-872-2750.

Another favorite hike in the Columbia River Gorge, on the Washington side of the Columbia, is **Dog Mountain**. This steep, switchbacking hike climbs a little over 3 miles to the top of a mountain with wonderful views of the river and gorge. The wildflowers here in the spring and early summer are fantastic. To reach the trailhead take Washington Highway 14 about 9 miles east of Carson. The parking area will be on your left (heading eastbound) facing the river. There are two routes up the mountain: one leads to your left — or south if you are standing with your back to the river — the other to your right. The southern approach is steeper going up, but it is my favorite because it is more open, and the views and wildflowers are prettier. You will hike along the cliff side, then through some forest before coming out into the open again on a steep, grassy slope. When you begin your descent, be prepared for steep downhill going and occasionally loose pebbles than can make for slippery footing. Again, this is a popular trail, so start early in the day. And it is one best enjoyed before the full heat of midsummer, although if you go early in the season, be prepared for much cooler or wetter weather on top. Keep an eye out for small wildlife. If you are lucky, you might see the slightly iridescent navy blue Western skink.

Mount Adams, the Dark Divide, and the Gifford Pinchot National Forest

To get a sense of some Cascade Range backcountry close to the Lewis and Clark Trail, consider hiking near **Mount Adams**, the snow-covered mountain Captain Clark spied from their expedition's camp near the Umatilla River. A lovely place for a day hike — which can be extended into a backpacking trip — is in the **Indian Heaven Wilderness Area** southwest of Mount Adams.

To reach the area, take Washington Highway 141 north from White Salmon, Washington, to Trout Lake, and then continue west about 15 miles on Highway 141 until it becomes Forest Road 24. Stay on this going north to the Cultus Creek campground where you'll find the trailhead. The trail leads south up toward Bird Mountain and past a basin of lakes. In late summer there are huckleberries galore here, and earlier in the season the wildflowers are wonderful. It is also very pretty in the fall. You can make a 6- to 7-mile day hike loop of this, stopping to picnic or, if you are brave, for a dip in a chilly lake — or connect with the Pacific Crest Trail for an extended expedition. Snow can linger surprisingly long in the spring around Trout Lake, so if you are thinking of heading out early in the season, you may want to call ahead to check conditions.

For more information and maps contact the Gifford Pinchot National Forest at the Mount Adams Ranger District in Trout Lake, Washington at 509-395-3400. Or see its Web site at http://www.fs.fed.us/gpnf.

Sadly, much of the surrounding Gifford Pinchot National Forest has been heavily logged, with great patches of Douglas fir, hemlock, and western red cedar having been clear-cut. But pieces of wilderness and roadless areas remain, harboring northern spotted owls, elk, trout streams, and habitat for many other kinds of wildlife. One such roadless area is the **Dark Divide** surrounding Quartz Creek to the north and west of the Indian Heaven Wilderness. You will not find the name Dark Divide on a map, so to find the area, follow the Lewis River upstream to find Quartz Creek, and then look south from the Cispus River to find the ridges containing Tongue Mountain, Juniper and Jumbo Peaks, Dark Mountain, Langille and McCoy Peaks, and Holdaway Butte to the west of McCoy Creek. An additional finger of roadless area containing substantial groves of old growth surrounds upper Clear Creek, which lies to the west of the Lewis River. The Dark Divide contains the largest unfragmented block of old-growth forest remaining in southwest Washington outside of a national park. There are steep, forested slopes and streambeds, waterfalls, and rugged alpine ridge tops. Nearby is a mysterious area of lava beds, where it is very easy to get lost, and local lore is full of Sasquatch sightings. For a charming account of this part of the country, see Robert Michael Pyle's book *Where Bigfoot Walks*.

A hike along Quartz Creek, with its stands of old growth and mossy canyon walls, is a good introduction to the Dark Divide. The easiest way to reach the trailhead is to take Forest Road 90 east from Cougar about 17 miles. (Cougar is on Washington Highway 503, which follows the Lewis River, and is reachable from I-5 at Woodland.) Stay on Forest Road 90 past Big Creek Falls and the Lower, Middle, and Upper Lewis River Falls. About half a mile past Upper Lewis River Falls, Forest Road 90 turns to the right, and there will be a sign for Quartz Creek Trail 5. Forest Road 90 crosses Quartz Creek. The trailhead is on the west side of the creek, and a parking area is on the east side. There are several streams to ford, so this hike is best done from June through the fall, when runoff from spring snowmelt will probably have subsided. Trail 5 — which is often steep — parallels Quartz Creek for about 10 miles until it meets Boundary Trail 1. Twenty miles round-trip is long for a day hike, so you will probably want to call it quits and head back at either Snagtooth Trail 4 or French Creek Trail 5C — or somewhere thereabouts. Because Quartz Creek Trail intersects with Boundary Trail 1, which heads west to Dark Mountain, or the Snagtooth Trail, which goes up to Snagtooth Mountain and Hat Rock, there are numerous backpacking possibilities — nearly all with natural loop trails — from this trailhead. To get a full sense of what the Dark Divide is like, you may want to plan both a lower-elevation old-growth hike and one that takes you out to the ridge tops.

The Gifford Pinchot National Forest map will be essential for accurate navigation, not only along trails but also on Forest Service roads, which can be confusing. (For those not accustomed to driving Forest Service roads, it is helpful to know that those with two-digit numbers are main roads, whereas those with three- and four-digit numbers tend to be minor roads.) The Forest Service Web site at http://www.fs.fed.us/gpnf/trails has good descriptions of hikes throughout this area, accompanied by trail maps.

Also in the vicinity and well worth exploring is the **Goat Rocks Wilderness Area** on the northwest side of Mount Adams. A wonderful overnight backpacking trip there is the hike across the Lily Basin to **Goat Lake,** a small glacial lake that often remains frozen year-round that sits atop a great cirque with a full-on view of Mount Adams.

To reach the trailhead take Washington Highway 12 almost to Packwood. About 2 miles southwest of Packwood turn east onto Forest Road 48. Stay on this road for about 10 miles, until you come to a clearly marked trailhead parking area. It is about 7 or 8 miles up to Goat Lake, and you will gain quite a bit of elevation — close to 1,000 feet — along the way. The views are wonderful, and at points you will feel like you are sitting in Mount Adams's lap. If you are lucky, you will be able to see Mount Rainier to the north as well. There are trickling streams, snowfields, and wildflowers. Because Goat Lake is essentially in a snowfield and on a ridge rim, camping spots are limited, and you may have to deal with strong winds circling up as the warm air rises through the night. But it is worth it. On your return to the trailhead you can retrace your route or make a loop trail by heading downhill around Snowgrass Flat and Goat Ridge.

For more information and maps call the Packwood Ranger District of the Gifford Pinchot National Forest at 360-494-0601 in Packwood, Washington.

Mount Hood

NOVEMBER 3D. 1805

The Fog so thick this morning that we could not see a man 50 Steps off, this fog detained us untill 10 oClock at which time we Set out, accompanied by our Indian friends who are from a village near the great falls

The Quick Sand river appears to pass through the low countrey at the foot of those high range of mountains in a Southerly direction. . . . A Mountain which we Suppose to be Mt. Hood, is S. 85° E about 47 miles distant from the mouth of quick sand river. This Mtn. is covered with Snow and in the range of mountains which we have passed through and is of a conical form but rugid.

The "Quick Sand" river was the Sandy River, which gathers its water from the snowmelt and glaciers of **Mount Hood** and flows into the Columbia just east of the present-day Portland, Oregon, city limits. Captain Clark's estimation of distance was remarkably accurate. A mileage marker on the outskirts of Portland puts the distance to a high point on Mount Hood as 48 miles. Today, the streams that run off Mount Hood provide drinking water for the city of Portland and surrounding communities. About 1 million acres of the forest on and around the mountain are encompassed by the Mount Hood National Forest, parts of which are designated as legislatively protected wilderness. Mount Hood, which

Mount Hood. Photo: Wayne Mumford.

rises to 11,245 feet, is the highest mountain in Oregon. Here protected old growth provides a home for endangered spotted owls,
but there are also clear-cuts. Streams that run off Mount Hood
provide essential spawning grounds for imperiled salmon. The
forest here contains huge Douglas fir, western and mountain hemlock and noble fir, and, at higher elevations, subalpine fir and
whitebark pine. The understory is full of vine maples, rhododen-
drons, salal, Oregon grape, and huckleberry, among many other
native plants. There are mountain meadows and lakes, and snowfields that persist year-round. Mount Hood is home to dozens of
mammal species, including deer, elk, coyote, black bear, cougar,
and marmot. On the dry, eastern side of the mountain — in the rain
shadow of the Cascades — the fir give way to huge ponderosa pine
and sage.

There are currently six areas of legislatively protected wilderness within the reach of Mount Hood and the Mount Hood
National Forest: the Badger Creek Wilderness, Columbia Wilderness, Bull-of-the-Woods Wilderness, Mount Hood Wilderness,
Salmon Huckleberry Wilderness, and part of the Mount Jefferson

Wilderness. Together these areas make up about 188,000 acres, less than 20 percent of the entire Mount Hood National Forest. Ongoing logging operations in the rest of the forest are damaging what is left of spotted owl habitat, contributing to degradation of streams vital to salmon and steelhead, and threatening the quality of drinking water sources. Oregon conservation groups are now working toward additional wilderness protection for Mount Hood's forests.

Countless hikes can be taken on Mount Hood — ones that approach the mountain from the west, east, north, and south. One of my favorites is the trail that leads up to **Elk Meadows** and **Gnarl Ridge,** which heads up the mountain from the southeast.

To reach the trailhead take Highway 35, which heads south to Mount Hood from the Columbia River city of Hood River, or from its junction with Highway 26 (heading eastbound from Portland) a few miles east of Government Camp. Take Highway 35 about 8 miles to the Clark Creek Sno-Park. The trail — which is used for cross-country skiing in the winter — climbs up to and then follows the creek west before meeting up with Trail 645, which heads up east to Elk Meadows. From there you can pick up Trail 652 or 652A and climb Gnarl Ridge, which rises above 6,000 feet, or take Trail 646 along Newton Creek up toward Lambeson Butte.

This network of trails also connects with **Timberline Trail,** which circumnavigates the summit of Mount Hood. For a 10-mile round-trip hike, head up to Gnarl Ridge and Elk Meadows and come back the way you came, or make a detour and hike up Elk Mountain, or return via Bluegrass Ridge or the Newton Creek Trail. The views are terrific whichever high point you pick. The Forest Service map of Mount Hood will help you plot your route. If you are backpacking, check with the Forest Service about where camping is currently permitted.

For more information contact the Mount Hood Information Center at 503-622-7674 in Welches, Oregon, or the Hood River Ranger District of the Mount Hood National Forest at 541-352-6002 in Mount Hood–Parkdale, Oregon. Or see the Forest Service's Mount Hood Web site at http://www.fs.fed.us/r6/mthood/.

Cross-Country Skiing and Snowshoeing on Mount Hood

Even the most ardent Luddites would probably admit that modern synthetic fabrics, lightweight metal, and plastics have improved the enjoyment of winter outdoors since the days of Lewis and Clark. Mount Hood has a vast network of cross-country skiing and snowshoe trails, and the snow season is generally dependable from mid-November until April.

A favorite trail that is a good introduction to skiing on Mount Hood is the 4.5-mile **Trillium Lake** loop that is accessible from a sizable parking area just east of Government Camp. This trail gets a lot of use, so be prepared for people, especially on the first long, steep downhill run. If you can do this on a weekday, it is ideal, but skiing around the lake among the huge, snow-draped fir trees is great fun even when your party is not the only one there.

Another popular and pretty set of trails is those around **Teacup Lake**, which is on the south side of the road across Highway 35 from Mount Hood Meadows and Clark Creek Sno-Park. There are several loops between 1.5 and about 3.5 miles long that can be done on their own or in combination. They are of varying degrees of difficulty and many include hills, which can make for some fun.

If you venture out on less-used trails or break your own on snow-covered roads, do keep an eye out for changing snow conditions. Mount Hood gets lots of snow, and snow slides or avalanches are not uncommon. Also be aware if you are skiing across creeks and watch for holes in the snow. For more information contact the Mount Hood Information Center at 503-622-7674 in Welches, Oregon. Sno-Park permits are required to park at maintained ski-trail areas from November 15 to April 15. These can be acquired at local sporting goods shops, ranger stations, and some national forest agency offices. Again, it is best to get one before you set out. There are a number of guidebooks devoted to regional cross-country and snowshoe trails, so if you are serious about such winter expeditions, I would recommend consulting those.

CHAPTER 9

The Lower Columbia River to the Pacific Ocean

Sauvie Island

NOVEMBER 4TH. MONDAY 1805

we proceeded on and met a large & a Small canoe from below with 12 men the large canoe was ornimented with Images carved in wood the figures of a Bear in front & a man in Stern, Painted & fixed verry netely on the canoe, rising to near the hight of a man two Indians verry finely Dressed & with hats on was in this canoe passed the lower point of the Island which is nine miles in length . . .

NOVEMBER 5TH. TUESDAY 1805

Rained all the after part of last night, rain continues this morning, I [s]lept but verry little last night for the noise Kept [up] dureing the whole of the night by the Swans, Geese, white & Grey Brant Ducks &c. on a Small Sand Island close under the Lard. Side; they were emensely noumerous, and their noise horrid.

Lewis and Clark called the island near which they saw this finely carved canoe "Image Canoe Island." On their return journey they called the same island "Wappato," after the root or bulb of the arrowhead plant, which the Chinookan Indians who lived there gathered and ate. The island sits in the Columbia at the confluence of the Columbia and Willamette Rivers — at the north end of the present-day city of Portland, Oregon — and is now called **Sauvie Island**. When Lewis and Clark described "wide and emence numbers of fowls flying in every direction, Such as Swan, geese, Brants, Cranes, Stalks [Storks], white guls, comerants & plevers &c. also great numbers of Sea Otter in the river," it was from just upstream of this point, near what is now Government Island at the east end of Portland.

While the industrial districts and suburbs of Portland and Vancouver, Washington, now sprawl along this stretch of the lower Columbia, Sauvie Island retains its rural character, and one can wander its wetlands for some first-class bird-watching. The island is about 4 miles wide — at its widest — and 15 miles long, encompassing about 24,000 acres. Bald eagles nest here in winter. Sandhill cranes stop here, and among the numerous resident and other visiting birds are red-tailed and rough-legged hawks, northern harriers, osprey, great blue herons, egrets, pileated woodpeckers, kingfishers, western grebes, cormorants, snow geese, Canada geese, kestrels, and many kinds of ducks — including green-winged teals, mergansers, cinnamon teals, northern shovelers, and wood ducks — as well as numerous songbirds. While you are there, watch for rabbits and beaver and listen for frogs in the spring.

The southern half of Sauvie Island is settled mostly by farms, many of which have seasonal "u-pick" harvests of berries, flowers, and pumpkins. The northern half of the island is sequestered as a wildlife area and thus contains remnants of the wetlands that once characterized the river region of the lower Columbia and Willamette Rivers. The island's flat roads make it popular for bike rides. There are several boat ramps from which you can launch a kayak or canoe to paddle the Multnomah Channel, Sturgeon Lake, and Gilbert River. This is a great way to bird-watch.

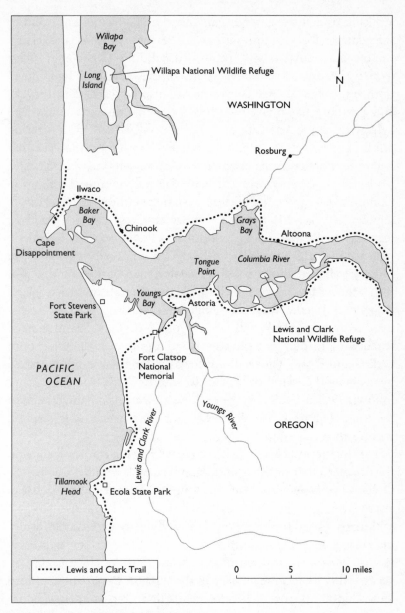

Map 9 The Mouth of the Columbia River.

Walking trails lead around Oak Island and Virginia Lake and to
the Warrior Rock Lighthouse at the very north tip of the island.

To reach Sauvie Island from Portland, take Highway 30 west
from downtown to the Sauvie Island Bridge, about 3.5 miles north
of the St. Johns Bridge. This route can also be traveled by bicycle,
and Portland has many bike shops that handle rentals and can
help with maps. The City of Portland's Office of Transportation
publishes "Bicycle Map and Resources," a useful leaflet (for that
and other Portland area biking information, call 503-823-CYCL).
Multnomah County and adjacent Clackamas and Washington
Counties also have good bike maps that are either free or relatively
inexpensive (for Multnomah County call 503-988-5050). Most
maps of the Portland metropolitan area include Sauvie Island.

Once over the Sauvie Island Bridge, if you turn right, you will
find a signboard with a good orientation map of the island. If you
turn left over the bridge and continue about a mile on Sauvie Island
Road past Reeder Road, Virginia Lake and the Wapato Access
Greenway State Park will be on your left. Oak Island can be
reached by turning onto Reeder Road and then turning left onto
Oak Island Road. The trailhead for Warrior Rock can be reached
by crossing the island by way of Reeder Road to Coon Point and
following Reeder Road to the parking area at the northwest end of
the road. The trails are all level. It is a little over 2 miles around
each of these lakes, and about 3 miles one way to Warrior Rock.

Parking permits are required to leave a vehicle at trailheads on
the northern half of the island, managed as a wildlife area by the
Oregon Department of Fish and Wildlife. These can be purchased
at the store just past the Sauvie Island side of the bridge. No permits are required for bicycling. The wildlife area is closed to walking during hunting season, usually from October through early
spring. For more information on precise dates of closures and on
accessibility of specific areas, call the Oregon Department of Fish
and Wildlife at 503-621-3488 in Portland, Oregon. Roads are
generally open throughout the year — as is the trail to Warrior
Rock — and closed areas should be well marked.

For those wanting to rent canoes or kayaks, there are several
conveniently located shops in Portland. Check the latest local

Yellow Pages for up-to-date listings. The Portland Bureau of Parks and Recreation conducts paddling tours of lower Columbia and Willamette waterways, as do various local river conservation groups and private outfitters.

For more information contact the Portland Bureau of Parks and Recreation at 503-823-7529 or see its Web site at http://www.portlandparks.org and look under "Outdoor Recreation."

Columbia River Estuary:
Paddling the Lower Columbia from Skamokawa

NOVEMBER 7TH. 1805

A cloudy foggey morning Some rain. we Set out early pro-
ceeded under the Stard. Side under a high rugid hills with Steep
assent the Shore boalt and rockey, the fog so thick we could
not see across the river . . . Encamped under a high hill on the
Stard. Side opposit to a rock Situated half a mile from the
shore, about 50 feet high and 20 feet in Deamieter; we with
dificuelty found a place clear of the tide and Sufficiently large
to lie on and the only place we could get was on round stones
on which we lay our mats rain continud. Moderately all
day . . . Great joy in camp we are in view of the Ocian this
great Pacific Octean which we been so long anxious to See.

This entry was written from near what is now the tiny town of Altoona, Washington, in Wahkiakum County, a county named for the Chinookan-speaking tribe that lived there when Lewis and Clark came down the river. Here the Columbia River widens dramatically. Tides and wind come sweeping in from the ocean, making it easy to see how Lewis and Clark could have mistaken the river and its great wide bays for the ocean itself.

The bay near where they camped on November 7 is now called Grays Bay. If you follow the narrow, winding, two-lane roads toward the river from Washington Highway 4, you can get a glimpse of some of the offshore rocks Lewis and Clark described — including the one noted in the journal entry from November 7.

Despite about two centuries of European American settlement, the communities of the lower Columbia are still rural and removed from the extensive development that has taken place in the valleys to the west of the Cascades, in what has come to be called the I-5 corridor (after the interstate that runs through Washington, Oregon, and California.) Wooded and forested hills rise steeply on either side of the river. Small rivers and streams that often swell to flooding in the rainy season course down to the Columbia. There are small farms, woodlots, and communities that once thrived on timber and fishing that are now trying to chart a future in which their prosperity does not depend on using natural resources as fast as possible. For much of the year rain buffets the banks of the Columbia. There is ocean salt in the marine air, and the wind often whips the river mouth bay into foaming whitecaps.

The Columbia River estuary is an important point of passage and nurturing for the Columbia basin's anadromous fish — particularly for salmon and steelhead. The estuary's health is also vital to the shellfish that are essential to the balance of the region's watery ecology. Both the fish and shellfish have long been part of the local economy; both have suffered as river conditions have been degraded.

The Columbia River shipping channel, which extends to the mouth of the river, is dredged regularly, an activity that has taken a significant toll on the estuary's ecological health and that of the surrounding riparian habitat. Islands of "dredge spoils" provide unnaturally expanded habitat for birds, particularly caspian terns, which prey on juvenile salmon and steelhead. Many of the young salmon and steelhead are now especially vulnerable to predators, since great numbers of them are deposited in the lower river by the barges and trucks that transport them around the dams upriver. The dredging itself can harm fish, and it has altered fragile shoreline habitat in detrimental ways. As of this writing there are plans to deepen the shipping channel by 3 feet, from the mouth of the river to the port of Portland (about 80 miles inland), to accommodate deep-draft vessels. The proposal is being fought by conservationists and by the fishing and shell-fishing community at the mouth of the river. The National Marine Fisheries Service — the federal agency responsible for protection of anadromous fish —

has acknowledged that this additional dredging would harm the river's imperiled fish.

The country immediately adjacent to the lower Columbia on both the Washington and the Oregon sides of the river is almost entirely private land, so the best way to explore this landscape is from the water. An excellent place from which to begin exploring the lower Columbia River estuary for the day, or better yet for a two- or three-day paddle, is Skamokawa, Washington.

Skamokawa is located on an inlet where several creeks run into the river, about 30 miles west of Longview, Washington, off Highway 4. It is an ideal place to begin paddling what has been dubbed the **Columbia River Heritage Canoe Trail** — though the water and wind conditions make it much better suited to sea kayak than canoe. There is a nice shop where you can rent kayaks in the tiny town center at Skamokawa near Vista Park, so if you rent there, that might be your launching point. There is also a friendly and helpful shop near the Youngs Bay bridge in Warrenton, Oregon, if you are coming that way and need to rent a boat, or you can rent in Portland.

If you are paddling for only a day, you may decide to explore the Washington shoreline and perhaps put in at Cathlamet, a few miles upstream. From there you can paddle the sloughs through the Julia Butler Hansen National Wildlife Refuge and downriver toward Skamokawa. If you are beginning an overnight trip from Skamokawa and plan to take out on the Oregon side of the river, you will want to organize a car shuttle. You can do this by taking the ferry across the Columbia to Westport, Oregon, from Puget Island, which is reachable by bridge from Cathlamet, Washington, and leave a vehicle at your takeout point — probably either at the John Day River (the one near Tongue Point) or at Aldrich Point near Knappa.

For an overnight trip, you will first want to get the appropriate maps from the United States Geological Survey (USGS) and charts from the National Oceanic and Atmospheric Administration (NOAA). A good way to organize an overnight trip is to camp the night before you put in at Vista Park, camp the second night somewhere across the river, and take out on the third day at the John

Day River. Bear in mind that there are not many places to camp on river islands; most are restricted from such use to protect riparian habitat and sensitive wetlands.

When you put in for a trip that takes you to the south, or Oregon, side of the river, one of the first things you will do is cross the Columbia's shipping channel. Take great care as you do to check that none of the enormous tankers or barges that ply the Columbia are steaming your way. Their wakes are huge and can easily swamp a boat, so stay well away or if possible simply get out of the water. Cross the river toward Fitzpatrick, Welsh, and Tenasillahe Islands. Then thread your way through the islands, tidal flats, and marshes of the 8,313-acre **Lewis and Clark National Wildlife Refuge**. There will be caspian terns, ravens, rookeries full of great blue herons, and a host of other birds, including bald eagles. You will want to pay attention to the tides. The water moves in and out rather dramatically, and low tide can leave you knuckle-dragging your boat through inch-deep water, especially in back channels between the islands. The Pacific Ocean and river currents intersect here, and the tidal surge of the Columbia River is strong enough to affect the river as far as 100 miles inland.

If the wind is strong coming upriver from the ocean, it can make for strenuous paddling. Explore the water around Woody Island, Goose Island, Horseshoe Island, Marsh Island, Karlson Island, Russian Island, and Svensen Island before ending your adventure at the boat ramp at the mouth of the John Day River across the water from Lois Island. The crosswinds can be strong approaching the wide river mouth, so other than when your route calls for a crossing, you will want to stick close to shore in the sheltered channels between islands. The mouth of the Columbia is notoriously treacherous water, and as a paddling friend puts it, "no fool" would paddle the mouth of the river itself.

There are no official campsites along this route, and camping is not permitted in the wildlife refuges, so you are on your own to figure that out. It can be done. You can also break this trip into sections that can be done as a one- or two-day trip. You will want to go in the summer because the other three seasons are usually very, very wet.

For more information contact the Lewis and Clark National Wildlife Refuge and Julia Butler Hansen National Wildlife Refuge at 360-795-4915 in Cathlamet, Washington. For maps contact the Oregon State Marine Board at 503-378-8587 or the National Ocean Service in Silver Spring, Maryland, at 301-713-3074. The National Ocean Service has an extensive Web site (http://www.nos.noaa.gov), which includes a great deal of map and chart information. A good source of maps (both marine and USGS) in the Pacific Northwest is Captain's Nautical Supplies in Portland at 503-227-1648.

For information on tides, check local newspaper weather page listings or see the Web site for NOAA's Center for Operational Oceanographic Products and Services at http://co-ops.nos.noaa.gov and follow the link for "Predictions," which will get you to tide tables listed by state. The local shops that rent and sell kayaks and canoes can help you out with advice, and most also offer guided trips or can recommend others who do. The Skamokawa Paddle Center, Pacific Wave in Warrenton, Oregon, Alder Creek and Ebb & Flow in Portland, and REI are good places to rent.

Paddling in Youngs Bay near Astoria and Fort Clatsop

FRIDAY NOVEMBER 22ND. 1805.

O! how horriable is the day waves brakeing with great violence against the Shore throwing the water into our Camp &c. all wet and confind to our shelters, Several Indian men and women crouding about the mens shelters to day, we purchased a fiew Wappato roots for which we gave Armban[d]s, & rings . . . those roots are equal to the Irish potato, and is a tolerable substitute for bread.

NOVEMBER 28TH. THURSDAY 1805

we could find no deer, several hunters attempted to penetrate the thick woods to the main South Side without suckcess the

*swan & gees wild and cannot be approached, and wind to
high to go either back or forward, and we have nothing to
eate but a little Pounded fish which we purchasd. At the Great
falls, This is our present situtaion! Truly disagreeable. aded
to this the robes of our selves and men are all rotten from
being continually wet . . . O! how Tremendious is the day.
This dredfull wind and rain continued with intervales of fair
weather, the greater part of the evening and night.*

These laments of wet weather were written from the shores of the
Columbia River near Astoria. After camping along the rainy,
windy northern banks of the Columbia, Lewis and Clark's party
crossed to the south side of the river, where they eventually made
their winter camp at Fort Clatsop.

If you wish to retrace Lewis and Clark's route by car, take
Washington Highway 4 to Skamokawa, and then follow the road
inland to Rosburg, where you can follow a narrow road down to
the water at Altoona. You will have to return the way you came to
rejoin Highway 4; then take Highway 401 south along the Naselle
River to the Columbia, where the road joins Highway 101 on the
Washington side of the Astoria bridge. To continue on to Ilwaco
and Cape Disappointment, follow Highway 101 west through the
town of Chinook along the north shore of Baker Bay. These are
towns that, like Astoria, once thrived on salmon fishing and can-
ning. A commercial fishery persists here, but it, along with the
coastal sportfishing, has suffered in recent years from the decline
in fish numbers. Inland from here, the timber industry was active,
but that, too, has quieted now, since heavy logging in the 1970s
and 1980s took most of the big trees. This is very much a place of
water, with numerous creeks running into the bays. Gulls and terns
wheel and screech overhead. The river mouth's big waves lap the
shoreline, and the place where the Columbia and the Pacific meet
and form the underwater sandbar known as the Columbia Bar is
still as treacherous a crossing for ships as it ever was.[1]

While much has changed since Lewis and Clark slogged their
way down the Columbia, the weather has not, so summer is the
season for extensive outdoor exploring — unless you are happy

spending long hours in the rain. Another good way to get a feel for this watery landscape is to paddle — again, sea kayak is the best way to go — the **Youngs River** and **Lewis and Clark River**, both of which empty into **Youngs Bay** at Astoria. While the wind on the bay can make for difficult paddling, the rivers are sheltered and so one can paddle them happily on a misty day. Both of these rivers are heavily influenced by the tide; if you will be setting out upriver, it is best to do so at high tide so you will not be paddling against the lunar pull.

If you want to paddle the whole navigable 9 miles of the Youngs River, you will want to organize a shuttle by leaving a vehicle at the boat ramp at the Astoria Yacht Club (not a fancy place!) just off Highway 101 at the foot of the Astoria side of the Youngs Bay bridge. Then take your boats and follow the Youngs River Loop Road, which can be reached by taking Alternate Business 101 from the Astoria Yacht Club across the river toward Miles Crossing. Youngs River Loop Road will be a direct left off Business 101. Follow Youngs River Loop Road upstream about 7 miles, until just past where the Klaskanine River joins the Youngs. You can park and put in there. If you reach the river's falls, you have gone too far.

The approach to the Lewis and Clark River is similar to that to the Youngs. Arrange a shuttle by leaving a vehicle at the Astoria Yacht Club, and then take Business 101 across the river to Miles Cross and follow Lewis and Clark Road past the Fort Clatsop turnoff, to Logan Road to a place where you can put in about 6 miles or so upstream. Both the Youngs and the Lewis and Clark Rivers pass through woods and farmland. If the wind is heading in from the west, be prepared for some stiff paddling. And once you reach Youngs Bay, take care to stick close to the shoreline until you make your final crossing, since the wind and tide can be strong.

If you want to paddle for only a couple of hours, put in at the Astoria Bay Yacht Club when the tide is favorable, hug the shoreline, and paddle upstream a bit on Youngs River for a little harbor tour. The USGS 7.5′ quad maps of Astoria and Olney will help you out here. There is also a NOAA maritime chart for this.

A Circumnavigation of Long Island in Willapa Bay North of Ilwaco and Cape Disappointment

NOVEMBER 18TH. MONDAY 1805

to the inner extremity of Cape Disapointment . . . there is a Small rock island . . . this Cape is an ellivated circlier [circular] point covered with thick timber on the inner side and open grassey exposure next to the Sea and rises with a Steep assent to the hight of about 150 or 160 feet above the level of the water this cape as also the Shore on the Bay & Sea coast is a dark brown rock.

NOVEMBER 19TH TUESDAY 1805

after takeing a Sumptious brackfast of Venison which was rosted on Stiks exposed to the fire, I proceeded on through ruged Country of high hills and Steep hollers on a course from the Cape N 20°W. 5 miles on a Direct line to the commencement of a Sandy coast which extended N. 10° W. from the top of the hill above the Sand Shore to a Point of high land distant near 20 miles . . . maney places open with small ponds in which there is great numbr. of fowl I am informed that the Chinnook Nation inhabit this low coutnrey and live in large wood houses on a river which passes through this bottom Parrilal to the Sea coast and falls into the Bay
I proceeded on the sandy coast 4 miles and marked my name on a Small pine, the Day of the month & year, &c . . . I saw a Sturgeon . . . and several joints of the back bone of a whale, which must have foundered on this part of the Coast.

These journal entries were written from what is now the coast of southwest Washington, where a lighthouse now stands above Fort Canby State Park. The lighthouse marks Cape Disappointment, a high bluff over the Pacific where waves crash, seals occasionally bark, and, if you are there at the right moment in winter, migrating gray whales can be spotted. The sandy coast Captain Clark described is now Long Beach, Washington, a long, sandy spit that reaches north with the Pacific on one side and Willapa Bay on the other. It is well worth the drive out to Cape Disappointment to wander around the headlands and watch the surf pound. And it is fun to walk out on the tip of the Long Beach Peninsula at the **Willapa National Wildlife Refuge** at **Leadbetter Point State Park**, an expedition best done outside the summer season if you want to avoid the vacation congestion. But the best way to get a sense of the elements of this landscape is from the water.

A good overnight paddling trip here — again, sea kayak is the vessel of choice — is the circumnavigation of Long Island, which is part of the Willapa National Wildlife Refuge. Willapa Bay and its adjacent estuary is one of the richest coastal ecosystems on the Pacific Coast. There are great blue herons, Pacific golden plovers, egrets, osprey, hawks, kestrels, cormorants, several species of sandpipers, brown pelicans, sooty shearwaters, bald eagles, and snowy plovers (these last two listed as threatened under the Endangered Species Act) — among many other species of water birds. Alas, the California condor, which Clark sketched in his journal, is a species now gone from this region, although there are hopes of reintroducing it to the area. Willapa Bay is also known for its oysters — an important local business. In recent years the invasion of nonnative sea grasses has posed problems for the bay's ecology — problems that have yet to be solved. Like other coastal communities, the town of Ilwaco has suffered with the downturn of fishing and fish numbers. But it is still very rich country to explore, and concerted efforts are being made to understand and solve current ecological problems.

To reach the launching point for a trip around Long Island, take Washington Highway 4 to where it meets Highway 101. Take 101 southwest across a small bridge over the Naselle River. About 2 miles from the bridge you will see parking areas for the Willapa National Wildlife Refuge on both sides of the road. You can leave a vehicle at the inland parking area and launch from the boat ramp across the road.

When I have done this, we headed west from the boat launch, generally hugging the shore of the island all the way around. There are established campsites at Smoky Hollow and just before you come to Jensen Point, as well as on the other side of the island near Lewis Slough and at the inner slough past Paradise Point.

At the north end of the island you will see oyster-harvesting operations; you will want to cross through this area at high tide so that you do not risk running aground on the mudflats in shallow water. In general, it helps with the paddling to time your circumnavigation of the island to take advantage of the tide rather than to fight it. When making the open-water crossing, be prepared for strong winds, and if the weather looks iffy, stick close to shore. If a storm blows in, wait it out onshore. On the inner side of the island the invasive spartina grass has encroached, creating deep, gluey mud, so take care if disembarking on such ground, since you will sink in quickly.

Hiking trails traverse Long Island, which is still home to black-tailed deer, black bear, Roosevelt elk, and many, many birds. Long Island has a stand of old-growth western red cedar, Sitka spruce, western hemlock, and Douglas fir. The oldest of these trees are around 1,200 years old, and most of the cedars date back some 900 years. Some foresters estimate that such a stand has existed here for at least 4,000 years. The island's only perennial freshwater stream runs through this grove, and old growth–dependent species of salamander and bat have been found here, along with forest-hunting raptors, flying squirrels, and Vaux's swifts. To visit the old-growth grove — a good all-day trip — traverse the short stretch of water between the boat launch described earlier off Highway 101 to the southeast side of Long Island. A clear road goes steeply into the basin. It curves west, then north, running alongside the old-growth stand. About 2 up-and-down miles in, there is a marked trailhead that takes off east into the stand. If you have camped at Smoky Hollow, you can reach the old-growth grove by following the old logging road south to the trailhead.

I have done this circumnavigation with a friend who brought along his five- and eight-year-old daughters. We all enjoyed ourselves immensely. (It is possible to rent a sea kayak with three hatches, so if you have a nonpaddling or very young companion, you might want to consider this option.)

For more information contact the Willapa Bay National Wildlife Refuge at 360-484-3482 in Ilwaco, Washington. There is a USGS 7.5′ quad map of Long Island that is very useful, as is the NOAA chart of Long Island and surrounding waters.

AQUATIC NUISANCE SPECIES

Not only is there the problem of invasive nonnative aquatic and upland species—zebra mussels, mitten crabs, hydrilla, knapweed, and others—being transported west and north; there is also the problem of invasives being transported east, so take equal care to wash and dry boats and boating and water gear, and to check shoes and pets before you leave your takeout point, and certainly before you put any of this equipment or clothing in another body of water. For more information contact the U.S. Fish and Wildlife Service at 877-786-7267 or see its Aquatic Nuisance Species Web site at http://ANSTaskForce.gov.

Oregon Coast: Ecola State Park and Tillamook Head

FRIDAY JANUARY 3D. 1806

At 11. A.M. we were visited by our near neighbours, Chief or Tiá. Co-mo-wool, alias Conia and six Clatsops. the[y] brought for sale some roots buries and three dogs also a small quantity of fresh blubber. This blubber they informed us they had obtained from their neighbours the Callamucks who inhabit the coast to the S.E. near whose vilage a whale had recently perished. this blubber the Indians eat and esteeme it excellent food . . . a smal Crow, the blue crested Corvus and the smaller corvus with a white brest, the little brown ren, a large brown sparrow, the bald Eagle and the beatifull Buzzard of the columbia still continue with us.

WEDNESDAY 8TH. JANUARY 1806

proceeded to the place the whale had perished, found only the Skelleton of this Monster on the Sand . . . I returned to the Village of 5 Cabins on the creek which I shall call E co-la or Whale Creek, found the nativs busily engaged boiling the blubber.

This first entry Captain Lewis wrote from the expedition's winter quarters at Fort Clatsop, which is near the present-day town of

Warrenton, Oregon. The "Buzzard of the columbia" is the California condor. There is a historic reconstruction of the fort at the site of the original Fort Clatsop, along with an interpretive center and short walking trails that lead down to the water.

The second entry here was written by Captain Clark, describing the spot where **Ecola State Park** is now located, near **Tillamook Head**, south of Seaside, Oregon. This is near the site of the expedition's salt making. Ecola State Park and Tillamook Head are better places from which to explore the coastline than Fort Clatsop. Ignore the typical beach town commerce of Seaside and Cannon Beach and concentrate on the stupendous cliffs and offshore rock formations. Watch for seals and sea lions (the sound of their bark is unforgettable), and if you are here in the winter or very early spring, watch for migrating whales. For information on whale watching see http://whalespoken.org/, the whale watching Web site maintained by the Oregon Parks and Recreation Department. The department can be reached in the coastal town of Waldport, Oregon, at 541-563-2002. The site has a wealth of whale information and links to Oregon State University's Hatfield Marine Science Center, which is located on the coast near Newport, Oregon.

To reach Ecola State Park take Highway 101 either south from Highway 26 toward Cannon Beach or north from Cannon Beach and follow the signs for the park road. Trailheads are located near Ecola Point and Indian Creek. You can take a hike of 5 miles or so along the bluff or shorter versions of the walk and admire the ocean views, but don't neglect to walk on the beach simply because it is so pretty. The trails are fairly level and follow a path used since long before Lewis and Clark arrived at the Pacific. If you are dressed for wind and rain, it is particularly pleasant to take this walk in the spring, fall, or winter and avoid the summer crowds. The Ecola State Park trails also connect with the Oregon Coast Trail, which extends along the length of the Oregon coast from the Columbia River to the California border — but does include close to 100 miles of walking along paved roads not designed for pedestrians.

For more information contact Ecola State Park in Cannon Beach, Oregon, at 503-436-2844. The Oregon State Parks and

Recreation Department has an official map of the Oregon Coast Trail and can be reached at 503-378-6305 in Salem, Oregon, or see the department's Web site at http://www.prd.state.or.us.

The Tillamook State Forest

SUNDAY MARCH 16TH 1806

The white Salmon trout which we had previously seen only at the great falls of the Columbia has now made it's appearance in the creeks near this place. One of them was brought us today by an Indian who had just taken it with his gig. . . . it was 2 feet 8 Inches long, and weighed 10 lbs.

SUNDAY 23RD. MARCH 1806

at this place we had wintered and remained from the 7th. of Decr. 1805 to this day and have lived as well as we had any right to expect . . . notwithstanding the repeated fall of rain which has fallen almost constantly since passed the long narrows.

Many of the creeks and rivers that Lewis and Clark would have explored during their winter at Fort Clatsop flow through what are now the Tillamook and Clatsop State Forests. Currently, seven of the Pacific Northwest's healthiest salmon runs depend on these rivers, including the north Oregon coast's healthiest populations of fall chinook and winter steelhead. The white salmon trout that Captain Lewis described here — and that Captain Clark sketched in his journal — was the silver or coho salmon. Coho salmon are now extinct in over half their historical range and qualify for listing as threatened under the Endangered Species Act all along the Oregon coast and south into northern and southern California.[2] Many other populations of salmon and steelhead in this region are also imperiled and considered at risk for extinction if conditions are not improved throughout their range. Yet coho, chum, spring and fall chinook, summer and winter steelhead, and sea-run cutthroat trout are still found here in these north coast rivers and streams.

The 810 square miles of the Tillamook and Clatsop State Forests make up the largest contiguous unprotected extent of mature coastal temperate rainforest between Canada and Mexico. The forests provide habitat for over seventy endangered species, including bald eagles, northern spotted owls, and marbled murrelets. These forests have been heavily logged since the mid–nineteenth century. This logging precipitated huge forest fires, which occurred here between the 1930s and the early 1950s, fires that came to be called the Tillamook Burn. In the wake of these fires the forest here was further logged, hampering its natural recovery. There was also extensive replanting, and many of those trees are now approaching maturity.

Today the future of the Tillamook and Clatsop State Forests is being hotly debated. It has yet to be determined whether heavy logging and clear-cutting will continue or whether substantial portions of the forests will be protected, set aside as refuges for salmon, steelhead, spotted owls, marbled murrelets, and other imperiled species. The rivers and streams here are also an important source of drinking water for surrounding communities. Water quality here is extremely good but is threatened by development, logging, and associated road-building activity — on both state and adjacent private land.

One classic hike near the Clatsop State Forest is up **Saddle Mountain,** about 65 miles east of Portland, Oregon, on Highway 26, or 12 miles from the coast. The trailhead is accessible from the clearly marked Saddle Mountain State Park, which will be on your right if you are heading west toward the coast from Portland. The trail is about 5 miles round-trip and switchbacks up through the woods before emerging onto the very steep basalt top of the mountain. The view from the top is terrific if you discount the clear-cuts all around. Be prepared for some steep, unsure footing at the very top. This is a popular hike, so go early in the day or on a weekday if you can. Remember that up top, at about 3,200 feet, things can be wet or muddy and slippery even when the weather seemed fine below.

Another well-known but occasionally extremely steep hike is up **Elk Mountain** off Highway 6 in the Tillamook State Forest.

Look for the sign for the Elk Creek campground a little more than 10 miles west of the junction with Highway 8. You will turn right onto a service road to reach the campground. Park there and look for the trailhead. You can follow the steep trail up the mountain via either the Kings Mountain Loop or Elk Mountain Trail. There is also a fairly level trail that begins by following the Old Wilson River Wagon Road along the creek bed. If you head up — and it *is* up — be prepared for slippery footing and some scrambling on this approximately 9-mile round-trip. You will quickly get a sense here of how rugged this terrain is and why it is such fertile country for both fir trees and salmon.

There are any number of other possible hikes to take in the Tillamook, but be aware that motorized recreational vehicles — dirt bikes and all-terrain vehicles — make prodigious use of the Tillamook and Clatsop State Forests.

Because these forests have been used primarily for logging, the most detailed maps you will find emphasize roads rather than recreational trails. The USGS maps of the Nehalem and Yamhill Rivers will home in on the territory you are after, but don't expect to see hiking trails marked. These maps are available through Nature of the Northwest Information Center at 503-872-2750 in Portland, Oregon. For more information, also see the Sierra Club's Tillamook State Forest Committee's recent book, *50 Hikes in the Tillamook,* and see the club's Web site at http://www.oregon.sierra club.org.

Animal Species Status List

In their journals, Lewis and Clark described 122 animal species not previously recorded in the annals of European American science. What follows is a list of these species and the others described or encountered by Lewis and Clark — along with a few other significant species in the range of their travels — annotated to reflect the current status of the species health: whether it is extinct or is listed by the federal or a state government as threatened, endangered, or of special conservation concern.

Of these 148 species and subspecies, 7 are now extinct, and 40 percent are officially protected in some fashion by federal or state government. There are, however, at least 55 additional species living within the range of Lewis and Clark's travels now officially protected by federal or state government. This means that, altogether, at least 55 percent of the species living within the range of Lewis and Clark's travels are now in serious decline. It should be noted that some species once on the brink of extinction have rebounded, but overall, native animal populations have not fared well over the past 200 years. Overhunting (or overfishing) was one of the first causes of these declines, but habitat loss and degradation are now the primary causes for species decline.

This list was compiled using the U.S. Fish and Wildlife Service and National Marine Fisheries Service lists of endangered species, official state wildlife agency species lists, and information compiled from these and other sources by the Center for Biological Diversity. Information from Lewis and Clark's journals was cross-referenced with *Lewis and Clark: Pioneering Naturalists* by Paul Cutright.

Names of species have evolved and changed since the days of Lewis and Clark. Where a scientific name was used to identify the animal by the name we use today, the Latin nomenclature is included — as it is to identify certain subspecies.

Endangered, threatened, candidate, or **extinct** in boldface type denotes status under the federal Endangered Species Act (ESA). Endangered species are those that are considered in imminent danger of extinction. Threatened species are those that will become endangered unless corrective measures are taken. Candidate species are those that the government recognizes as qualifying for listing as either threatened or endangered.

Badger[2]	The skin and bones of one killed near the Grand River in Arikara country of South Dakota was sent back to "the United States."
Bald eagle[2]	**Threatened** — Population declines throughout the lower 48 states, due to loss of habitat and toxics ingested via eagles' primary food fish led the bald eagle to be listed in most states in 1978 as **endangered.** The 1972 ban on DDT has helped numbers to rebound, and the status to be upgraded to **threatened** in 1995.
Beaver[3]	By the end of the nineteenth century, trapping had decimated beaver populations, but subsequent protective management regulations have helped beaver numbers to rebound.
Bighorn sheep[1]	Audubon bighorn, the sheep seen by Lewis and Clark in the western Dakotas and eastern Montana, are **extinct.** Rocky Mountain bighorn (*Ovis canadensis*) and California bighorn (*Ovis canadensis*

1. Species described for science by Lewis and Clark.
2. Other species mentioned in the journals of Lewis and Clark.
3. Species within the range of Lewis and Clark's travels.

californiana), seen farther west, are now **endangered.**

Bison[2]
At the time of European settlement, an estimated 50 to 100 million bison roamed North America. By 1889, the American population had been reduced to about 1,000. Only the herds in Yellowstone National Park are descended directly from the original herds that roamed the Great Plains. Missouri state endangered; Wyoming state sensitive species.

Black bear[2]
American black bear (*Ursus americanus*) — **threatened** — also called the cinnamon bear and now found throughout the Rocky Mountain West, west of the Cascades, and in the Northeast south through the Appalachians as well as in Florida, Louisiana, eastern Arkansas, and Missouri.

Black-billed magpie[1]
Found throughout the American West, generally from the Great Plains to the crest of the Cascades.

Black-footed ferret[3]
Endangered — Dependent on prairie dogs for prey, ferret populations had declined precipitously by the 1960s with the eradication of prairie dog colonies as grasslands were plowed and planted for farms and ranches. Assumed extinct in 1979, but rediscovered in the 1980s. The ferrets are slowly, through captive breeding and reintroduction, being reestablished.

Bonaparte's gull[1]
This small, ternlike gull of the Pacific coast has a black head in summer.

Brewer's blackbird[1]
This small, common blackbird is found throughout the western and north central United States.

Broad-tailed hummingbird[1]
This species is found primarily in the Rocky Mountain region. Males have a red throat.

Bull snake[1]
This subspecies of gopher snake is found from Illinois to Colorado and the Rocky

Mountains. Due to loss of plains grasslands to agriculture, there is some concern
about habitat loss.

Bull trout[3]

Threatened — Populations have declined
due to habitat degradation from logging,
mining, dams, and road construction.

Bushy-tailed wood
rat; pack rat[1]

Likes high mountains, rimrock, and pines.
It is found from the western edge of the
Dakotas to the Pacific coast.

Cabanis's woodpecker[1]

This speckled woodpecker was seen
by Lewis on the Lolo Trail in Idaho on
June 15, 1806.

California condor[2]

Endangered — The number of condors is
estimated to have been in the hundreds
around 1800. By 1939 the number was
reduced to barely 100. Now, thanks to
captive breeding programs, there are over
150 condors alive, and about 50 have been
released into the wild.

California newt[1]

The warty salamander (*Triturus torosus
torosus*) was seen near the Columbia River
Cascades.

Carolina parakeet[2]

Extinct — Lewis and Clark were the first
European Americans to describe observing
this bird west of the Mississippi River.

Catfish, blue and
channel[1]

Both occur widely throughout the United
States and live both in deep-water pools
and in shallow water.

Chinook salmon[2]

Threatened in Idaho, Washington, Oregon, and California. Sacramento River
winter runs are **endangered**.

Chum salmon[3]

Threatened — Populations relatively
healthy in Washington, except for Puget
Sound and the lower Columbia. They are
in serious decline in Oregon, where many
runs are **extinct**, as are those in most of
California.

Clark's nutcracker[1]

This bird is found throughout much of the
western United States and lives in high
mountains, often near the tree line.

Coho salmon[2]	**Threatened** where runs still exist in Washington, Oregon, and California but now **extinct** in over half their historical range. Snake River coho are now **extinct**.
Columbia black-tailed deer[1]	Originally considered a distinct species, these deer are now considered a subspecies of mule deer.
Columbia River chub[1]	*Mylocheilus caurinus*, a kind of minnow now called a peamouth, which is common; not to be confused with the Oregon chub (*Oregonicthys crameri*), which is **endangered**.
Columbian ground squirrel[1]	This squirrel has reddish feet and legs and is found from western Montana to eastern Washington and northeastern Oregon.
Columbian sharp-tailed grouse[1]	The rarest of seven recognized subspecies of sharp-tailed grouse, these birds occupy less than 10 percent of their former range in Idaho, Montana, Utah, and Wyoming and 10–50 percent in Colorado and Washington. Idaho and Washington state species of concern.
Columbian toad[1]	*Bufo boreas*, now known as the Boreal or Western toad, seen by Lewis and Clark on the Clearwater River. The southern Rocky Mountain population of these frogs is now a **candidate** for ESA listing. Idaho state species of concern; Washington state candidate species; Wyoming state sensitive species.
Coyote[1]	Found throughout the United States except for parts of northern New England and possibly the southeast.
Crow, common, western common, and northwestern[1]	The northwestern crow lives on the north Pacific coast, the common crow throughout the West.
Cutthroat trout[1]	The westslope cutthroat, *Oncorhynchus clarki lewisi*, is found in the Upper Missouri River Basin and was the trout first seen by Lewis at the Great Falls of the

	Missouri River; several petitions have been submitted for ESA listing: Wyoming state sensitive species; Montana state imperiled species. Coastal cutthroat, *Oncorhynchus clarki clarki* (found west of the Cascade Mountains): proposed **threatened**; candidate for listing in Oregon. Yellowstone cutthroat, *Oncorhynchus clarki bouvieri:* Montana state species of special concern; Wyoming state sensitive species.
Desert cottontail[1]	Lives in the desert Southwest but also in Wyoming, southeastern Montana, and western Dakotas.
Double-crested cormorant[1]	Lives throughout North America. Idaho state protected species.
Douglas's squirrel; chickaree[1]	Lives in the evergreen forests of the West, primarily west of the Cascades.
Dusky horned owl[1]	A subspecies of great horned owl, seen by Lewis and Clark on the Clearwater River in Idaho.
Eagle, golden[2]	Found throughout North America. Washington state candidate species; North Dakota watch/sensitive species list.
Eastern rattlesnake or massasauga[2]	**Candidate** and Missouri state endangered species. This small species of rattlesnake lives in the floodplain, wet prairies, marshes, and meadows of northern Missouri. Its habitat has been greatly reduced by conversion to agriculture.
Eastern wood rat[1]	Seen by Lewis and Clark near the Osage River in Missouri.
Elk[2]	Missouri state endangered; North Dakota watch/sensitive species list but plentiful throughout the Rocky Mountain West and into forested areas east of the Cascades. The largest elk herd now lives in the Hells Canyon area.
Ermine[1]	Also called the short-tailed weasel, this animal is dark brown with light underparts, turning white or light brown in winter.

Eulachon or candlefish[1]	This Pacific fish of the smelt family is particularly prized by Northwest Indians for its oil.
Fisher[3]	*Martes pennati,* federal species of concern. This species lives in extensive mixed hardwood forests and is an Idaho, Wyoming state species of concern; Washington state endangered species; North Dakota state endangered species.
Forster's tern[1]	This species has been the most widespread tern in the West. Idaho and Montana state protected species; Wyoming state species of concern; North Dakota watch/sensitive species.
Franklin's grouse[1]	This species lives in the northern Rockies and Cascades and is similar to the spruce grouse except that the males have large white spots on their tail feathers. It is sometimes described as a "dusky" grouse.
Glaucous-winged gull[1]	This Pacific coast gull is resident from northwest Oregon north.
Goldeye[1]	This fish of the mooneye family resembles shad, as noted by Lewis, who saw it in the Marias River.
Gray wolf[1]	The gray wolves (*Canis lupus*) that exist today in the West as a result of migration and reintroductions are **endangered**, with the reintroduced wolves having a special status as an experimental population (this gives them less, not more, protection). The subspecies first described by Lewis and Clark, *Canis lupus nubilus*, the Great Plains wolf, was **extinct** by 1926, and *Canus lupus fuscus*, a brownish wolf that lives in the Cascades, was **extinct** by 1940. *Canis lupus irremotus*, the northern Rocky Mountain subspecies, is **extinct** in Alberta, Idaho, Oregon, Montana, and Wyoming.
Great blue whale[2]	*Balaenoptera musculus* — **endangered**. This whale is the largest animal known. It can

	grow to 100 feet long and weigh up to 150 tons.
Great-tailed fox[1]	Also called a red fox and widespread throughout much of North America. Wyoming state species of concern.
Grizzly bear[1]	*Ursus horribilus* — **threatened**. About 1,000 grizzlies remain in the lower 48 states, primarily in five wildland populations, including Glacier and Yellowstone National Parks.
Harbor seal[1]	The common seal is found on both North American coasts. It was first seen by Lewis and Clark on the Columbia River about 100 miles inland from the Pacific.
Harris's woodpecker[1]	Now called the hairy woodpecker, this bird is found in wooded areas of the West and elsewhere in North America.
Hutchins's goose[1]	This subspecies of Canada goose was seen by Lewis on May 5, 1805, above the mouth of the Poplar River in Montana.
Least tern[1]	*Sterna antillarum* — **endangered**. This bird nests on inland rivers such as the Platte, Niobrara, and Missouri, where habitat has been degraded and diminished by dams.
Lesser Canada goose[1]	*Branta canadensis leucopareira*, Aleutian Canada goose. Listed as **endangered** in 1967, later **threatened** as populations rebounded, and **delisted** in February 2001. It is heavily preyed upon by foxes introduced for fur to the Aleutian Islands where the goose breeds. None were seen between 1938 and 1962, and in the 1970s they numbered only in the 100s. Washington state threatened species; Oregon state endangered species.
Lesser snow goose[2]	Feeds in marshes and wetlands. Was seen by Clark near the Missouri River in South Dakota.
Lewis's woodpecker[1]	This bird is large and dark, with a pink belly. It was first seen by Lewis on July 25,

1805, near the Gates of the Mountains near Helena, Montana. Washington state candidate species; Wyoming state species of concern.

Long-billed curlew[1]
This species lives in high plains country, where its habitat is declining due to agriculture. Idaho state protected species; Wyoming state species of concern; North Dakota state threatened species.

Long-tailed weasel[1]
Found throughout much of North America; Lewis and Clark sent one of these weasels to President Jefferson from Fort Mandan in April 1805.

Lynx[2]
Lynx canadensis — **threatened**. Clark wrote that he had gloves lined with lynx fur during the winter the party spent with the Mandan in what is now North Dakota, but there is a chance it may have been mistaken for bobcat fur.

Marbled murrelet[3]
Threatened throughout its current range in California, Oregon, and Washington, this small seabird flies inland to nest in old-growth trees of the coastal temperate rain-forest such as those near Fort Clatsop.

McCown's longspur[1]
This small bird resembles a sparrow and a chickadee, but like horned larks, it lives in open prairie grassland country. Wyoming state species of concern; North Dakota state threatened species.

Montana horned owl[1]
This is a subspecies of the great horned owl reported by Lewis on April 14, 1805, near the Missouri River in North Dakota.

Moose[2]
Moose are found in northern forests near lakes and wetlands. North Dakota state watch/sensitive species list.

Mountain beaver[1]
Also called aplodontia, this burrowing rodent of the Pacific coast was noted by Lewis at Fort Clatsop.

Mountain goat[1]
Favors rocky crags and cliffs at high elevation, now mostly in northern Idaho and Montana.

Mountain lion, cougar[1]	This species had the most extensive range of any large North American mammal. Bounty hunting and habitat loss reduced its numbers severely, but with current conservation measures populations are now increasing. Missouri state endangered; state threatened in South Dakota and North Dakota.
Mountain quail[3]	This is a state species of special concern in Idaho, where the bird has lost about 50 percent of its habitat. It was listed as a federal **candidate** category 2 species from 1990 until 1996, when that listing distinction of the ESA program was discontinued.
Mountain sucker[1]	This fish is found in the upper Missouri, Columbia, Sacramento, and Colorado River systems. It likes clear mountain streams.
Mule deer; black-tailed deer[1]	Found throughout western North America. This deer was first noted by Lewis and Clark near Chamberlain, South Dakota.
Northern flicker[1]	The subspecies noted by Lewis and Clark was the yellow-shafted flicker, *Colaptes auratus luteus*. This subspecies has been declining, likely due to habitat loss and the use of pesticides on lawns and other feeding areas.
Northern spotted owl[3]	**Threatened** — This owl nests in old-growth trees of Pacific Northwest forests of Oregon, Washington, California, and British Columbia. The 1993 Northwest Forest Plan was created in part to protect northern spotted owl habitat.
Northern squawfish[1]	Found in the Columbia River and other Pacific watersheds. This fish was first seen by Lewis in the Walla Walla River.
Nuttall's poor-will[1]	This bird is now called the common poor-will. It was first seen by Lewis near the

mouth of the Cannonball River in North
Dakota. North Dakota peripheral/species
of concern.

Oregon bobcat,
northern bobcat[3]

Lynx rufus fasciatus, a subspecies of *Lynx rufus*, which is the bobcat that lives along the Pacific Northwest coast; and *Lynx rufus pallenscens*, which lives in the vicinity of the Rocky Mountains.

Oregon jay[1]

Perisoreus canadensis, now called the gray jay, of which Lewis and Clark probably identified a subspecies.

Oregon ruffed grouse[1]

Bonasa umbellus sabini, a subspecies of ruffed grouse. It lives in the northern United States, Canada, and Alaska.

Pacific fulmar[1]

This is a Pacific subspecies of the northern fulmar, which is found on northern oceans. It was described by Lewis at Fort Clatsop.

Pacific loon[1]

Gavia artica pacifica, the arctic loon, which used to be considered the same species as the Pacific loon.

Pacific nighthawk[2]

Chordeiles minor hesperis, a subspecies of common nighthawk.

Pacific tree frog[1]

According to *Peterson's Field Guide to Western Reptiles and Amphibians*, this is the most commonly heard frog on the Pacific coast.

Pale goldfinch[1]

Also called the western goldfinch, this is likely a subspecies of the American goldfinch. It was first seen by Lewis on the Marias River in Montana.

Passenger pigeon[2]

Extinct — Once so prolific that their flocks darkened the skies. The last passenger pigeon died in the Cincinnati Zoo in 1914.

Piñon jay[1]

This bird is found primarily in Great Basin juniper, and sage habitat. Idaho state protected species.

Piping plover[3]

Threatened — This bird has breeding grounds in the central United States on the Missouri River and prairie wetlands and

	feeds on river islands. The damming of the Missouri River has eliminated and degraded its habitat.
Plains horned toad[1]	What Lewis and Clark called the plains horned toad (*Phrynosoma cornutum*) is now called the Texas horned lizard. Lewis and Clark saw this toad at the north end of its range.
Pocket gopher[1]	*Thomomys talpoides rufescens*, probably a subspecies of the Northern pocket gopher, was seen by Lewis above the mouth of the Knife River in North Dakota.
Prairie chicken[3]	**Endangered** — Attwater's greater prairie chicken (*Tympanuchus cupido attwateri*); lesser prairie chicken (*Tympanuchus pallidicinctus*), **candidate**; greater prairie chicken, North Dakota threatened species.
Prairie dog, black-tailed[1]	**Candidate** — Eradication, alteration, and elimination of habitat have reduced populations by 90–95 percent of what they were historically.
Prairie horned lark[1]	*Eremophila alpestris leucolaema*, a Great Plains subspecies of horned lark.
Prairie sharp-tailed grouse[1]	Federal species of **concern**. Washington state threatened species; Idaho state species of concern.
Pronghorn, Oregon pronghorn[1]	By 1900, pronghorn populations had declined radically because of hunting and alterations to habitat. Since then, protective management regulations have helped populations to rebound. North Dakota watch/sensitive species list.
Pygmy rabbit[3]	**Endangered** — This is North America's smallest rabbit. It lives in the sagebrush sea country of Idaho, Montana, Oregon, and Washington.
Pygmy horned toad[1]	(*Phrynosoma douglassii*), now called the short-horned lizard, lives in sagebrush, shortgrass prairie, and piñon-pine-juniper country.

Raccoon[1]	Lewis and Clark encountered three previously unfamiliar western subspecies in Missouri, in Idaho, and near the John Day River in Oregon.
Rattlesnake, prairie and (northern) Pacific[1]	The prairie rattler was seen by Lewis near the Great Falls of the Missouri River, and the Pacific rattler north of the Columbia River in what is now Klickitat County, Washington.
Raven, western American[1]	This is native to but no longer reproduces in North Dakota. It is a different subspecies from that known by Lewis and Clark in the East.
Red-necked grebe[1]	This bird winters along the Pacific coast and was described by Lewis at Fort Clatsop. Idaho state protected species; North Dakota watch/sensitive species list.
Richardson's blue grouse[1]	*Dendragapus obscurus richardsonii*, a subspecies of blue grouse that was first seen by Lewis near the headwaters of the Missouri River near Three Forks, Montana.
Richardson's red squirrel[1]	*Tamasciurus hudsonicus richardsoni*, a subspecies of red squirrel that lives in sagebrush grasslands and Rocky Mountain country.
Ring-necked duck[1]	Similar to a scaup, males have a vertical white mark on their wings. It is found in the northern United States and Canada.
River otter[2]	State endangered in Nebraska and North Dakota; state threatened in South Dakota; Wyoming state species of concern.
Roosevelt's elk[1]	This subspecies of elk lives west of the Cascade Mountains.
Sage grouse[1]	**Candidate** — Western sage grouse and Gunnison sage grouse. Some populations of sage grouse have now declined as much as 80 percent from their historic levels due to elimination and alteration of habitat. Washington state threatened species.

Sauger[1]	This species is primarily found in the Mississippi River Basin, Great Lakes, and St. Lawrence. Lewis described one he found in the Marias River in Montana.
Sea otter[1]	*Enhydra lutis nereis*, **threatened** — Lewis and Clark admired the furs but never saw a live one.
Shiras's moose[1]	This is also now referred to as the Wyoming or Rocky Mountain moose. It has restricted hunting seasons in Wyoming.
Shorttail shrew[1]	This species is found from the central Dakotas, Nebraska, and Kansas east. It was among the specimens shipped to President Jefferson from Fort Mandan.
Sockeye salmon[2]	**Endangered** in the Snake River, where some runs have disappeared; sockeye are severely depleted in the Columbia River. A few still return to the Deschutes River; otherwise, there are no self-sustaining runs in Oregon or California. Some Washington runs are listed as **threatened**.
Starry flounder[1]	Described by Lewis at Fort Clatsop in March 1806.
Steelhead[3]	**Endangered** in southern California and the upper Columbia and **threatened** in the Snake River, lower Columbia River, upper Willamette River, and elsewhere in California.
Steller's jay[1]	This strikingly blue, black-headed, crested jay is found in the conifer, pine, and oak forests of the West.
Striped skunk[1]	Found throughout North America. The subspecies of skunk Lewis identified lived near Celilo Falls on the Columbia.
Sturgeon[1]	White sturgeon (*Acipenser transmontanus*) — **endangered** — Clark saw white sturgeon on the Pacific coast. Pallid sturgeon, which live in the Missouri River, are now also **endangered**.

Swift fox[1]	Probably a subspecies of Northern swift fox (*Velpes velox hebes*), it is now **endangered**. State threatened species in Nebraska and South Dakota; Montana state imperiled species; Wyoming state species of concern.
Thirteen-striped ground squirrel[1]	This squirrel was first seen by Lewis near the Great Falls of the Missouri River. Wyoming state species of concern; North Dakota state endangered species.
Townsend's chipmunk[1]	This large brown chipmunk lives from west of the Cascades to the Pacific coast.
Townsend's mole[1]	This mole lives from west of the Cascades to the Pacific coast.
Trumpeter swan[2]	Hunted nearly to extinction by 1900, trumpeter swans were once abundant in North America. Only two major populations remain, one near the Pacific, ranging from Alaska to northern Oregon, and one ranging from the Northwest Territories to the Greater Yellowstone region. It probably was observed by Lewis and Clark near the Yellowstone River. Idaho state protected species; Wyoming state species of concern.
Turtle, soft-shelled[1]	What Lewis and Clark saw near the confluence of the Tongue and Yellowstone Rivers is now known as the Western spiny soft-shelled turtle. Montana state species of concern.
Water terrapin[1]	The turtle Lewis noted near the Great Falls of the Missouri was, if indeed the *Trachemys elegans* noted in the historic literature, likely a western subspecies of what is known today as the red-eared slider. If not, it was a western painted turtle.
Western and Northwestern garter snake[1]	Both snakes are found from the Oregon Cascades northwest into British Columbia, as well as in northwestern California.

Western badger[1]

This is state listed in the Midwest, but not where Lewis and Clark saw it on the Pacific coast.

Western fence lizard[1]

The subspecies Lewis saw in what is now Klickitat County, Washington, was the northwestern fence lizard.

Western frog[1]

Rana pretiosa, now called the Oregon spotted frog — **candidate** — Found from the northwestern reaches of the Great Basin northwest to Alaska. It is **threatened**, particularly in Oregon and Washington, by nonnative bullfrogs.

Western gray squirrel[1]

This squirrel is found from the Washington Cascades south into much of California. Washington state threatened species.

Western grebe[1]

This subspecies, with white around its eyes and an orange yellow rather than greenish yellow bill, has been renamed Clark's grebe. Idaho state protected species; Washington state candidate species; Montana state protected species.

Western gull[1]

This gull lives on the Pacific coast from Baja California to northwest Washington.

Western hognose snake[1]

Lewis and Clark saw the subspecies called the plains hognose snake in Montana.

Western meadowlark[1]

First seen by Lewis at the Great Falls of the Missouri River, where he differentiated this bird from the eastern meadowlark by its distinctive call. The meadowlark is Oregon's state bird.

Western mourning dove[1]

Widespread throughout the West. Lewis noted this dove near the Bitterroot River in Montana.

Western pileated woodpecker[1]

The large (nearly 20-inch) red-crested woodpecker was seen by Lewis near Fort Clatsop. He declared it a western subspecies of the eastern woodpecker it resembles.

Western snowy plover[3] — *Charadrinus alexandrinus nivosus* — **threatened** — This bird lives on the Pacific coast.

Western tanager[1] — Bright yellow bird with black wings and tail; the males have a striking vermilion head. It was first seen by Lewis on the Clearwater River. North Dakota state peripheral/species of concern.

Western willet[1] — This species likes marshes, wet meadows, mudflats, and beaches. North Dakota watch/sensitive species.

Western winter wren[1] — This very small dark wren was noted by Lewis at Fort Clatsop.

Whistling swan[1] — *Cygnus columbianus*, also known as the tundra swan, was described by Lewis at Fort Clatsop.

White pelican[2] — Idaho state species of concern; Washington state endangered species; Wyoming state species of concern.

White-fronted goose[1] — This gray goose has a pink bill and a white patch on the front of its face.

White-rumped shrike[1] — Also known as the loggerhead shrike. North Dakota watch/sensitive species; Idaho state species of special concern; Washington state candidate species.

White-tailed deer[1] — Lewis and Clark saw four subspecies of white-tailed deer. They saw what is now called *Odoceilus virginianus macroura* on the plains and prairies of Missouri, Kansas, and Nebraska. On the Great Plains of the Dakotas and Montana, they saw *O.v. dakotensis*, and they saw *O.v. ochroura* west of the Continental Divide. The Pacific coast's Columbian white-tailed deer, *Odocoileus virginianus leuecerus* is now **endangered**.

White-tailed jack rabbit[1] — Missouri state endangered; Washington state candidate species.

Whooping crane[2] — **Endangered** — These cranes had nearly disappeared by the late 1940s but thanks to

	conservation measures have begun to rebound. Current populations stop in the Great Plains wetlands during migration between wintering grounds in Texas and summer grounds in northern Canada.
Wild turkey[2]	Lewis and Clark and their party killed and ate a number of these during their journey. Wild turkeys are found throughout much of the United States.
Wolverine[3]	Federal species of **concern**; Washington state candidate species; Oregon state threatened species; Montana state imperiled species; Wyoming state species of concern. The largest current populations of wolverines are in Montana.
Woodland caribou[3]	**Endangered** — This caribou relies on stands of low-elevation old-growth conifers. It is now one of the most imperiled large mammals in the lower 48 states, with the remaining population of less than 50 found in the Selkirk Mountains.
Yellow-bellied marmot[1]	*Marmota flaviventris avara* were seen near the John Day River, and *M.f. nosophora* near the Lemhi River.
Yellow-haired porcupine[1]	This species is found in the Northeast and from the Upper Missouri River west. It was noted by Lewis and Clark in Montana on what they called the Porcupine River, now called the Poplar River.

Conservation Groups, Campaigns, and Tribal Organizations

To make this appendix easy to use, organizations are listed here alphabetically by state, followed — under the heading "National Groups" — by national groups and organization headquarters not necessarily located within these states. For reasons of space, it is not possible to provide an accurate, comprehensive list of all the individual tribes and Indian nations in the vicinity of the Lewis and Clark Trail, so instead I have listed tribal organizations that together include nearly all these tribes and nations. I apologize in advance for any inadvertent omissions. Finally, in addition to organizations, I have included some conservation campaigns — generally efforts of an established group or coalition of groups — focused on a particular issue of concern to this region. Again, for reasons of space, this overall listing is not comprehensive but is meant to serve as an introductory resource. Offices move, and organizations evolve, but this information is correct as this book goes to press.

Idaho

Committee for Idaho's High
   Desert
P.O. Box 2863
Boise, ID 83701
208-429-1679
http://www.cihd.org

Idaho Conservation League
P.O. Box 844
Boise, ID 83701
208-345-6933
http://www.wildidaho.org

Idaho Rivers United
P.O. Box 633
Boise, ID 83701
208-343-7481
http://www.idahorivers.org

Save Our Wild Salmon
   Coalition
1511 North Eleventh
Boise, ID 83702
208-345-9067
http://wildsalmon.org

Sierra Club Northern Rockies
   Chapter
P.O. Box 552
Boise, ID 83701
208-384-1023
http://idaho.sierraclub.org/

Western Watersheds Project
P.O. Box 1770
Hailey, ID 83333
208-788-2290
http://www.westernwatersheds.
   org

The Wolf Education and
   Research Center
418 Nez Perce
P.O. Box 217
Winchester, ID 83555
208-924-6960
http://www.wolfcenter.org/

Illinois

Sierra Club Illinois Chapter
200 North Michigan Avenue,
   Suite 505
Chicago, IL 60601-5908
312-251-1680
http://illinois.sierraclub.org
See the Web site for links to
local chapters.

Iowa

Iowa Environmental Council
711 East Locust Street
Des Moines, IA 50309
515-244-1194
http://www.earthweshare.org

Loess Hills Audubon Society
P.O. Box 5133
Sioux City, IA 51102
515-727-4271
http://www.avalon.net/~yiams/
See http://www.audubon.org/
for links to other Audubon state
chapters.

Sierra Club Iowa Chapter
3839 Merle Hay Road,
  Suite 280
Des Moines, IA 50310
515-277-8868
http://iowa.sierraclub.org/
See the Web site for links to
local chapters.

Kansas

Kansas Chapter of the Sierra
  Club
9844 Georgia
Kansas City, KS 66109-4326
913-299-4443
http://www.kssierra.org

Missouri

Audubon Missouri
2620 Forum Boulevard,
  Suite C-1
Columbia, MO 65203
573-447-2249
http://www.audubon.org/
  chapter/mo/mo
Contact the society or see links
for local Audubon-affiliated
groups around the state.

Missouri Coalition for the
  Environment
6267 Delmar Boulevard, 2E
St. Louis, MO 61630
314-727-0600
http://www.moenviron.org

Missouri Prairie Foundation
Box 200
Columbia, MO 65205
http://www.moprairie.org

Missouri River Communities
  Network
200 Old Business 63 South,
  Suite 205
Columbia, MO 65201
573-256-2602
http://www.moriver.org

Sierra Club Ozark Missouri
  Chapter
1007 North College, Suite 1
Columbia, MO 65201
573-815-9250
http://missouri.sierraclub.org
Contact the Sierra Club or see
links for its Eastern Missouri
and Osage Groups.

Montana

Alliance for the Wild Rockies
P.O. Box 8731
Missoula, MT 59807
http://www.wildrockiesalliance
  .org

American Rivers
215 Woodland Estates
Great Falls, MT
406-454-2076
http://www.amrivers.org

Clark Fork-Pend Oreille
  Coalition
P.O. Box 7594
Missoula, MT 59807
406-542-0539
http://www.clarkfork.org

Greater Yellowstone Coalition
13 South Wilson
Bozeman, MT 59715
406-586-1593
http://www.greateryellowstone
   .org

Montana Wilderness Association
P.O. Box 635
Helena, MT 59624
406-443-7350
http://wildmontana.org

Predator Conservation Alliance
P.O. Box 6733
Bozeman, MT 59771
406-587-3389
http://www.predatorconservation
   .org

Sierra Club Montana Office
P.O. Box 1290
Or 111 South Grand, West
   Wing
Bozeman, MT 59771
406-582-8365
For other regional information
also contact the
Sierra Club Northern Plains
   Field Office
23 North Scott, Room 27
Sheridan, WY 82801-6338
307-672-0425

Nebraska

American Rivers
Mill Towne Building
650 J Street, Suite 400
Lincoln, NE 68508
402-477-7910
http://www.amrivers.org

Audubon Nebraska
P.O. Box 117
Denton, NE 68339
402-797-2301
http://www.audubon.org/
   chapter/ne

Nebraska Wildlife Federation
P.O. Box 81437
Lincoln, NE 68501-1437
402-476-9081
http://www.omaha.org/newf/

Sierra Club Nebraska Office
941 "O" Street, Suite 206
Lincoln, NE 68508
402-475-2292
http://nebraska.sierraclub.org/

North Dakota

Audubon Society North Dakota
   State Office
118 Broadway, Suite 802
Fargo, ND 58102
701-298-3373
http://www.audubon.org/
   chapter/nd/

Mandan, Hidatsa, and Arikara
   Nation
Three Affiliated Tribes
404 Frontage Road
New Town, ND 58763
701-627-4781
http://www.mhanation.com

North Dakota Wildlife
  Federation
1605 East Capitol Avenue
Bismarck, ND 58507
701-827-5227
http://www.ndwf.org

Sierra Club North Dakota Office
311 East Thayer Avenue, #113
Bismarck, ND 58504
701-530-9288
http://www.sierraclub.org/nd/

Oregon

American Rivers
320 SW Stark Street, Suite 418
Portland, OR 97204
503-827-8648
http://www.amrivers.org

Audubon Society of Portland
5151 NW Cornell Road
Portland, OR 97210
503-292-6855
http://www.audubonportland.org

Columbia River Inter-tribal Fish
  Commission
729 NE Oregon, Suite 200
Portland, OR 97232
503-238-0667
http://www.critfc.org/

Fish Passage Center
2501 SW First Avenue,
  Suite 230
Portland, OR 97201
503-230-4099
http://www.fpc.org

Friends of the Columbia River
  Gorge
522 SW Fifth Avenue, Suite 820
Portland, OR 97204
503-241-3762 or in Hood
  River, OR, at 541-386-5268
http://www.gorgefriends.org
*Friends of the Columbia River
Gorge, the Sierra Club's
Columbia and Loo Wit groups,
and the Trust for Public Land
(http://www.tpl.org) have
launched a Lewis and Clark
Landscape Project to extend
public acquisition and
permanent protection of land
within the Columbia River
Gorge.*

Hells Canyon Preservation
  Council
P.O. Box 2768
LaGrande, OR 97850
541-963-3950
http://www.hellscanyon.org

Oregon Natural Resources
  Council
5825 North Greeley
Portland, OR 97217
503-283-6343
http://www.onrc.org

Pacific Coast Federation of
  Fishermen's Associations
P.O. Box 1170
Eugene, OR 97440
541-689-2000
http://www.pcffa.org/

Save Our Wild Salmon
  Coalition
2031 SE Belmont
Portland, OR 97214
503-230-0421
http://www.wildsalmon.org

Sierra Club Oregon Chapter
2950 SE Stark Street, Suite 100
Portland, OR 97214
503-243-6656
http://www.oregon.sierraclub.org/

Trout Unlimited
213 SW Ash Street, Suite 205
Portland, OR 97205
503-827-5700
http://www.tu.org

Willamette Riverkeeper
380 SE Spokane Street
Portland, OR 97202
503-223-6418
http://www.willamette-river
  keeper.org

South Dakota

American Rivers South Dakota
  Field Office
P.O. Box 1029
Aberdeen, SD 57402
695-229-4978
http://www.amrivers.org/
  contactus/southdakotaoffice
  .htm

Intertribal Bison Cooperative
1560 Concourse Drive
Rapid City, SD 57703
605-394-9730
http://www.intertribalbison.org/

Missouri Breaks Audubon
P.O. Box 832
Pierre, SD 57501
http://mywebpage.netscape.com/
  mobreaksas/index.html or
through links at http://www
  .audubon.org/chapter/sd/

Sierra Club South Dakota
  Chapter
P.O. Box 1624
Rapid City, SD 57709
605-348-1345
http://southdakota.sierraclub.org/

South Dakota Wildlife
  Federation
P.O. Box 7075
Pierre, SD 52501
605-224-7524
http://www.sdwf.org

Washington

Affiliated Tribes of Northwest
  Indians
18139 Midvale Avenue North,
  Suite C
Shoreline, WA 98133
206-542-5115
http://www.atniedc.com

American Rivers
150 Nickerson Street, Suite 311
Seattle, WA 98109
206-213-0330
http://www.amrivers.org

Save Our Wild Salmon
  Coalition
1525 West Seventh Ave.
Spokane, WA 99204
509-747-2030
http://www.wildsalmon.org
and
424 Third Avenue West,
  Suite 100
Seattle, WA 98114
206-286-4455

Sierra Club Northwest Field
  Office
180 Nickerson Street, Suite 202
Seattle, WA 98109-1631
206-378-0114
http://www.sierraclub.org/wa/
and
Sierra Club Inland Northwest
  Office
10 North Post Street, Suite 447
Spokane, WA 99201
509-456-8802

Washington Wilderness
  Coalition
4649 Sunnyside Avenue North,
  Suite 520
Seattle, WA 98103
206-633-1992
http://www.wawild.org

National Groups

American Lands Alliance
726 Seventh Street SE
Washington, DC 20003
202-547-9400
http://www.americanlands.org

American Rivers' Missouri
  River Campaign
Mill Towne Building
650 J Street, Suite 400
Lincoln, NE 68508
402-477-7910
http://www.savethemissouri.org
or http://www.amrivers.org

Center for Biological Diversity
P.O. Box 710
Tucson, AZ 85702-0710
520-623-5252
http://www.sw-center.org/
  swcbd/ or http://www
  .biologicaldiversity.org

Defenders of Wildlife
1101 Fourteenth Street NW
  No. 1400
Washington, DC 20005
202-682-9400
http://www.defenders.org

Earthjustice Legal Defense Fund
426 Seventeenth Street,
  6th Floor
Oakland, CA 94612-2820
510-550-6700
http://www.earthjustice.org

Endangered Species Coalition
1101 Fourteenth Street NW
  Suite 1400
Washington, DC 20005
202-756-2804
http://www.stopextinction.org

Friends of the Earth
1025 Vermont Avenue NW
Washington, D.C. 20005
877-843-8687 or 202-783-7400
http://www.foe.org

League of Conservation Voters
1920 L Street NW Suite 800
Washington, DC 20036
202-785-8683
http://www.lcv.org

National Congress of American
   Indians
1301 Connecticut Avenue NW
   Suite 200
Washington, DC 20036
202-466-7767
http://www.ncai.org

National Public Lands Grazing
   Campaign
http://www.publiclandsranching.
   org

Natural Resources Defense
   Council
40 West Twentieth Street,
New York, NY 10011
212-727-2700
http://www.nrdc.org

Sierra Club
85 Second Street, 2nd Floor
San Francisco, CA 94105
415-977-5500
http://www.sierraclub.org
*For the Sierra Club's Lewis and
Clark campaign "Protecting the
Wildlands of Lewis and Clark,"
see http://www.sierraclub.org/
lewisandclark. Or contact the
Sierra Club's office in Bozeman,
Montana, or Seattle, Washington, for further information.*

Sierra Club Northern Plains
   Field Office
23 North Scott, Room 27
Sheridan, WY 82801-6338
307-672-0425
http://www.sierraclub.org/wy/

The Wilderness Society
1615 M Street NW
Washington, DC 20036
800-THE-WILD
http://www.wilderness.org

Public Agencies, Sources of Maps, and Other Useful Information

This appendix begins with a section listing sources of national information, and sources of information about the Lewis and Clark Trail. Following that, the information is listed alphabetically by state. Web site addresses change, but this information is current as this book goes to press.

Lewis and Clark National Historic Trail

For the National Park Service's Lewis and Clark National Historical Trail map and related information see http://www.nps.gov/lecl or contact the park service at:
Lewis and Clark National Historic Trail
1709 Jackson Street
Omaha, NE 68102
402-514-9311

For additional Lewis and Clark Trail information, contact the U.S. Forest Service's Lewis and Clark National Historic Trail Interpretive Center.
4201 Giant Springs Road
Great Falls, MT 59403-1806
406-727-8733
http://www.fs.fed.us/r1/lewisclark/lcic.htm

The Army Corps of Engineers (http://www.usace.army.mil) manages most of the dams on the Missouri River and those on the lower Snake and Columbia Rivers. It should be contacted for information about water releases from those dams and any passage through its locks. Regional contact information can be found through the "Where We Are" link on its Web site, which also has information about obtaining maps.

The 100th Meridian Initiative is aimed at preventing the westward spread of invasive species, particularly zebra mussels, which are now found in the eastern United States.
877-786-7267
http://fisheries.fws.gov/FWSMA/Mazebra.htm
or http://ANSTaskForce.gov

The National Ocean Service at http://www.nos.noaa.gov has a great deal of map and chart information.
1305 East West Highway
Silver Spring, MD 20910
301-713-3074

The National Park Service can be reached at its national headquarters: 202-208-6843, or through http://www.nps.gov. Information about the national Wild and Scenic River System can also be found through the National Park Service Web site at http://www.nps.gov/rivers.

The U.S. Bureau of Land Management at http://www.blm.gov or 202-452-5125 can provide national information and help locating district offices, which sell maps of local and nearby areas. The Bureau of Land Management is part of the Department of the Interior. Many (but not all) of the newer national monuments are managed by the Bureau of Land Management, and information on those can be found through the BLM Web site.

The U.S. Fish and Wildlife Service, which manages many national wildlife refuges, can be reached at http://www.fws.gov or 800-344-9453 for national programs. The Fish and Wildlife Service is also the agency responsible for managing most endangered species, although the National Marine Fisheries Service (http://www.nmfs.noaa.gov) is responsible for management of anadromous and marine fish — such as salmon — listed under the Endangered Species Act.

U.S. Forest Service (http://www.fs.fed.us); see individual listings below. In addition to managing national forests, the U.S. Forest Service, which is part of the U.S. Department of Agriculture, also manages national grasslands.

The U.S. Geological Survey can be reached at 888-ASK-USGS or see its Web site at http://www.usgs.gov or http://mapping.usgs.gov.

Idaho

Clearwater National Forest
  office
12730 Highway 12
Orofino, ID 83544
208-476-4541
http://www.fs.fed.us/r1/
  clearwater

Cobalt Ranger District
Salmon National Forest
RR2, Box 600
Highway 935
Salmon, ID 83467
208-756-5100

Hells Canyon National
  Recreation Area
Headquarters:
88401 Highway 82
Enterprise, OR
541-426-4978
Satellite offices:
Riggins, ID: 208-628-3916
Clarkston, WA: 509-758-0616
 http://www.fs.fed.us/r6/w-w/
  hcnra.htm

Idaho state tourism Web site
  with link for maps
800-VISIT-ID
http://www.visit.id.or/map/
  mapgallery.html

Idaho state Web site
http://www.state.id.us

Lost River Ranger District
Challis National Forest
P.O. Box 507
Mackay, ID 83251
208-588-3400

Sawtooth National Recreation
  Area Visitor Center
HC 64, Box 8291
Ketchum, ID 83340
208-727-5000 or 208-727-5013
http://www.fs.fed.us/r4/sawtooth

Snake River Wild and Scenic
  River information
From the Hells Canyon
National Recreation Area
offices: 509-758-0616, 208-
628-3916 or 541-426-4978.
For reservations for river
permits call 509-758-1957 or
888-758-8037. Also see the
National Park Service Web site
at http://www.nps.gov/rivers/
wsr-snake.html.

Illinois

Cahokia Mounds State Historic
  Site
30 Ramey Street
Collinsville, IL 62234
618-346-5160
http://www.cahokiamounds.com

Horseshoe Lake State Park
Illinois Department of Natural
  Resources
3321 Highway 111
Granite City, IL 60240
618-931-0270
http://dnr.state.il.us/lands/
landmgt/parks/r4/horsesp
.htm

Illinois Department of
  Transportation
217-782-6953
http://www.dot.state.il.us/
  idot.html

Illinois state tourism
800-2CONNECT

http://www100.state.il.us/
  visiting

Iowa

De Soto National Wildlife
  Refuge
1434 316th Lane
Missouri Valley, IA 51555
712-642-4121
http://midwest.fws.gov/DeSoto/
  dsotobro.html

Iowa Department of
  Transportation
515-239-1101
http://www.dot.state.ia.us

Iowa state Web site
888-472-6035 for tourist
  information
http://www.state.ia.us

Kansas

Kansas Department of
  Transportation
785-296-3566
http://www.ink.org/public/kdot

Kansas state Web site
800-2KANSAS for tourist
  information
http://www.accesskansas.org

Missouri

Arrow Rock State Historic Site
P.O. Box 121B
Arrow Rock, MO 65320
660-837-3330
http://www.mostateparks.com/
  arrowrock.htm

Katy Trail State Park
660-882-8196
http://www.mostateparks.com/
katytrail.htm
Information on the Katy Trail is
also available through the
Missouri Department of
Natural Resources at 800-334-
6946. The Greater St. Charles
Convention and Visitors Bureau
publishes a very helpful "Gateway to the Katy Trail" brochure, complete with mileage
chart and listing of services
along the trail.

Missouri Department of
Natural Resources (800-334-
6946) maintains information
about Missouri state parks and
historical sites on its Web site:
http://www.dnr.state.mo.us or
http://www.mostateparks.com.

Missouri Department of
Transportation
888-ASK-MODOT
http://www.modot.state.mo.us
Follow Web site links for maps.

Missouri Division of Tourism
800-810-5500
http://www.missouritourism.org

Missouri state Web site
http://www.state.mo.us

Squaw Creek National Wildlife
Refuge
P.O. Box 158
Mound City, MO 64470
660-442-3187
http://midwest.fws.gov/
SquawCreek/

Van Meter State Park
Route 1, Box 47
Miami, MO 65344
660-886-7537
http://www.mostateparks.com/
vanmeter.htm

Montana

Beartooth Ranger District
Custer National Forest
Red Lodge, MT 59068
406-446-2103

Bozeman Ranger District
Gallatin National Forest
Bozeman, MT 59715
406-522-2520

Custer National Forest
406-657-6200
http://www.fs.fed.us/r1/custer/

Glacier National Park
West Glacier, MT 59936
406-888-7800
http://www.nps.gov/gla

Libby Ranger District
Kootenai National Forest
Libby, MT 59923
406-293-7773

Montana Department of Fish,
  Wildlife and Parks
1420 East Sixth Avenue
P.O. Box 200701
Helena, MT 59620-0701
406-444-2535
http://www.fwp.state.mt.us/
  parks

Montana State Department of
  Transportation
406-444-6200
http://www.mdt.state.mt.us

Montana State Highway
  Department
800-226-ROAD

Montana state tourism
800-VISIT-MT (800-847-4848)
  or 406-444-2654
http://travel.state.mt.us

Montana state Web site
http://www.state.mt.us/

Charles M. Russell National
  Wildlife Refuge
P.O. Box 110
Airport Road
Lewistown, MT 59457
406-538-8706
http://www.r6.fws.gov/cmr/

Seely Lake Ranger District
Lolo National Forest
HC 31, Box 3200
18 Mile Marker, Highway 83 N
Seely Lake, MT 59868
406-677-2233

Stevensville Ranger District
Bitterroot National Forest
Stevensville, MT 59870
406-777-7423

Swan Lake Ranger District
Flathead National Forest
Bigfork, MT 59911
406-837-5081

Three Rivers Ranger District
Kootenai National Forest
Troy, MT 59935
406-295-4693

Ulm Pishkun State Park
406-866-2217
Limited information is available
through the state parks link on
the Montana Department of
Fish, Wildlife and Parks Web
site.

Upper Missouri National Wild
  and Scenic River
Bureau of Land Management
Lewistown Field Office
P.O. Box 1160
Lewistown, MT 59457
406-538-7461
Contact the BLM for river
maps or see the BLM's Upper
Missouri River Breaks National
Monument Web site at http://
www.mt.blm.gov/ldo/um.

Yellowstone River: The BLM publishes a "Floaters Guide to the Yellowstone" for the upper reaches of the Yellowstone River above Billings and Park City, Montana, as well as a series of "Recreation Guide Maps" (about $4 each), which include landownership and river access points for the whole length of the river. These are available from the BLM office in Billings, MT, at 406-896-5000.

Nebraska

Fort Niobrara Wildlife Refuge
Hidden Timber Route
HC 14, Box 67
Valentine, NE 69201
402-376-3789
http://www.r6.fws.gov/
REFUGES/niobrara/
NIOBRARA.HTM

Missouri National Recreational River
P.O. Box 591
O'Neill, NE 68763
402-336-3970
http://www.nps.gov/rivers/wsr-missouri-nebraska1.htm (for the Missouri River from Gavins Point Dam to Ponca State Park)
http://www.nps.gov/rivers/wsr-missouri-nebraska2.htm (for the Missouri River from Fort Randall Dam to Lewis and Clark Lake)

Nebraska Canoe Trails Web site
http://www.ngpc.state.ne.us/
boating/canoetrails.html

Nebraska Department of Roads
Box 94759
Lincoln, NE 68509
402-471-4567

Nebraska Division of Travel and Tourism includes Web site links for maps
877-NEBRASKA
http://www.visitnebraska.org

Nebraska Game and Parks Commission
2200 N. 33rd Street
Lincoln, NE 68503
402-471-0641
http://www.ngpc.state.ne.us/
parks

Nebraska state Web site
http://www.state.ne.us

Niobrara State Park
P.O. Box 226
Highway 12
Niobrara, NE 68760
402-857-3373
http://www.ngpc.state.ne.us/
parksearch/parks/html/
90511s.htm

Ponca State Park
P.O. Box 688
Ponca, NE 68770-0688
402-755-2284
http://www.ngpc.state.ne.us/
parks/ponca.html

Smith Falls State Park
HC 13, Box 25
Valentine, NE 69201
402-376-1306
http://www.ngpc.state.ne.us/
    parks/smith.html

North Dakota

The Army Corps of Engineers
for river conditions, water
levels, and releases from
Garrison Dam.
701-654-7441
http://www.nd.water.usgs.gov

Cross Ranch State Park
1403 River Road
Center, ND 58530
701-794-3731
http://www.state.nd.us/ndparks/
    Parks/CRSP.htm
Follow links for "Nature
Preserves" for the Cross Ranch
Nature Preserve (701-794-
8741), and links for "Canoeing
Rivers" for river information at
http://www.state.nd.us/ndparks/
Trails/canoeing.htm or call 701-
745-3380.

Fort Union Trading Post
    National Historic Site
15550 Highway 1804
Williston, ND 58801-8680
701-572-9083 or 701-572-7622
http://www.nps.gov/fous

Knife River Indian Villages
    National Historic Site
P.O. Box 9
Stanton, ND 58571-0009
701-745-3309 or 701-743-3300
http://www.nps.gov/knri

Little Missouri National
    Grassland maps
Southern half: U.S. Forest
    Service Medora Ranger
    District
161 Twenty-first Street, West
Dickinson, ND 58601
701-225-5151
Northern half: McKenzie
    Ranger District
1901 South Main Street
Watford City, ND 58854
701-842-2393
These maps are available only
by mail or at the district offices.

Maah Daah Hey Trail
U.S. Forest Service, Medora
    District
161 Twenty-first Street West
Dickinson, ND 58601
701-225-5151
http://www.nps.gov/thro/
tr_mdh.htm
Maah Daah Hey information is
also available from Sully Creek
State Park at 701-663-9571 and
from:

North Dakota Parks and
    Recreation Department
1835 Bismarck Expressway
Bismarck, ND 58504

North Dakota State Department
 of Transportation
701-328-7623
http://www.state.nd.us/dot/road
 .html

North Dakota state tourism Web
 site includes link for maps
800-HELLO-ND
http://ndtourism.com/maps.html

North Dakota state Web site
http://www.state.nd.us

Theodore Roosevelt National
 Park
P.O. Box 7
Medora, ND 58645-0007
North Unit: 701-842-2333
South Unit: 701-623-4466
http://www.nps.gov/thro

Oregon

Captain's Nautical Supplies
333 NW Broadway
Portland, OR 97209
503-227-1648
This is a good source of maps
(both marine and USGS) in the
Pacific Northwest.
Eagle Cap Ranger District and
 Hells Canyon National
 Recreation Area
Wallowa-Whitman National
 Forest
88401 Highway 82
Enterprise, OR 97814
541-426-4978

Ecola State Park
Cannon Beach, OR
503-436-2844 or 800-551-6949
http://www.oregonstateparks
 .org

Mount Hood Information
 Center
65000 E. Highway 26
Welches, OR 97067
503-622-4822 or 800-622-4822
http://www.mthood.org

Mount Hood National Forest
 Headquarters
Recreation information: 888-
 622-4822 or 503-622-4822
Other information: 503-668-
 1700
http://www.fs.fed.us/r6/mthood/

Nature of the Northwest
 Information Center
800 NE Oregon, Suite 177
Portland, OR 97232
503-731-4444

Oregon Coast Trail
An official map is available
through the Oregon State Parks
and Recreation Department.
503-378-6305 in Salem,
 Oregon, or see their Web site
 at http://www.prd.state.or.us.

Oregon Department of
 Transportation information
800-977-6368 or 503-588-2941
http://www.odot.state.or.us

Oregon State Marine Board
P.O. Box 14145
Salem, OR 97309
503-378-8587
http://www.marinebd.osmb.
  state.or.us/
For boating and marine map
information.

Oregon state tourism
800-547-7842
http://www.traveloregon.com

Oregon state Web site
http://www.oregon.gov

Portland Bureau of Parks and
  Recreation
503-823-7529
http://www.portlandparks.org;
follow links under "Outdoor
Recreation"

South Dakota

The Army Corps of Engineers
for information about Gavins
Point Dam and the impound-
ment known as Lewis and Clark
Lake:
Gavins Point Project Office
P.O. Box 710
Yankton, SD 57078
402-667-7873

Farm Island Recreation Area
1301 Farm Island Road
Pierre, SD 57501-5829
605-224-5605
http://www.state.sd.us/gfp/
sdparks/fmisland/fmisland.htm

National Park Service for
Missouri National Recreation
River from Gavins Point Dam
to Ponca State Park and from
Fort Randall Dam to Lewis and
Clark Lake, and part of the
Niobrara River information.
Yankton, SD
402-667-5530

South Dakota Department of
  Game, Fish and Parks
523 East Capitol Avenue
Pierre, SD 57501
605-773-3391
http://www.state.sd.us/gfp

South Dakota Department of
Transportation. Web site
includes link for maps
605-773-3265
http://www.sddot.com/pub.cfm

South Dakota state tourism
  information
800-732-5682
http://www.travelsd.com

South Dakota state Web site
http://www.state.sd.us

USDA Forest Service
Fort Pierre National Grassland
124 South Euclid Avenue — Box
  417
Pierre, SD 57501
605-224-5517
http://www.fs.fed.us/r2/nebraska/
units/fp/ftpierre.html

Washington

Adams Ranger District
Gifford Pinchot National Forest
2455 Highway 121
Trout Lake, WA 98650-9724
509-395-3400
http://www.fs.fed.us/gpnf

Hanford Reach of the Columbia
River and Hanford Reach
National Monument
http://pacific.fws.gov/hanford or
http://www.hanfordreach.org
Or call the U.S. Fish and Wildlife Service at 509-371-1801.

Juniper Dunes
Bureau of Land Management
Spokane District
1103 N. Fancher
Spokane, WA 99212
509-536-1200
http://www.or.blm.gov/Spokane/
recreation/internet/juniper.pdf

Lewis and Clark National
Wildlife Refuge and Julia
Butler Hansen National
Wildlife Refuge
P.O. Box 566
Cathlamet, WA 98612
360-795-4915
http://pacific.fws.gov/visitor/
washington.html

Packwood Ranger District
Gifford Pinchot National Forest
U.S. Highway 12
Packwood, WA 98361
360-494-0601

Washington Department of
Transportation
360-705-7000; for road conditions: 800-695-ROAD
http://www.wsdot.wa.gov
For maps see: http://www.wsdot
.wa.gov/mapsdata.htm

Washington state Web site
http://www.access.wa.gov

Wenaha-Tucannon Wilderness
Umatilla National Forest
Pomeroy Ranger District
71 West Main
Pomeroy, WA 99347
509-843-1891
http://www.fs.fed.us/r6/uma/
wenaha.htm

Willapa Bay National Wildlife
Refuge
HC 01, Box 910
Ilwaco, WA 98624-9707
360-484-3482
http://pacific.fws.gov/visitor/
washington.html

Notes

Excerpts from the journals of Lewis and Clark are taken from *The Original Journals of the Lewis and Clark Expedition 1804–1806*, edited by Reuben Gold Thwaites and published by Dodd Mead and Co.

Introduction: Why This book?

1. Sierra Club, *Wild America: Protecting the Lands of Lewis and Clark* (San Francisco: Sierra Club, 2000), 3.
2. Scott Faber and Chad Smith for American Rivers, *Voyage of Recovery: The Missouri River* (Washington, D.C.: American Rivers, 2001), 14.
3. http://biology.usgs.gov/pubs/ecosys.htm.
4. John C. Ryan, *State of the Northwest: Revised 2000 Edition* (Seattle: Northwest Environment Watch, 2000), 35.
5. Ibid., 38.
6. Ibid., 55.
7. Ibid., 38.

1. Introducing the Lewis and Clark Expedition

1. Frank Bergon, ed., *The Journals of Lewis and Clark* (New York: Viking Penguin, 1989) xiv.
2. Ibid.
3. William Clark is referred to throughout the journals and histories of the expedition as "Captain," although it was not until January 2001 that this status was officially conferred upon him by President Bill Clinton.

3. Following the Trail Today

1. The Wild and Scenic Rivers Act (Title 16, Chapter 28, sec. 1271 of the *U.S. Code*) was passed by Congress in 1968. For more infor-

mation see the National Wilderness Preservation System Web site at
http://www.wilderness.net/nwps/legis/rivers_legis.cfm. The opening
section of the act reads as follows: "It is hereby declared to be the policy of the United States that certain selected rivers of the Nation
which, with their immediate environments, possess outstandingly
remarkable scenic, recreational, geologic, fish and wildlife, historic,
cultural, or other similar values, shall be preserved in free-flowing
condition, and that they and their immediate environments shall be
protected for the benefit and enjoyment of present and future generations. The Congress declares that the established national policy of
dam and other construction at appropriate sections of the rivers of the
United States needs to be complemented by a policy that would preserve other selected rivers or sections thereof in their free-flowing
condition to protect the water quality of such rivers and to fulfill
other vital national conservation purposes."

2. Philip N. Jones, *Canoe and Kayak Routes of Northwest Oregon* (Seattle: The Mountaineers, 1997), 10.

4. Missouri, Nebraska, and South Dakota

1. Smithsonian Guides to Natural America, *The Heartland: Illinois, Iowa, Nebraska, Kansas, and Missouri* (Washington, D.C.:
Smithsonian Books; New York: Random House, 1997), 46.

2. U.S. Geological Survey, "The Missouri River Story," at
http://infolink.cr.usgs.gov. For more information contact the Missouri
River Natural Resources Committee of the U.S. Fish and Wildlife
Service at DeSoto National Wildlife Refuge, 1434 316th Lane, Missouri Valley, IA 51555, phone: 712-642-4121.

3. Ibid.

4. Faber and Smith for American Rivers, *Voyage of Recovery*, 14.

5. U.S. Geological Survey, "The Missouri River Story."

6. Arow Rock State Historic Site Visitor Center Museum exhibit.

7. Richard Manning, *Grassland: The History, Biology, Politics,
and Promise of the American Prairie* (New York: Penguin Books,
1997), 2.

8. Ibid., 69; also see the Intertribal Bison Cooperative Web site at
http://www.intertribalbison.org.

5. North Dakota and Eastern Montana

1. *Ovis canadensis californiana* was chosen as the reintroduction
species because it was thought to be closer to the native Audubon
bighorn than other subspecies. Some biologists prefer to lump all the

bighorn species together under the name of Rocky Mountain bighorn, while others prefer to differentiate by subspecies, of which *Ovis canadensis californiana* is one. Subspecies can evolve as different populations of a species adapt to a particular landscape over time, augmenting the overall diversity of a species. The bighorn is currently considered by the U.S. Fish and Wildlife Service to be a "desired nonnative," an official status that affords less protection than that given to endangered, threatened, or sensitive native species.

2. Bill Cunningham, *Wild Montana: A Guide to 55 Roadless Recreation Areas* (Helena, Mont.: Falcon Publishing, 1995), 279.

3. BLM. 2000. Use of weed-free forage on public lands in Nevada. *Federal Register*, 65-54544, USDI-BLM.

4. For a good description of rattlesnake "do's and don'ts," see Andy Kerr, *Oregon Desert Guide: 70 Hikes* (Seattle: The Mountaineers, 2000), 31–33.

6. Central and Western Montana and across Lolo pass into Idaho

1. Rick Bass, personal communication, July 31, 2002.

7. Idaho and Eastern Washington

1. It is important to note that it is domestic livestock grazing that poses a threat to the ecological integrity of the landscape, and not that of natural populations of elk, pronghorn, deer, and other wild ungulates.

2. Ken Olsen, "Unbearable Conditions," *Spokane (Wash.) Spokesman-Review,* November 29 and 30, 1998. This was a four-part series regarding the role of salmon in sustaining grizzly bears and old-growth forests.

3. Alvin M. Josephy Jr., *The Nez Perce Indians and the Opening of the Northwest,* abridged edition (Lincoln: University of Nebraska Press, 1979), 14. For a compelling account of the Nez Perce's ordeal during white settlement of the Northwest, read further in Josephy's book.

4. Ibid., 620.

5. Gretchen R. Oosterhout and Phillip R. Mundy for Trout Unlimited, "The Doomsday Clock 2001: An Update on the Status and Projected Time to Extinction for Snake River Wild Spring/Summer Chinook Stocks." Portland, Ore., April 16, 2001. For copies of the report contact Trout Unlimited at 503-827-5700 or through its Web site at http://www.tu.org.

8. The Columbia Basin and Columbia River Gorge

1. Elizabeth Woody, "Recalling Celilo," in *Salmon Nation*, ed. Edward C. Wolf and Seth Zuckerman (Portland, Ore.: Ecotrust, 1999), 9–10.

2. Richard L. Hill, "A New Look at an Old Landslide," *Oregonian*, September 29, 1999.

9. The Lower Columbia River to the Pacific Ocean

1. Sam McKinney, *Reach of Tide, Ring of History* (Portland, Ore.: Oregon Historical Society, 1987), 9–14.

2. There has been litigation over whether or not Oregon coastal coho should be listed under the Endangered Species Act, since the National Marine Fisheries Service included hatchery fish in its initial analysis of coastal coho. The fact is that although hatchery fish and wild fish share a genetic makeup, the conditions under which they are reared make their life strategies and chances of survival markedly different. Among other problems, hatchery fish can be more susceptible to predators and often suffer as a result of being fed in captivity rather than feeding naturally. In addition, the Endangered Species Act was designed to protect self-sustaining populations and the habitat on which they depend.

There has also been litigation challenging the Oregon Department of Forestry's Forest Practices Act for allowing logging and road building in places and ways that degrade habitat essential to the survival of imperiled coho salmon.

Bibliography and Recommended Reading

Alden, Peter, and John Grassy. *National Audubon Society Field Guide to the Rocky Mountain States*. New York: Alfred A. Knopf, 1998.

Alden, Peter, and Dennis Paulson. *National Audubon Society Field Guide to the Pacific Northwest*. New York: Alfred A. Knopf, 1998.

Ambrose, Stephen E. *Undaunted Courage: Meriwether Lewis, Thomas Jefferson, and the Opening of the American West*. New York: Simon and Schuster, 1996.

Arno, Stephen F., and Ramona P. Hammerly. *Northwest Trees*. Seattle: The Mountaineers, 1977.

Bass, Rick. *The Book of Yaak*. Boston: Houghton Mifflin. 1996.

Beatte, Brian, and Brett Dufur. *River Valley Companion: A Nature Guide*. Columbia, Mo.: Pebble Publishing, 1997.

Bergon, Frank, ed. *The Journals of Lewis and Clark*. New York: Viking Penguin, 1989.

Biddle, Nicholas, ed. *The Journals of the Expedition under the Command of Capts. Lewis and Clark*. New York: New York Heritage Press, 1962.

Burt, William H., and Richard P. Grossenheider. *Peterson Field Guides: Mammals*. Boston: Houghton Mifflin, 1980.

Carson, Rachel. *Silent Spring*. New York: Fawcett World Library, 1962.

Columbia Group Sierra Club: Tillamook State Forest Committee. *50 Hikes in the Tillamook State Forest*. Portland, Ore.: Columbia Group Sierra Club, 2001.

Cone, Joseph. *Common Fate: Endangered Salmon and the People of the Pacific Northwest*. Corvallis, Ore.: Oregon State University Press, 1996.

Craighead, John J., Frank C. Craighead, and Ray J. Davis. *Peterson Field Guides: Rocky Mountain Wildflowers*. Boston: Houghton Mifflin, 1963.

Cunningham, Bill. *Wild Montana: A Guide to 55 Roadless Recreation Areas*. Helena, Mont.: Falcon Publishing. 1995.

Cutright, Paul Russell. *Lewis and Clark: Pioneering Naturalists*. Lincoln: University of Nebraska Press, 1989.

De Voto, Bernard, ed. *The Journals of Lewis and Clark*. Boston: Houghton Mifflin, 1953.

DeLorme. *Idaho Atlas & Gazetteer*. Yarmouth, Maine, 1998.

———. *Illinois Atlas & Gazetteer*. Yarmouth, Maine, 1996.

———. *Kansas Atlas & Gazetteer*. Yarmouth, Maine, 1997.

———. *Missouri Atlas & Gazetteer*. Yarmouth, Maine, 1998.

———. *Montana Atlas & Gazetteer*. Yarmouth, Maine, 1999.

———. *Nebraska Atlas & Gazetteer*. Freeport, Maine, 1996.

———. *North Dakota Atlas & Gazetteer*. Yarmouth, Maine, 1999.

———. *Oregon Atlas & Gazetteer*. Freeport, Maine, 1991.

———. *South Dakota Atlas & Gazetteer*. Yarmouth, Maine, 1997.

———. *Washington Atlas & Gazetteer*. Freeport, Maine, 1995.

Dufur, Brett. *The Complete Katy Trail Guidebook*. Rocheport, Mo.: Pebble Publishing, 1999.

Durbin, Kathie. *Tree Huggers: Victory, Defeat and Renewal in the Pacific Northwest Ancient Forest Campaign*. Seattle: The Mountaineers, 1996.

Ewing, Susan. *The Great Rocky Mountain Nature Factbook*. Portland, Ore.: West Winds Press, 1999.

Faber, Scott, and Chad Smith. *Voyage of Recovery: The Missouri River*. Washington, D.C.: American Rivers, 2001.

Fischer, Hank, and Carol Fischer. *Paddling Montana*. Helena, Mont.: Falcon Publishing, 1999.

Hart, John. *Walking Softly in the Wilderness: The Sierra Club Guide to Backpacking*. San Francisco: Sierra Club Books, 1998.

Houck, Michael C., and M. J. Cody, eds, *Wild in the City: A Guide to Portland's Natural Areas*. Portland, Ore.: Oregon Historical Society Press, 2000.

Jones, Philip N. *Canoe and Kayak Routes of Northwest Oregon*. Seattle: The Mountaineers, 1997.

Josephy, Alvin M., Jr. *The Nez Perce Indians and the Opening of the Northwest*. Abridged edition. Lincoln: University of Nebraska Press, 1979.

Judd, Ron C., and Dan A. Nelson. *Pacific Northwest Hiking*. San Francisco: Foghorn Press, 1995.

Kerr, Andy. *Oregon Desert Guide: 70 Hikes.* Seattle: The Mountaineers, 2000.

Kricher, John C., and Gordon Morrison. *Peterson Field Guides: Ecology of Western Forests.* Boston: Houghton Mifflin, 1993.

Lichatowich, Jim. *Salmon without Rivers: A History of the Pacific Salmon Crisis.* Washington, D.C., and Covelo, Calif.: Island Press, 1999.

Limerick, Patricia Nelson. *The Legacy of Conquest: The Unbroken Past of the American West.* New York: W. W. Norton, 1987.

———. *Something in the Soil: Legacies and Reckonings in the New West.* New York: W. W. Norton, 2000.

Ludlum, David. *National Audubon Society Field Guide to North American Weather.* New York: Alfred A. Knopf, 1991.

Lundeen, Dan, and Allen Pinkham. *Salmon and His People: Fish and Fishing in Nez Perce Culture.* Lewiston, Idaho: Confluence Press, 1999.

Manning, Richard. *Grassland: The History, Biology, Politics, and Promise of the American Prairie.* New York: Penguin Books, 1995.

———. *One Round River: The Curse of Gold and the Fight for the Big Blackfoot.* New York: Henry Holt, 1997.

Maser, Chris. *Forest Primeval: The Natural History of an Ancient Forest.* Corvallis, Ore.: Oregon State University Press, 2001.

Mathews, Daniel. *Cascade Olympic Natural History: A Trailside Reference.* Raven Editions in conjunction with the Portland Audubon Society. Portland, Ore., 1992.

Matthiessen, Peter. *Wildlife in America.* New York: Penguin Books, 1978.

Maughan, Ralph, and Jackie Johnson Maughan. *Hiking Idaho.* Helena, Mont.: Falcon Publishing, 1995.

McConnaughey, Bayard H., and Evelyn McConnaughey. *National Audubon Society Nature Guides: Pacific Coast.* New York: Alfred A. Knopf, 1997.

McKinney, Sam. *Reach of Tide, Ring of History.* Portland, Ore.: Oregon Historical Society, 1987.

McPhee, John. *Annals of the Former World.* New York: Farrar, Straus and Giroux, 1998.

McRae, W. C., and Judy Jewell. *Montana Handbook.* Chico, Calif.: Moon Publications, 1992.

Merchants Exchange and the Columbia Snake River Marketing Group. *The Great Waterway: The Guide to Marine Facilities and Industrial Properties on the Columbia and Snake River System.* Portland, Ore., 1999.

Molvar, Erik. *Wild Wyoming*. Guilford, Conn.: Globe Pequot Press, 2001.

Murie, Olaus J. *Peterson Field Guides: Animal Tracks*. Boston: Houghton Mifflin, 1974.

Nabokov, Peter, ed. *Native American Testimony: A Chronicle of Indian-White Relations from Prophecy to the Present, 1492– 1992*. New York: Penguin Books, 1991.

Niehaus, Theodore F., and Charles L. Ripper. *Peterson Field Guides: Pacific States Wildflowers*. Boston: Houghton Mifflin, 1976.

Page, Lawrence M., and Brooks M. Burr. *A Field Guide to Freshwater Fishes: North American North of Mexico*. Boston: Houghton Mifflin, 1991.

Palmer, Tim. *America by Rivers*. Washington, D.C., and Covelo, Calif.: Island Press, 1996.

Petersen, Keith C. *River of Life, Channel of Death: Fish and Dams on the Lower Snake*. Lewiston, Idaho: Confluence Press, 1995.

Peterson, Roger Tory. *Peterson Field Guides: Western Birds*. Boston: Houghton Mifflin, 1990.

Peterson, Roger Tory, and Margaret McKenny. *Peterson Field Guides: Wildflowers, Northeastern, Northcentral North America*. Boston: Houghton Mifflin, 1968.

Pojar, Jim, and Andy MacKinnon. *Plants of the Pacific Northwest Coast: Washington, Oregon, British Columbia and Alaska*. Redmond, Wash.: Lone Pine Publishing, 1994.

Ronda, James P. *Lewis and Clark among the Indians*. Lincoln: University of Nebraska Press, 1984.

Ryan, John C. *State of the Northwest. Revised 2000 Edition*. Seattle: Northwest Environment Watch, 2000.

Ryser, Fred A., Jr. *Birds of the Great Basin: A Natural History*. Reno: University of Nevada Press, 1985.

Schmidt, Thomas. *National Geographic's Guide to the Lewis and Clark Trail*. Washington, D.C.: National Geographic Society, 1998.

Schneider, Bill. *The Hikers Guide to Montana*. Helena, Mont.: Falcon Press, 1994.

Shaw, Richard J., and Danny On. *Plants of Waterton-Glacier National Parks and the Northern Rockies*. Missoula, Mont.: Mountain Press, 1979.

Shepard, Lansing. *Smithsonian Guides to Natural America: The Northern Plains*. Photographs by Tom Bean. Preface by Thomas E. Lovejoy. Washington, D.C.: Smithsonian Books; New York: Random House, 1996.

Sierra Club. *Wild America: Protecting the Lands of Lewis and Clark.* San Francisco: Sierra Club, 2000.

Smithsonian Guides to Natural America. *The Heartland: Illinois, Iowa, Nebraska, Kansas, and Missouri.* Washington, D.C.: Smithsonian Books; New York: Random House, 1997.

Stebbins, Robert C. *Peterson Field Guides: Western Reptiles and Amphibians.* Boston: Houghton Mifflin, 1985.

Stegner, Wallace. *The American West as Living Space.* Ann Arbor: University of Michigan Press, 1987.

Strickler, Dee. *Wayside Wildflowers of the Pacific Northwest.* Columbia Falls, Mont.: Flower Press, 1993.

Taylor, Ronald J. *Sagebrush Country: A Wildflower Sanctuary.* Missoula, Mont.: Mountain Press, 1992.

Thom, James Alexander. *Camping along the Lewis and Clark Trail.* Vols. 1 and 2. Billings, Mont.: Discovery Publishing, 2000.

Thwaites, Reuben Gold. *Original Journals of the Lewis and Clark Expedition 1804–1806.* New York: Dodd, Mead and Co., 1904–5.

Ulrich, Roberta. *Empty Nets: Indians, Dams and the Columbia River.* Corvallis: Oregon State University Press, 1999.

Ulrich, Tom J. *Mammals of the Northern Rockies.* Missoula, Mont.: Mountain Press, 1986.

Vielbig, Klindt. *Cross-Country Ski Routes: Oregon.* Seattle: The Mountaineers, 1994.

Vitt, Dale H., Janet E. Marsh, and Robin B. Bovey. *Mosses, Lichens and Ferns of Northwest North America.* Edmonton, Alberta, Vancouver, B.C., and Redmond, Wash.: Lone Pine Publishing, 1988.

White, Richard. *The Organic Machine: The Remaking of the Columbia River.* New York: Hill and Wang, 1995.

Whitehill, Karen, and Terry Whitehill. *Nature Walks in and around Portland.* Seattle: The Mountaineers, 1998.

Winckler, Suzanne. *Smithsonian Guides to Natural America: The Heartland.* Photographs by Willard Clay, Michael Forsberg, Charles Gurce, and Tom Till. Preface by Thomas E. Lovejoy. Washington, D.C.: Smithsonian Books; New York: Random House, 1997.

Wolf, Edward C. *A Tidewater Place: Portrait of the Willapa Ecosystem.* Long Beach, Wash.: The Willapa Alliance, 1993.

Wolf, Edward C., and Seth Zuckerman, eds. *Salmon Nation: People and Fish at the Edge.* Portland, Ore.: An Ecotrust Book, 1999.

Wood, Wendell. *A Walking Guide to Oregon's Ancient Forests.* Portland, Ore.: Oregon Natural Resources Council, 1991.

Index